8/2/20

Please return on or before the latest date above.
You can renew online at www.kent.gov.uk/libs
or by phone 08458 247 200

D1426494

C153060767

AIR WAR MALTA

AIR WAR
MALTA

June 1940 to November 1942

Diane Canwell and Jon Sutherland

Pen & Sword
AVIATION

First published in Great Britain in 2008 by
Pen & Sword Aviation
an imprint of
Pen & Sword Books Ltd
47 Church Street
Barnsley
South Yorkshire
S70 2AS

ISBN 978-1-84415-740-2

A CIP catalogue record for this book is
available from the British Library

Typeset in Sabon 11/13pt by
Concept, Huddersfield

Printed and bound in England by CPI UK

Pen & Sword Books Ltd incorporates the Imprints of Pen & Sword
Aviation, Pen & Sword Maritime, Pen & Sword Military, Wharncliffe
Local History, Pen & Sword Select, Pen & Sword Military Classics,
Leo Cooper, Remember When, Seaforth Publishing and Frontline
Publishing.

For a complete list of Pen & Sword titles please contact
PEN & SWORD BOOKS LIMITED
47 Church Street, Barnsley, South Yorkshire, S70 2AS, England
E-mail: enquiries@pen-and-sword.co.uk
Website: www.pen-and-sword.co.uk

CONTENTS

ACKNOWLEDGEMENT

The authors are very grateful to Paul Lazell for supplying the photographs used in this book. Paul's late father, Sergeant William (Bill) John Lazell, of the 7th Regiment, 27th Battalion, Royal Artillery, was sent to Malta, arriving on 24 July 1941. He remained on the island operating radar and heavy anti-aircraft guns until his departure on 5 March 1944. During his stay on Malta, Bill took literally hundreds of 35mm photographs. His collection of photographs, along with his extensive daily diary, provides a fascinating account of life on Malta during the Second World War.

Paul Lazell can be contacted at paulsdadsphotos@aol.com. His website is at www.paulsww2photographs.webeden.co.uk.

INTRODUCTION

The island of Malta is situated at the 'crossroads' of the Mediterranean and is almost at the heart of the Mediterranean, 1,100 miles to the east of Gibraltar and 911 miles west of Alexandria. However, it is closest to North Africa and to Sicily, being just 185 miles east of Tunisia and 200 miles from Tripoli. Sicily lies just 60 miles to the north.

There are, in fact, three inhabited islands: Malta, Gozo and Comino with a combined land area of just 122 sq miles. Malta, the largest island, is just 17 miles long and 9 miles at its widest point. There are no lakes or rivers and it is on the eastern shore where the majority of the harbours are located. Gozo is just 9 miles long and no more than 4.5 miles wide at the most. The most significant harbour in the Maltese islands is the Grand Harbour, on the eastern coast of Malta. In fact it is two harbours divided by a peninsula, dominated by the capital, Valletta. To the north of Valletta is Marsamxet, another harbour, and on the south coast is the only other harbour of any significance, Marsaxlokk. Neither Gozo nor Comino has a harbour as such, but they do have bays and havens for shipping.

In its strategic position Malta can trace human habitation back to prehistoric times. The first major settlers on the island were the Phoenicians. Malta then became part of the Carthaginian Empire and after the Punic Wars passed to the hands of the Romans. The islands then passed successively into the hands of the Vandals, the Byzantines and the Arabs. The Arabs were succeeded by the Normans and in the Middle Ages Malta was sold and resold to various barons and lords until it eventually became part of the Spanish Empire. In 1530 the islands were handed over to the Knights of St John by Charles V. The Knights had been driven out of Rhodes and now established themselves on Malta, where they would remain for nearly 300 years.

In 1565 Suleiman the Magnificent laid siege to Malta, bringing with him over 40,000 men. The siege lasted from May to September before the Ottomans retreated before the onset of winter. The deprivations suffered under the Ottomans' siege were equal to the ordeal of hunger, terror and bombardment at the hands of the Italians and Germans during World War Two.

The islands were briefly controlled by the French after Napoleon Bonaparte seized the islands in 1798. Two years later, after a blockade by Horatio Nelson, the French garrison surrendered and Malta became part of the British Empire. From this point on the islands, somewhat overpopulated, became almost wholly reliant on the British and their military expenditure in order to survive.

Prior to the outbreak of World War Two, Valletta had become the Royal Navy's Mediterranean Fleet Headquarters, although the head-quarters was moved to Alexandria in Egypt at the beginning of World War Two. By the time Italy declared war in June 1940 there were 300,000 civilians on the islands, fewer than 4,000 British troops, just over forty anti-aircraft guns, four Gladiators, three pilots and just five weeks of food supplies.

Inevitably, the island was going to become the focus of Italian attention in the Mediterranean. It was an isolated, British colony, close to the Italian mainland. The Italians feared that it would be used by the British to launch attacks. It became one of Mussolini's priorities, to beat the islands into submission by air and pave the way for its occupation.

The events that would take place between June 1940 and the generally accepted end of the siege by air and sea in late 1942 would have few parallels during World War Two. Ton for ton the Italians and the Germans dropped more bombs on Malta than the *Luftwaffe* dropped on London during the blitz. Almost daily there were interceptions and dogfights around and above the island. Hundreds of air alerts shattered the calm of the islands and sent civilians and military personnel alike scurrying for shelter. Hour-by-hour, the attrition on the island, its resources, population and often scant air cover threatened to over-whelm its ability to defend itself.

To begin with, the island's antiquated biplanes were all that stood in the way of the Italians flattening the island and forcing the civilians and the garrison into submission. Gradually, over the months, the Gladiators were reinforced by Hawker Hurricanes and then Spitfires and a host of other military aircraft, until defence became offence and it was the Italians and the Germans who were subjected to incessant bombing and attack.

On 15 April, 1942, King George VI awarded the island the George Cross. It was an award that was usually given to individuals, rather than a whole population. But, as the monarch said:

> To honour her brave people, I award the George Cross to the Island Fortress of Malta to bear witness to a heroism and devotion that will long be famous in history.

Undoubtedly Malta was one of the most intensively bombed areas during World War Two. There were around 3,000 raids, nearly 1,500 civilians were killed and nearly 3,700 injured. It is notoriously difficult to be certain as to the aircraft losses on either side. The Royal Air Force claim around 860 Italian and German aircraft, although this figure may, in fact, be closer to 600. Around 290 Spitfires and Hurricanes were lost between June 1940 and December 1942, although in all over 840 Allied aircraft were lost, both in the air and on land. The German *Luftwaffe* claim over 440 Allied aircraft shot down.

The siege of Malta was almost entirely a siege by air. In the period up to the end of 1940, air activities were almost exclusively Italian. However in early 1941, matching the fortunes of the Germans in North Africa, the *Luftwaffe* reinforced the Italians and made a determined attempt to overwhelm the island's defences. With the changing fortunes in North Africa and Germany's obsession with the invasion of Russia, there was a lull before the *Luftwaffe* returned in 1942 and nearly overwhelmed Malta's scant defences and pounded the island almost at will.

After April 1942 it was the Allies that were to turn to the offensive, intercepting aircraft attacks before they even crossed the coast. Daily Rommel's supply vessels were intercepted and destroyed by aircraft operating out of Malta. No German or Italian vessel was safe along the whole of the African coast or from Italy to Greece.

Just prior to the launching of Montgomery's much awaited North African Offensive at El Alamein, the *Luftwaffe* returned for one last time to try to overwhelm Malta. They assembled half of their bomber strength in the Mediterranean. By now sufficient reinforcements had arrived on Malta and the island was able to hold out while the 8th Army drove along the North African coast, overrunning German airbases.

By the end of 1942 the siege was over and the island could now be turned into an offensive arm of the Allied effort against the Italian mainland. Aircraft from the island covered the amphibious invasion of Sicily and continued to be instrumental in ensuring air superiority across the whole of the Mediterranean.

CHAPTER ONE
THE OUTPOST OF THE BRAVE

When war was declared in September 1939 Malta seemed to be far from the probable battlefields of the new World War. Around it were either friendly or neutral countries. The Mediterranean was controlled by the British and the French and when Admiral Sir Andrew Cunningham moved the Mediterranean Royal Navy command to Alexandria, leaving just a pair of cruisers, two destroyers and a flotilla of submarines in Malta, the island seemed to be even less in danger of attack. Mussolini had already declared that he would remain neutral in the war between Britain, France and Germany.

However, Mussolini, by June 1940, was seriously considering his position. Italy had seen Germany overwhelm Poland and then strike west, sweeping all before them and forcing Holland, Belgium and then France to buckle under the *blitzkrieg* spearheaded by the *Luftwaffe*.

On 10 June 1940, addressing an adoring crowd in Rome, Mussolini declared war on France and Britain. He believed the time was ripe to bring his country into the war before Germany claimed all the spoils. He had already ordered elements of the Italian air force south into Sicily and had prepared outline plans for attacks on Malta. With France on the verge of collapse the whole of the Mediterranean strategy carefully constructed by the British and the French was about to unravel and the vast Mediterranean would have to be policed by Cunningham's naval forces alone. What had been a friendly, non-belligerent coastline, just 60 miles from Malta, was now occupied by an ambitious Italian air force, eager to display its prowess and its modern machines.

The Italian navy was ready to step into the void that was left by the defeated French. How could the tiny garrison on Malta be expected to hold out? How would it be possible to sustain 300,000 people who could only grow 30 per cent of the food they needed? It was an island that produced little meat and milk and was desperately short of water, except in the rainy season. All the air assets that could stand in the way of the Italian air force were three remaining Fleet Air Arm Gloucester Gladiator biplanes, Faith, Hope and Charity. The biplanes were still in packing cases at Kalafrana and had been left behind when HMS *Glorious* had left the island. Permission was needed to even unpack the cases: permission was received and then rescinded. There were more delays and finally the aircraft could be pieced together. Six volunteer RAF pilots were hurriedly trained to fly them.

Nothing could have prepared the island for the ordeal that it was about to face. Over twenty years after the battle for the supremacy of the air above the islands former war correspondent, Alan Moorehead, wrote:

> The greatest of the battles for supply fell upon Malta. This was now turned into a hell. Malta was a base for British submarines and aircraft preying on the Axis' lines of supply to Libya. In the spring of 1942, the Axis decided to obliterate that base and they wanted to starve it as well. Right through the spring they turned such a blitz upon Malta as no other island or city had seen in the war. It was a siege of annihilation. One after another all the other great sieges were eclipsed – England and Odessa, Sebastopol and Tobruk. Malta became the most bombed place on earth.

Literally, years of neglect had left Malta without any credible air defences. In June 1940 all British air assets were being carefully protected for what would become the battle of Britain. Britain could not spare a single Hurricane or Spitfire, nor could they risk any other aircraft to defend the skies over the islands. Yet if Malta was to fall into the hands of the Italians or Germans the Mediterranean route between Britain and Egypt would be compromised. Axis aircraft, submarines and surface vessels could then interdict any convoys or attempts to reinforce Egypt. Any fight for Malta would be a fight to the end. If the Maltese or the garrison led by the Governor, Lieutenant-General William Dobbie, had any illusions that the conflict would pass Malta by, this was shattered at dawn on 11 June 1940, just six hours after Italy declared war on Britain and France.

What preparations were possible had been made, even before war had broken out in 1939. Sir Charles Bonham-Carter had been the Governor of the island in 1939. He had encouraged the creation of District Committees across the islands, so there would be some form of local government and these committees could recruit air raid wardens, organize air raid shelters, first-aid stations and casualty clearing centres. Air raid wardens were trained and allocated particular areas. They were expected to send delegates to provide monthly reports to a central committee set up by the governor. The committee was also concerned with food and rationing. By the end of 1939, 365 men and 236 women had become air raid wardens. Gas masks had been distributed: this was a necessary step, particularly considering the indiscriminate use of gas that the Italians had made against tribesmen in Abyssinia.

Old passageways and tunnels were opened up in ancient defence works. These would provide useful shelter during air raids. Areas of housing directly close to the dockyards would have to be evacuated and additional military personnel would need billets. Systematically the authorities began hoarding food and ammunition. An early decision was made to concentrate the defence on the island of Malta itself and effectively leave Gozo and Comino undefended.

A blackout practice was carried out on the night of 2 to 3 May 1940. It lasted from 22.00 hours until the following dawn. On 11 May air raid warning practice commenced at 19.00 hours. Residents cleared the streets of Valletta in minutes, they observed blackout regulations and cars were parked and left.

The previous day Sir William Dobbie, now Acting Governor, called for volunteers for a force of special constables. On 20 May 'licensed sportsmen and other persons capable of using a gun' were asked to join the Home Defence Force. It seemed that if the enemy were to arrive then it would probably be by parachute. Amazingly, within three days of the call for the Home Defence Force volunteers, 3,000 people had presented themselves. The volunteers would become known as the Malta Volunteer Defence Force. They were issued with steel helmets and given brassards with the letter 'v' on them.

On 27 May a curfew was imposed from 23.00 to 05.00 hours. The Central Hospital at Floriana and Blue Sisters at St Julian's were prepared to accept casualties from air raids. Two other hospitals were set up, one at the Mater Boni Consilii School at Paola and the other at the Bugeja Technical Institute at Hamrun.

Malta had every reason to fear the Italian air force (*Regia Aeronautica*). It boasted 5,400 aircraft, most of which were either in Italy or North Africa. Around 2,000 of the aircraft were being used for flight practice and training, but they had a front line strength of 975 bombers and 803 fighters and fighter bombers. In addition they had 400 reconnaissance aircraft, eighty transports, 285 maritime reconnaissance aircraft and a further 400 older, mainly biplanes, based in Italian East Africa.

At this point in the war the primary Italian bomber was the Savoia-Marchettism 79 (Hawk). It was a three-engine aircraft capable of being used in a straightforward bomber role, carrying 2,200 lb of bombs, or in an anti-shipping role, carrying two torpedoes. It had a cruising speed of 200 mph and a maximum speed of 225 mph. It was powered by three, Alfa Romeo RC34, 750 hp engines. The best fighter was the Macchi C200, with a maximum speed of 300 mph. It was powered by a Fiat A74, 840 hp engine and had a pair of 12.7 mm machine guns. In addition to this the Italians deployed CR42 and CR50 fighters and Fiat BR20M bombers.

On the ground at Malta, to resist a potential invasion, were the 2nd Battalion Devonshire Regiment, the 2nd Battalion Queens Own Royal West Kent Regiment, the 1st Battalion Dorsetshire Regiment and the 2nd Battalion Royal Irish Fusiliers. A further battalion of Maltese infantry would soon become the 1st Battalion of the Queens Own Malta Regiment. Completing the defence force for September 1939 was the 7th Anti-aircraft Regiment of the Royal Artillery. In addition, just a month before the first Italian attack, the 8th Battalion Manchester Regiment arrived in May 1940. On paper the ground force was now classed as a division. Anti-aircraft defences were also beefed up, with the arrival of the 27th Heavy Anti-Aircraft Regiment.

It was just before 07.00 on 11 June 1940 that ten S79s appeared over the coast, making for Hal Far. Almost immediately a second wave of fifteen S79s made for the dockyard and Valletta's two main harbours. A third wave seemed to be making for the seaplane base at Kalafrana. The bombers were escorted by Macchi 200s.

Flight Lieutenant George Burges was sitting on the lavatory when the alert was sounded. He ran out to his Gladiator, along with two of his colleagues. Unfortunately they could not get high enough before the bombs started dropping over the Grand Harbour. Aloft Burges could see Hal Far, his own airfield, in smoke from the first wave of bombs. Burges chased a second wave of bombers, but when the Italians saw him they just sped up and left the Gladiator in their wake. The Italians had hit Valletta, Hal Far, Portes-des-Bombes, Marsa, Sliema and other targets. They had managed to kill seven servicemen, eleven civilians and injure 130 more.

The Italians returned in the afternoon with more attacks on Hal Far, Valletta and the Grand Harbour. The Hal Far based Gladiators again tried to respond and the anti-aircraft defences tried to engage the enemy. By the end of the day there had been eight air raid alerts, of which five had become bombing raids. The Italians had been flying at heights of between 10,000 and 15,000 ft, making it difficult for the Gladiators to engage them.

Finally the all clear was sounded and that evening all service personnel were told to report immediately for duty. The bars and clubs in Valletta were swept by military police, who ordered the servicemen back to their units.

Governor Dobbie issued an Order of the Day:

> The decision of His Majesty's Government to fight until our enemies are defeated will be heard with the greatest satisfaction by all ranks of the Garrison of Malta. It may be that hard times lie ahead of us, but I know that however hard they may be, the courage and determination of all ranks will not falter, and that with God's help we will maintain the security of this fortress. I call on all officers and other ranks humbly to seek God's help, and then in reliance on Him to do their duty unflinchingly.

The experience of the first attack played heavily on the minds of the servicemen and civilians of the island. The night before the attack Air Chief Marshal Sir Robert Brooke-Popham had attended an official dinner party laid on by the Governor, when he was interrupted by Flight Lieutenant Burges, who informed him that the Italians had declared war. Brooke-Popham's assistant, Air Commodore Sammy Maynard, had hoped that they would have at least forty-eight fighters, or four squadrons, to defend Malta. Maynard was a New Zealander and he had only happened on the Gladiators in their packing cases by chance back in March 1940.

After the first day's attack Maynard put it to the Gladiator pilots that new tactics were needed in order to deal with any future attacks. Squadron Leader Jock Martin, who was in command of the Gladiator flight, agreed with him that the Gladiators' only chance to intercept the Italians was to be above the bombers as they approached. The solution seemed to be that the pilots would have to take it in turns to sit in their cockpits on the ground, ready to take off as soon as the enemy had been spotted. However, with an inadequate number of crew members properly trained to cover the daylight hours from 05.00 to 20.00 hours meant that each man would have to spend four hours sitting in a cockpit, followed by four hours of rest.

The ground crews would also need to work night and day, not only to keep the Gladiators aloft, but also to ensure that the airfield remained open. They would have to cannibalise whatever parts they could lay their hands on from the stores. They utilised parts from a Royal Navy Swordfish (the Gladiator was renamed a Gladfish). They also fitted three-bladed propellers to the Gladiators to improve their climb. Maintenance crews would also have to use parts from Blenheim bombers just to keep Faith, Hope and Charity flying.

The exodus of civilians from Valletta began the day after the first attack. As J. Storace recalled at the time:

> Women with bundles on their heads or with bundles hanging from their arms, carrying babies, with one or two children holding onto their skirts, with a boy or girl pushing a pram loaded with the most essential belongings, crowded the road, walking without a destination in view, but leaving their beloved homes, abandoning their city, going anywhere as far away as possible from this target area. Buses, touring cars, cabs and other horse drawn vehicles carrying the more fortunate families who either owned a vehicle or could afford to hire one, moved in this crowd of walking and less fortunate humanity in the direction of Zabbar.

A solitary Italian reconnaissance plane flew over Malta on 12 June. It was promptly shot down. But on the following day there were four air raid warnings, two developing into bombing raids. The first hit Kalafrana, killing two and wounding four others. The second was intercepted by the three Gladiators. The Italian bombers panicked and dropped their bombs prematurely, most of them falling into the sea or onto empty fields. Seventeen casualties were inflicted by the bombing on 12 June and the authorities clamped down on blackout violations, prosecuting several people.

On 13 June Dobbie contacted the War Office. He had heard that there were some Hurricanes heading for Egypt and he desperately wanted these. To his amazement the War Office agreed.

The first air raid alarm sounded at 08.35 on 14 June. Italian bombers were dropping bombs on Grand Harbour, Fort St Angelo and then over St John's Co-Cathedral. There were only a handful of casualties, but there were seven more raids on 14 June, the last focusing on Cospicua, close to the dockyards. This time the Italians used both high explosives and incendiaries. This was a particularly vulnerable part of the island, as it was one of the most crowded.

The refugee situation was becoming impossible and many refugee settlement centres were set up in the villages, in order to deal with the exodus of inhabitants from Valletta.

On 15 June a single air raid claimed one life at Hanrun. Even Sunday 16th was not without incident. The first alarm heralded the arrival of three formations of enemy aircraft, thought to be around thirteen in strength, and they dropped bombs around Kalafrana. Another formation of Macchi 200 fighters was also spotted and in the afternoon more bombs were dropped near Mosta. Luckily there were only two casualties.

The Italians struck early on the morning of 17 June with an air raid at 06.15 hours. Five Italian bombers and a pair of fighters dropped munitions harmlessly into the countryside in the centre of the island. Governor Dobbie's order for the day read:

> Whatever may be the outcome of the negotiations in France it will not affect the determination of His Majesty's Government to continue the war and defeat our enemies. Here the task of the fighting forces of maintaining the integrity and safety of Malta remains unchanged and will be resolutely carried out. I know I can rely on the support and cooperation of all the people and that they will cheerfully do whatever may be required of them to assist in this glorious task. May God help us to do our duty to the full and finally give us victory.

From this proclamation it was clear to servicemen and civilians alike that all did not bode well in France. But they could not be prepared for the prospect of the Allied effort losing six million fighting men when France would drop out of the war in little more than a week's time. It would also place potential new enemies close at hand, in the form of the Vichy French.

The Italians launched their first night raid on Malta on Thursday 20 June. The islanders heard that the Germans had already captured Paris, but this brought with it a glimmer of hope for Malta itself. Two Royal Navy training squadrons, Nos 767 and 769, had been based at the French Naval airfield of Olayvestre on the south coast of France. On 18 June they were withdrawn to Algeria and then split into two sections of twelve Swordfish aircraft. Twelve of the best crew members left Tunis for Hal Far, where they would arrive on 20 June. Ultimately they would become No. 830 Squadron Fleet Air Arm (1 July).

Meanwhile the three Gladiators still doggedly defied the Italian air force over Malta. Two more crated Gladiators had been unpacked, but no sooner had the three become five than Malta's air force was once again reduced to three. One of the new Gladiators crashed while taking off. The pilot was unhurt, but the Gladiator was wrecked. In the afternoon a second Gladiator hit a packing case when it landed and flipped over. Once again the Gladiator was a write off, but the pilot emerged safely from the wreckage.

A day later, on 22 June, Malta would claim its first kill.

CHAPTER TWO
THE ITALIAN OFFENSIVE

Towards the end of the first week of the war for Malta, Berlin radio proudly announced that the Italian air force had 'completely destroyed the British naval base at Malta'. In order to provide photographic proof of their 'victory', the Italians sent a Savoia Marchetti 79 (SM79) to take shots of the airfield and the Grand Harbour. Waiting for the bomber aloft was Flight Lieutenant Burges in Faith and Flying Officer Timber Woods in Hope. Burges described the encounter in his own words in his combat report:

> Ordered to intercept enemy aircraft reported approaching Malta. Enemy sighted at 13,000 ft when we were at 12,000 ft. Altered course to intercept and climbed to 15,000 ft, and carried out stern attack from above enemy. Port engine and then starboard engine of enemy caught fire and attack was discontinued.

Far below, promenaders in Valletta and Sliema saw the Italian aircraft drop into the sea, followed by two crew members who had managed to bale out. The pilot, Francesco Solimena and the observer, Alfredo Balsamo, were picked up by the destroyer, HMS *Diamond*. The second pilot and two others were killed. These were the first enemy airmen shot down over Malta and they became prisoners of war.

The message that Dobbie had written to the War Office on 12 June saw the welcome arrival of five Hurricanes. They landed on Malta on 13 June, but instructions for them to remain on the island had not got through and to Air Commodore Maynard's distress, after refuelling they took off again. Two more Hurricanes arrived; again their intention was to fly onto Egypt. Six more arrived on 22 June. The aircraft were flown by Ferry Pool pilots: all were shocked to discover that they were to become part of Malta Fighter Flight. Just one of the pilots had combat experience. The defence of Malta now primarily passed over to the Hurricanes, rather than the Gladiators.

On the very same day, at 18.50, the French signed an armistice with the Germans at Compiegne. Henceforth the Germans would occupy

Northern France. The remainder of France and the colonies, including those in North Africa, would remain 'free' to be governed by the French. French North Africa, consisting of Morocco, Algeria and Tunisia, was effectively enemy-held territory. Less than a fortnight before the entire coastline of the Mediterranean had either been in Allied hands or had been neutral. Now over 60 per cent of it was in enemy hands. The only ports open to the British were Malta, Palestine, Gibraltar and Egypt. Malta's strategic position was now even more crucial. Winston Churchill saw Malta as being the potentially vital base from which to launch offensive operations. Malta was now isolated, potentially difficult to resupply, yet a vital link between Britain, Gibraltar and the Middle East.

Burges's attack on the Italian aircraft caused the Italians to reconsider their flights over Malta and, from this point on, the bombers were protected by fighters. Once again, Burges was aloft on 23 June, intercepting bombers when a Macchi 200 came straight for him. Burges made a turn and fired a burst of machine-gun fire into the enemy fighter's tail. The Italian aircraft turned and came back at him: once again Burges turned and shot into the tail. The Italian made the same manoeuvre for a third time and this time Burges after opening fire again saw black smoke belching from the enemy aircraft's engine. The pilot, Lamberto Molinelli, baled out, dropped into the sea and was picked up by a naval craft. Burges visited the Italian in the Mtarfa capital's military hospital. The Italian was plainly angered by the fact that his modern aircraft had been shot down by an ageing biplane.

On Malta the need to strengthen air raid precautions and build shelters was obvious if the island was to withstand constant raids by the Italians. There was a stretch of railway tunnel at Floriana; the only other large shelter was in the dockyards. The first step was to create a Home Defence Force and Special Constabulary: around 5,000 people volunteered. The Home Guard would take care of enemy parachutists but adequate air raid warnings were necessary. For many the first they knew that there was an attack was when the anti-aircraft defences opened fire. Shelters were dug into the bastion walls and tunnels dug, many of them interconnecting for emergency escape. Most of them were excavated by the people themselves, or voluntary workers. Quarrymen were required to register. The workers had the advantage that they were cutting into limestone: this was easy to tunnel into and once exposed to sea air it became hard and far less prone to collapse. Also working underground was a listening post at Lascaris, near Valletta. Here signals were intercepted, indicating enemy movement both in North Africa and in Sicily.

Areas that had not been previously used for growing crops were turned over to food production. Both the golf course and the polo ground became market gardens. Elsewhere, the life of the island tried to continue on a normal basis, albeit with rationed fuel, power and food and drink stocks. The authorities also extended the curfew hours. Initially the curfew ran from 20.30 to 05.00, although by the end of August it was changed to 22.00 to 06.00.

An inventory of vehicles was also made. The island's 585 buses were invariably commandeered for military use. There were 816 lorries, 170 vans, 1,875 private cars, 671 hire cars and 341 motorcycles. By mid-July the bulk of the vehicles were banned to conserve fuel. By October even the taxis and hire cars were banned and bus schedules were cut back, causing enormous inconvenience to people, as they had been evacuated from the main areas of business and had to commute into work.

There were further Italian air attacks on Wednesday 26 June when a number of civilians were killed at Birkirkara, Gzira, Marsa, Mqabba, Paola, Qormi, Valletta, Vittoriosa and Zejtun. The following day Malta suffered its twenty-eighth air raid, at 21.15.

On Saturday 29 June, nine Italian bombers in groups of three approached the island. The Malta Flight scrambled to intercept them and one of the enemy aircraft seemed to be badly damaged and, belching smoke from its tail, disappeared into low cloud. By the end of June there had been twenty-one air raid alerts and the Italians had dropped approximately 170 tons of bombs on the island. The RAF station at Kalafrana had been bombed on two occasions but as yet there had been no casualties.

On 3 July a pair of SM79s, protected by nine Fiat CR42s, approached the island in the morning on a reconnaissance mission. A Hurricane, which was already aloft, intercepted and managed to shoot down one of the SM79s around 5 miles out of Kalafrana. The crew was seen to bale out but none were picked up. On 4 July the Italians mounted a low level attack on Kalafrana. The raider flew over the base and then headed towards Hal Far. The station's air defences opened up but failed to hit the raider. On Saturday and Sunday, 6 and 7 July, there were a number of air raids, widespread across the island. Many of the victims were children.

On the previous Friday a French Latecoere 298B torpedo float plane had arrived at Kalafrana at 23.00 hours from Bizerta in Tunisia. The two crew members volunteered to join the RAF. The aircraft would prove to be extremely useful in the future and would be used for reconnaissance missions over Sicily and North Africa. Ultimately its crew would be attached to No. 230 Squadron, at Kalafrana.

On 8 July a fleet under Admiral Sir Andrew Browne Cunningham in his flagship HMS *Warspite* left Alexandria, bound for Malta. The Italian battle fleet had been spotted 200 miles to the east of Malta, heading south. Aircraft from Malta were ordered to shadow the enemy vessels. However it was the Italians who found the British first and Italian reconnaissance planes, closely followed by bombers, began attacking the fleet. A British flying boat spotted the Italian fleet moving back towards Italy and Cunningham changed course hoping to cut the Italian ships off from their base. By the morning of 8 July he was just 90 miles to the west of them. Although the British were outnumbered and out-gunned, he moved to engage. The fleet came within range at 15.00 hours. HMS *Warspite* began trading shots with the enemy cruisers at a range of 13 miles. The Italians retreated under a smoke screen. Cunningham pressed on and *Warspite* opened up on two Italian battleships just before 16.00. At precisely 16.00 there was a massive explosion on the Italian flagship funnel and a huge cloud of black smoke. The Italian Admiral Riccardi again pulled back under thick smoke.

The Italians were clearly in confusion and had even been bombed by their own aircraft. Cunningham threw his destroyers and cruisers forward and as he did so the Italian air force appeared overhead. There were hundreds of aircraft swarming to attack the British fleet. They attempted to bracket the *Warspite* on five occasions, but Cunningham was undaunted and by that evening was just 25 miles south of the Italian coast having achieved his objective of protecting the convoys heading to Alexandria. He took the fleet south but ran into air attacks from Italian aircraft based in Libya. His mission accomplished he took the decision to head back towards Alexandria but despite once again coming under attack from Italian aircraft the *Warspite* returned unscathed.

By 9 July George Burges was now flying a Hurricane. He was on morning watch and had spent two hours sitting on the airfield waiting to take off should there be an air-raid alert. He suddenly heard the order to scramble and minutes later he was aloft accompanied by a second Hurricane. Three enemy aircraft had been spotted 10 miles out from St Paul's Bay, at a height of 15,000 ft. The Hurricanes encountered a single bomber escorted by Fiat biplanes. Burges got behind the bomber and shot it down. The other pilot managed to get one of the Italian biplanes. Rome Radio later reported that they had engaged a pair of Spitfires over Malta and had shot one of them down.

On 13 July Burges was awarded the Distinguished Flying Cross for his courageous action so far in the defence of Malta. On the same day, a dozen CR42s were intercepted by a single Hurricane and a Gladiator. By this stage the island had a single operational Hurricane and a pair of Gladiators. They were desperately hoping for more aircraft. It seemed that the Italians were intent on wearing down the island's fighter cover, as each group of bombers was now protected by large formations of fighters.

Flight Lieutenant Keeble was the first RAF pilot lost over the island on 16 July. He had engaged a CR42 and the two pilots had managed to shoot one another down; they were both killed.

The Gladiator's charmed lives came to an end on the last day of July. The pilot managed to bale out into the sea, but he was suffering from extensive burns. By the end of the month twelve Italian aircraft had been shot down but the Malta Fighter Flight now just had three serviceable aircraft. Churchill was adamant that they needed to be reinforced. HMS *Argus* steamed into the Mediterranean on 31 July with twelve Hurricanes onboard. They were to be escorted by a pair of Skuas and all the aircraft arrived safely on 2 August.

The pilots were experienced, having already flown during the battle of Britain. The men had reported to RAF Uxbridge and it was not until they had actually reached the Mediterranean that they were told that they would be operating out of Malta. The men had been given to believe that they would simply be ferrying the Hurricanes to the island and that they would be taken back to Gibraltar by flying boat and then onward back to England. None of them had taken anything with them and now they would be operating as the new Malta Fighter Flight out of Luqa. They would become No. 261 Squadron on 16 August. Luckily they were to have a period of orientation, without any significant Italian aircraft presence, as raids had virtually stopped after the fleet action that Cunningham had fought at the beginning of July.

The day before, on 15 August, ten SM79s and nineteen CR42s had approached Hal Far. Four Hurricanes went aloft to intercept and managed to shoot down one of the CR42s, but a Hurricane, flown by Sergeant Roy O'Donnell, was shot down and his body was not recovered.

Nine days later, on 24 August, Kalafrana and Hal Far were raided by six SM79s covered by seventeen CR42s. Again four Hurricanes intercepted and a CR42, flown by Renzo Bocconi, was shot down. He managed to bale out and was picked up and taken as a prisoner of war.

A tempting target for the Italians left Alexandria bound for Malta at 23.00 hours on 29 August. There were three supply ships with a close escort of four destroyers. To protect these, an aircraft carrier, two battleships, five cruisers and nine destroyers shadowed the convoy. The fleet was attacked by Five SM79s which struck at noon on 31 August; there were three hits on one of the supply ships, the *Cornwall* which caused it to list and the convoy slowed down but pressed on for Malta. The island was in sight on 2 September and they managed to sail into the Grand Harbour and deliver 40,000 tons of supplies.

HMS *Illustrious* left Gibraltar for Alexandria on 30 August. She would be escorted by Gibraltar-based surface vessels as far as Sicily, where she would then be picked up by the Mediterranean Fleet. This was part of a grand plan by Cunningham and Rear Admiral Lyster to attack the Italian fleet and to seize control of the Mediterranean. As if to announce its arrival, half a dozen Swordfish flew into Malta on 2 September from HMS *Illustrious*. Two days later, on 4 September, German aircraft made their first appearance over Malta. However, they were not piloted by members of the *Luftwaffe*, but by Italian crews. This was the first raid of this type and they had come to attack shipping in the Grand Harbour, but, due to lack of targets, they bombed Kalafrana instead at around 18.00: luckily they caused little or no damage.

Another new arrival appeared on 6 September, with the appearance of three Marylands touching down at Luqa after seven hours flight from England. They had flown straight over France and had photographed Sardinia *en route*. They would become a vital photographic reconnaissance flight. Each of the Marylands had a crew of three. They were American built aircraft and spares were clearly going to be a problem. The three aircraft became No. 431 Reconnaissance Flight.

The island was also soon to have a submarine base established there. Cunningham was concerned about the lack of submarine cover in the Mediterranean and the submarines being used were far too old. Consequently, on 7 September Commander George Simpson was ordered to Malta to become the commander of the new submarine base. The base would be in the middle of Marsamxett Harbour on an island that had been a former quarantine hospital. One of its inhabitants had been Lord Byron, who had stayed there in 1811. His name was amongst the hundreds carved into the walls. In charge of preparing the base was Lieutenant Commander R G Giddings. The Admiralty proposed that submarines would begin operating out of Malta from the beginning of 1941.

Meanwhile the Italian attacks on the island continued unabated. On 14 September Italian bombers hit Valletta and Kalafrana, on the following day Ju87s, escorted by fighters, attacked Hal Far airfield. On the 17th another twelve Ju87s, supported by twenty-one CR42s and six Macchi 200s struck Luqa airfield. On this occasion the Hurricanes scrambled to intercept the raid and as the Italians made off a Ju87, piloted by Luigi Catani, was shot down off Filfla and his gunner was killed. The RAF Air Sea Rescue boat ST280 rescued the remaining crew and they became prisoners of war. Catani explained his experiences under interrogation:

> I was in the Ju87B and was brought down after a combat with two fighters. We, the dive bombers, came from Pantelleria and met the fighters over Malta, at least that is my impression as I was one of a crowd and followed my leaders. We left Pantelleria at 9.30 CET. There were about twelve of us and I do not know how many fighters there were. This was my first trip to Malta. It is only a week since I became a dive-bomber pilot. We arrived over Malta at 4,000 m and I came down to under 800 m. My motor was not working at its best and as I was the last I became separated from the others.

Throughout September there had been twenty-five air raid alerts over Malta and the Italians had dropped 163 tons of bombs. Malta had appeared as a major feature in *The Times* back in England:

> Malta as a fortress is, perhaps, stronger than it ever was, and it would be a bold enemy who would attempt its reduction and capture. But it is one of the most thickly populated places in the world, and thus an attractive target to an enemy who counts terrorism among his weapons. Malta stands or falls by sea power, and the spirit of its people, while Britain holds command of the sea, the prowess of the garrison on land and the staunchness of the people are assured of constant support, which is all they need to beat off any foe.

Indeed, Cunningham had not been idle. He had ferried 2,000 troops to Malta by the end of September and was aiming to deal a sizeable blow to the Italian fleet. On 11 October HMS *Ajax* had sunk two enemy destroyers and badly damaged a third. The following day an Italian destroyer was finished off by HMS *York*. Meanwhile, Italian-held Leros in the Dodecanese had been attacked by Swordfish operating off HMS *Eagle* and HMS *Illustrious*.

Cunningham's intended target, however, was the Italian fleet at anchor in Taranto. The photo reconnaissance mission was launched from Malta on 9 October. Each of the key Italian targets were positively identified and confirmed. The attack would take place on the next suitable moon, which was 11 November.

Meanwhile, over Malta, on 9 October a night-fighter Hurricane intercepted five SM79s attacking Kalafrana. The pilot of the Hurricane was assisted by searchlights on Malta which helped pick out the Italian attackers resulting in an SM79 being shot down. There were no survivors, but one of the bodies was washed ashore on 15 October.

Two days later another convoy arrived in Malta from Port Said consisting of four supply ships. Also, HMS *Illustrious* helped reinforce Malta's air defences with the arrival of Fairey Fulmar fighters. They were a big improvement on HMS *Eagle*'s Sea Gladiators. HMS *Illustrious* had also brought in some replacement aircraft to reinforce 830 Naval Air Squadron.

No. 431 Reconnaissance Flight overflew Taranto almost every day. On 7 November one of these aircraft, piloted by Adrian Warburton, was chased back to Malta by four Macchi 200s. Three days later he photographed five battleships, fourteen cruisers and twenty-seven destroyers in Taranto Harbour. He also confirmed the arrival of another battleship on 11 November. By this stage Cunningham was about to give final approval to the attack on Taranto from HMS *Illustrious*. By 20.00 on 11 November she was in position 170 miles from Taranto. The first squadron took off at 20.35 and they arrived over the harbour and attacked just before 23.00. A second squadron engaged their targets just before midnight. From the squadrons just two Swordfish were lost but the Swordfish had managed to sink or badly damage three battleships, while a cruiser and two destroyers had also been damaged. The damage was confirmed by No. 431 Reconnaissance Flight when 'Titch' Whiteley overflew Taranto the following morning. As a consequence of this attack the Italians withdrew their fleet to Naples. Cunningham was delighted with the results. The balance of sea power in the Mediterranean was now firmly back with the British.

The attack had been made possible by the reconnaissance flights flown out of Malta. Air Commodore Maynard received a letter dated 14 November from Cunningham himself:

> I hasten to write to you a line to thank you for the most valuable reconnaissance work carried out by your squadrons, without which the successful attack on Taranto would have

been impossible. I well know what long monotonous flying time they have had to put in and I am very grateful to them. The work over Taranto has been particularly valuable and gave us all we wanted to know. Good luck and my grateful thanks again for your cooperation.

On 9 November another supply convoy from Port Said arrived at Malta and three days later a Maltese-based Hurricane shot down a Macchi 200 just off St Thomas Bay. A Maltese-based trawler recovered the body of the pilot.

A much needed delivery of Hurricanes arrived on 17 November. Twelve Hurricanes had taken off from HMS *Argus*, but unfortunately only four reached Malta; the others ran out of fuel and ditched into the Mediterranean. A Sunderland managed to pick up one of the pilots, Sergeant Spyer. Thankfully, there were other successful reinforcements throughout November. Around 20,000 tons of supplies arrived, along with new ground crew, anti-aircraft guns and the 4th Battalion of the Royal East Kent Regiment. In all, around 3,500 service personnel had been sent to reinforce the island.

Warburton continued his reconnaissance flights and wrote of one of his early experiences after Taranto, towards the end of 1940:

> I was entering the Bay of Naples from the southwest at 1,500 ft when I saw an SM79 with brown mottled camouflage heading across my track. The clouds were at 2,000 ft in a solid bank, so if fighters appeared I could retire. I therefore made a stern attack; some pieces of the tail flew off and my rounds started going into the fuselage. I closed the range and concentrated on the starboard engine which started to smoke and eventually stopped. My rear gunner wanted to try the new turret, so I broke away and drew parallel to the SM79, slightly above and about 100 yards to his starboard. My rear gunner put in a burst of about twenty rounds which ignited the petrol, and the SM79 burst into a mass of flames and dived into the sea from 1,000 ft, disappearing immediately. I then carried on with my recce of Naples and returned to Luqa.

On 18 November a new type of warfare was then begun over Malta. The Italians were now risking single aircraft attacks. One was intercepted by a Hurricane pilot who was flying at 15,000 ft. He clearly saw the SM79 illuminated by search lights operating around the Grand

Harbour and Kalafrana. He dived down to 10,000 ft and engaged the bomber. He saw it fall in flames into the sea two miles out of Kalafrana.

Three Macchi 200s were on a reconnaissance patrol on 26 November. One was shot down by a Hurricane. The pilot's body was recovered by Air Sea Rescue launch HSL107. In the same engagement the Hurricane pilot, Sergeant Dennis Ashton was shot down to the south of Malta and killed.

Additional supplies came in on 26 and 29 November. The convoy on 29 November was accompanied by an aircraft carrier and a battle cruiser. Throughout the month Sunderlands belonging to Nos 228 and 230 Squadrons had flown upwards of thirty patrols and had also carried out nine flights between England, Gibraltar and the Middle East, carrying both passengers and mail. Throughout the month there had been thirty-two air raids and the Italian bomb tonnage had dropped to just 64 tons.

The eagerly awaited submarine reinforcements for the island left Portsmouth harbour on 10 December. HMS *Upholder*, commanded by First Lieutenant Michael Crawford, was bound for the island. It was a brand new Unity class submarine, around 540 tons. It was smaller than German and Italian U-boats and much slower. There was a complement of around thirty and it was tightly packed inside with barely enough room for the crew.

By the end of the month of December there had been eighteen air raids and 18 tons of bombs dropped on Malta. However, the *Luftwaffe* had begun to arrive in Sicily. It was inevitable that operations would intensify against Malta. This was primarily in order to subdue the island to ensure that men and supplies could safely reach Rommel in North Africa. The Italians turned over a number of airbases to the *Luftwaffe*, primarily at Comisco, Catania, Gela, Gerbini, Palermo and Trapani. Rather than just facing Italian aircraft, the air defenders of Malta would now face Heinkels, Junkers and Messerschmitts.

CHAPTER THREE
THE *ILLUSTRIOUS* BLITZ

The Germans had originally intended to leave Malta in the hands of the Italians whilst they concentrated on the Russian offensive, which was to be launched in the summer of 1941. However Italian inaction and reversals forced them to adopt a more positive role.

By January 1941 Italian ground troops were in retreat in North Africa and with their losses at Taranto they had proved to be incapable of commanding the Mediterranean waters. A complete coastal air group, *Fliegerkorps* X, was transferred from Norway to Sicily. They had 260 frontline aircraft, the majority of which were Stuka dive bombers and Me109 fighters.

On Malta, by the beginning of 1941 the defensive and offensive capabilities had been enhanced: there were sixteen Wellington bombers and two squadrons of Blenheims but there were just sixteen Hurricanes. However, 830 Squadron's Swordfish were active and a constant threat to the Italian navy. Despite the Italian bombing, the dockyards were still in working order and after the attack on Taranto, with the Italians losing half of their battleships in one night, the Italian navy had effectively lost control of the Sicily channel. Any of their vessels using Sicily, Taranto or Naples were under extreme threat. Their land forces, reliant on their supply port of Tripoli, were prey to constant Allied air attack. Shipping routes to North Africa were in danger from numerous magnetic mines. The Italian position was woeful and the Germans could not afford to have their position undermined by the Italian failures.

The obvious solution for the Germans was to launch an invasion of Malta. This was proposed by Admiral Raeder, who was the commander in chief of the German navy. Although he and Herman Goering did not get on, they both agreed that Malta needed to be neutralized and the British Mediterranean Fleet crippled. The first step would be to destroy HMS *Illustrious*. It had been HMS *Illustrious*'s Swordfish that had inflicted heavy damage on the Italian fleet in Taranto harbour in November 1940.

When the Germans moved their 10th Air Corps to Sicily, just 60 miles from Malta, they had a greater striking power than all the RAF and Fleet Air Arm assets in the Mediterranean. Added to this, the British forces had to cover the whole of the Mediterranean from Gibraltar to Alexandria, a distance of 2,000 miles. The new German arrivals boasted 150 HE111s and Ju88s. There was a similar number of Ju87s. To protect and escort them were around fifty Me109s. Rather than focusing on attacking Malta, the first priority would be to destroy British shipping starting with the Mediterranean Fleet then HMS *Illustrious* and then any other targets of opportunity.

An opportunity to strike against HMS *Illustrious* would soon come. The British were about to initiate Operation Excess. This was a convoy of merchant ships whose cargoes included twelve Hurricanes in crates, 4,000 tons of ammunition and 3,000 tons of seed potatoes, which were specifically earmarked for Malta onboard the cargo ship *Essex*. Four other vessels were due to sail onto Alexandria. The convoy left British waters along with a larger convoy that was heading for South Africa. The convoy encountered the German heavy cruiser, *Hipper*, on Christmas Day, *en route* to Gibraltar. Force H (a naval formation based in Gibraltar that had been assembled from vessels taken from the Home Fleet) was dispatched from Gibraltar and managed to bring all but one of the ships to safety (the lost ship had been bound for Alexandria and was driven ashore). The convoy left Gibraltar on 6 January 1941. Force H would cover the convoy as far as Sicily and from then on its protection would be in the hands of the Mediterranean Fleet, including HMS *Illustrious*.

Cunningham left Alexandria on 7 January onboard HMS *Warspite*. By 10 January he was to the north-west of Malta, ready to meet the convoy. Covering the fleet from the air were Fulmars of HMS *Illustrious*. Although Force H was supposed to protect the convoy until the Mediterranean Fleet arrived, in fact, Force H left the convoy at dusk on 9 January. Two cruisers, HMS *Gloucester* and HMS *Southampton*, along with a pair of destroyers, waited with the convoy.

Suddenly, above Cunningham's fleet, at 12.30, a pair of Italian torpedo bombers was spotted. They moved in for an attack and the Fulmars descended to engage. However, the two Italian aircraft were the least of Cunningham's problems, as an enormous number of German aircraft appeared. More Fulmars took off from HMS *Illustrious* as the Germans moved in to attack the aircraft carrier. Cunningham's fleet filled the sky with anti-aircraft fire, but forty Stukas, peeling off one at a time, dived in to attack from around 2,000 ft.

Cunningham had taken an enormous risk by bringing the *Illustrious* so close to the operational area of the newly arrived German air force. He clearly believed that the aircraft carrier would not only provide cover for the fleet, but also the fleet itself would be perfectly capable of protecting the aircraft carrier but he had never encountered dive-bomb attacks before. The Stuka attacks lasted for 6½ minutes and in that time HMS *Illustrious* was hit six times, the bridge was narrowly missed and an explosion in the hangar set fire to aircraft parked there. Two more bombs fell through the aircraft lift and soon there were fires across the whole of the vessel and thick, black smoke everywhere. HMS *Illustrious* had to get to a safe haven for vital repairs to take place. She had been hit by 1,000 lb bombs and her armour plating was only really capable of dealing with 500 lb bombs. Fireproof screens in the hangar had been torn to pieces, part of the ship's anti-aircraft batteries had been knocked out, yet her commanding officer, Captain Denis Boyd, managed to continue to manoeuvre before the steering was crippled. Boyd refused to flood the magazines and in 3 hours he had managed to nurse her back to 17 knots and was *en route* to Malta.

The *Illustrious*'s remaining Fulmars also headed for Malta, landing at Hal Far to rearm and refuel. But, HMS *Illustrious* was not yet out of danger: just off Malta she was attacked by Italian torpedo bombers. Some of her anti-aircraft batteries were still in operation and the Italian aircraft decided that discretion was the better part of valour and peeled away. Another twenty-five dive bombers attacked, but by now the Fulmars had been refuelled and they managed to shoot down six Stukas, allowing the badly listing HMS *Illustrious* to pull into the Grand Harbour at 21.45 on 10 January.

Tugs and minesweepers helped her into the port and she berthed at Parlatorio Wharf. A total of 126 of her crew had been killed and a further ninety-one wounded. The cargo ship *Essex* had reached Malta in safety and the three ships that were bound for Alexandria had also got away. Sixty of the wounded were sent to Imtarfa Hospital. Beds had been made ready and medical staff was *en route* to help out. Many of the men were badly burned. Everyone knew that it would only be a matter of time before the Germans returned to try and finish off HMS *Illustrious*. Hundreds of dockyard workers appeared at daybreak, desperate to help and repair and refit the vessel. Despite the casualties onboard *HMS Illustrious*, the ship and the rest of her crew had been extremely fortunate in that the fires had not set off ammunition or fuel.

Of equal importance was the unloading of the merchantman *Essex*. There were twelve Hurricanes onboard and the ammunition that she carried would undoubtedly be needed to beat off any enemy air attack. The anti-aircraft guns onboard were found to be buried under 3,000 tons of potatoes.

Amazingly the Germans did not return on 11 January; just a handful of Italian bombers. This was a great surprise as the Italians had been extremely active on 9 January, when sixteen Macchi 200s had attacked Luqa airfield. Nine Italian Ju87s, with an escort of ten CR42s, had bombed ships in Marsaxlokk Bay and then bombed Kalafrana. A Hurricane had shot down one of the Macchi 200s and the Italian pilot now found himself in Mtarfa Hospital, surrounded by some of the wounded and injured from HMS *Illustrious*.

The Germans reappeared, supported by the Italians, on 16 January. It was just before 14.00 hours. The Germans had sent forty-four Stukas, seventeen Ju88s, ten Me110s and the Italians ten CR42s and some Macchi 200s. The main target was, of course, HMS *Illustrious*. The anti-aircraft guns opened up first and the Stukas had to dive through the wall of fire. A second attack followed then another, fifteen minutes later. Each time the waters around HMS *Illustrious* were churned and lifted in enormous spouts. The aircraft carrier vanished in the spray, but her guns never stopped firing back. The Germans managed to hit her just once on the quarterdeck, but near misses left the dockyard around cratered and in flames. A handful of Hurricanes and Fulmars were aloft, trying to break up the German and Italian attack. Another bomb hit the cargo ship *Essex*, killing fifteen and wounding twenty-three.

A Royal Artillery officer said of the action:

> I was on a light anti-aircraft gun position in the harbour area for one of these attacks, and I can still see clearly a German bomber diving through that terrific curtain of steel, followed by a Fulmar. The bomber dropped his bomb and proceeded to sneak his way through the harbour entrance only a few inches above the water. He was so low that he had to rise to clear the breakwater, which is only some 15 ft high. He was obviously wobbling badly, and as he rose the Fulmar pilot shot him down into the sea on the far side of the breakwater. The Fulmar pilot then landed at his airfield, and I later received a message from him to say that he didn't think much of our barrage! However, he never flew that particular plane again, so badly was it damaged.

The Stukas were ably flown and the pilots were undoubtedly brave in facing the barrage of anti-aircraft fire. The Ju87s were carrying 2,500 lb bombs and with that amount of weight took 90 minutes to reach 10,000 ft. Casualties around the dockyard were heavy: over fifty Maltese civilians were killed and there was significant damage to houses in Senglea, on the other side of the Grand Harbour. Rescuers struggled to dig people out of their homes and some of the streets were buried in as much as 10 ft of rubble. Between them the anti-aircraft positions and the fighters claimed ten German aircraft.

Poor weather prevented the Germans from attacking until 18 January. This time the primary focus was on Luqa and Hal Far airfields. The Germans' idea was clearly to eliminate the fighters so that they could finish off HMS *Illustrious* without hindrance. Eighty German aircraft attacked the two airfields, putting Luqa out of service for some time.

The following day, at 08.30, the Germans struck again. It was a heavy raid. The British claimed that they had shot down thirty-nine, plus five probable and nine damaged. The Hurricanes and Fulmars claimed seventeen of the losses. The Germans admitted to ten and the Italians to four. British losses were two. By 19 January fighter cover over Malta amounted to six Hurricanes, a single Fulmar and one Gladiator. A sergeant in the Royal Marines, manning a battery of Fort St Angelo, said:

> The Sunday raids were interesting and exciting. We had two visits from Gerry. Bombs were dropped in around all the creeks, causing terrific clouds of dust, flying masonry and iron. Although I did not see it myself, it was stated that a complete motorcar went sailing over the top of us. The dust and spray often blinded our view but the dive bombers always came on. As they broke through the dust they seemed like hawks looking for prey. The sight was one never to be forgotten, the bursts of the heavies, the red tracers of the Bofors and light machine guns, and the illumination made by the crashing planes all adding to the splendour of the day. Since these attacks I have witnessed many more dive bombing attacks from the same position and more concentrated on us. Although tragic, I must say that it is very exciting and good sport to be having a crack at a dive bomber. You lose all sense of fear and self preservation while it lasts. You get the same feeling as being at a football final.

On the morning of the 19th an Italian Cant Z506B, belonging to the Italian Red Cross, began looking for a downed Ju88. The Italian crew spotted wreckage off Valletta. It was immediately pounced on by a pair of Hurricanes, who promptly shot it down. In the afternoon a second

Cant came out to look for the Red Cross plane, but only spotted wreckage. Another Ju88, having attacked the Grand Harbour, flew south towards Kalafrana. A Hurricane shot it down and crashed into a bay near Zonqor Point. A fourth raid saw a Hurricane shoot down an Italian CR42.

On 20 January Winston Churchill sent a message to Dobbie:

> I send you, on behalf of the War Cabinet, heartfelt congratulations upon the magnificent and ever memorable defence of your heroic garrison and citizens, assisted by the Royal Navy and, above all, the Royal Air Force, that you are making against the German and Italian attacks. The eyes of all Britain, indeed, the whole British Empire, are watching Malta in her struggle, day by day and we are sure that success as well as glory will reward your efforts.

In recounting Churchill's stirring words, Dobbie broadcast to the Maltese people:

> We are living in stirring times, and Malta, like other parts of the British Empire, is taking its share in the momentous happenings.

In the first three weeks of January alone 950 enemy aircraft had attacked Malta with an average of 150 sorties a week but, luckily, bad weather, including gales, electrical storms and low cloud cover, had impeded the enemy. The race was on to make sure that HMS *Illustrious* was seaworthy in order for her to leave the Grand Harbour for the comparative safety of Alexandria.

On 23 January, sailing under her own power at a speed of 23 knots, the principal target of the *Luftwaffe* left Malta. The Italians were certain that as a fighting vessel she was finished, proudly proclaiming:

> The damage suffered is of such proportions that she will be out of service for the duration of the war.

Although the blitz on the *Illustrious* was over, this was not the end of air operations in January 1941. Gustav Ulrich, the pilot of a Ju88, became a victim of one of Malta's Gladiators on 24 January when he and his crew were shot down on a reconnaissance sortie. Earlier that day a Cant on patrol was also shot down by a Maltese-based fighter. Spirits were lifted on 28 January when six new Hurricanes arrived from Egypt accompanied by a Wellington, which also carried three replacement fighter pilots. On the 29th another six pilots arrived in a Sunderland.

Several New Zealand pilots were already operating as members of the RAF. One such was Flight Sergeant Hyde who had arrived in August 1940 and served nine months with No. 261 Squadron. Another New Zealand pilot, Pilot Officer Langdon, was killed in air operations in February 1941, having transferred to the RAF in June 1940 from the Royal New Zealand Air Force.

Throughout the month of January there were actually sixteen bombing raids out of the fifty-seven air raid alerts. The majority of the bombs were dropped in an attempt to sink HMS *Illustrious*. Between them the Germans and Italians dropped 423 tons of bombs. The blitz on the *Illustrious*, for many, meant the beginning of the siege proper. They were unaware of the fact that the frenzied attempts by the Germans in particular to silence the island would be short-lived. They would not be able to sustain the kind of attacks that they had launched against HMS *Illustrious* and, in any case, the Russian campaign beckoned. However for now the impetus was with the Germans and for the short period of time that they would still be operational in this theatre they were determined to make their mark.

CHAPTER FOUR

LUFTWAFFE ONSLAUGHT

Air Vice Marshal Maynard said at the beginning of February 1941: 'They don't like us.' The Germans were certainly throwing as many aircraft as possible at the island in an attempt to subdue the defenders. Day and night there were large scale raids and attempts to lay mines in the waters around the Grand Harbour.

The first major air raid of the month was launched on 4 February. Upwards of 100 enemy aircraft struck against Hal Far, Luqa and Kalafrana. Whenever possible the Germans and the Italians were still dropping their parachute mines and although a system of mine watching and sweeping was brought in, many of the mines struck the sides of the dockyards, cratering and blasting the area. If anything, the air war above Malta was beginning to intensify.

On 8 February half a dozen Hurricanes were scrambled to intercept the night raiders. A Hurricane chanced on an HE111, flying at about 10,000 ft above Rabat. The German aircraft crashed into the sea. The following day Me109s of 7 *Staffel* (*Jagdgeschwader* 26) arrived in Sicily. Most of the pilots were very experienced, having fought in the battle of Britain in the previous year. The *Luftwaffe* was clearly attempting to achieve air superiority and this would only add pressure to the dwindling numbers of Hurricanes and their pilots.

Three days later the Me109s appeared in the skies over the island of Malta. At the same time Hurricanes belonging to B Flight No. 126 Squadron scrambled to intercept a trio of Ju88s, reported to be flying at 20,000 ft. As the Hurricanes climbed to intercept they were pounced on by the Me109s. Pilot Officer D J Thacker's aircraft was badly hit and lost height. He managed to get over St Paul's Bay at around 5,000 ft, when suddenly the Hurricane's engine cut and he was forced to bale out. He was only in the water for around three quarters of an hour before HSL107 picked him up. Two other Hurricanes were also roughly dealt with by the Me109s. Flight Lieutenant Gerald Watson lost his life when his Hurricane flipped over as he hit the sea. His body was never found. Flight Lieutenant Bradbury was more fortunate: he managed to coax his badly shot-up Hurricane back to the airfield, where he managed to make a forced landing.

It was clear that the Hurricanes were no match for the Me109s. On 16 February the experience of an encounter between the Hurricane Mark Is and the Me109s was described in a combat report written by Flight Lieutenant MacLachlan:

> While on patrol over Luqa at 20,000 ft, we were attacked from above and astern by six Me109s. As previously arranged the flight broke away to the right and formed a defensive circle. As I took my place in the circle I saw four more Me109s coming down out of the sun. Just as they came within range I turned back towards them and they all overshot me without firing. I looked very carefully but could see no more enemy aircraft above me, so I turned back to the tail of the nearest 109. I was turning well inside him and was just about to open fire when I was hit in the left arm by a cannon shell. My dashboard was completely smashed, so I baled out and landed safely by parachute.

MacLachlan lost his arm when it had to be amputated at Imtarfa Military Hospital. The loss of his arm did not prevent the Flight Lieutenant from getting back into a Hurricane. Soon after his recovery from the amputation a colleague took him up for a test flight: he managed to land the aircraft by himself. A few days later he flew a Hurricane and then asked whether he could rejoin the squadron. Ultimately he was returned to Britain, where he did indeed continue to fly with great success.

There were continual raids through the first and second week of February 1941 and 17 February saw the island being raided for the eleventh night in succession. The Germans had so far failed to prevent the British from continuing to use the harbour and the airfields were still operational.

The island suffered a succession of alerts on 25 February, during which two German bombers were shot down. In the afternoon Canadian Pilot Officer John Walsh was on patrol over the island. He was attacked whilst he was flying at around 27,000 ft, over St Paul's Bay. He was forced to bale out, but managed to land a few hundred metres from a naval vessel. One of Walsh's legs had been broken in four places and he also had a broken arm. It was likely that he had hit his own tail plane when he baled out. Unfortunately Walsh died of pneumonia.

On 26 February one of the biggest raids on the island so far was launched. Around thirty-eight Ju87s, twelve Ju88s, ten Dorniers and ten

HE111s were escorted by up to thirty enemy fighters. They seemed to be making for Luqa as their primary target when they were spotted at around 13.00 hours. Anti-aircraft defences opened up on them and eight Hurricanes took off to intercept. However, the main force of bombers passing over the island at between 6,000 and 8,000 ft covered Luqa airfield in bombs. Half a dozen Wellingtons were burned out and seven more were badly damaged. There was also damage to some Marylands that were parked on the airfield. The airfield itself was badly cratered, with severe damage to hangars and workshops and would be out of service for 48 hours. The anti-aircraft crews claimed five of the Ju87 dive bombers, with four probable and one damaged. The Hurricanes had two confirmed kills and eleven probable. However, the RAF losses for the day were five Hurricanes, and three pilots were lost.

This was not the end of the action for the day: two German airmen from a Ju87 were picked up by an Air Sea Rescue launch HSL107. The men had been hanging onto a lifebuoy. An Me109 also attacked a pair of fishing boats off Gozo. Later in the afternoon, a Red Cross sea-plane was spotted, escorted by German aircraft, hunting downed crew members. The Germans attempted another major attack later, with dive bombers coming in, dodging the bursting shells of the anti-aircraft batteries.

With the losses on the ground and in the air, it was becoming clear that the Germans were slowly gaining air superiority. The larger formations appearing over the island showed that they were prepared to be bolder than the Italians had been in the past. Systematically they were attempting to neutralise Malta's fighter defences and to cause long-term damage to the airfields. In the course of ten days in February, all the Royal Air Force's flight leaders had been lost. Throughout the month of February there had been at least 109 air alerts, sixty-two of which had developed into raids. The Germans were being extremely selective, striking primarily at Hal Far, Luqa and the dockyards. Of the 376 tons of bombs dropped on the island, all but two tons had landed on these targets.

Malta's shrinking air resources were a major problem and would become even more so as the German air offensive intensified. A signal from Malta at the beginning of March outlined the danger the island now faced:

> Blitz raid of several formations totalling certainly no less than one hundred aircraft, of which sixty bombers attacked Hal Far. A few of these aircraft dropped bombs and machine

gunned Kalafrana. Damage to Kalafrana was slight both to buildings and aircraft. One Sunderland unserviceable for few days. Damage Hal Far still being assessed. Preliminary report as follows: three Swordfish and one Gladiator burnt out. All other aircraft temporarily unserviceable. All barrack blocks unserviceable and one demolished. Water and power cut off. Hangars considerably damaged. Airfield temporarily unserviceable. Eleven fighters up. Enemy casualties by our fighters, two Ju88s, two Ju87s, one Do215, two Me109s, confirmed. One Ju88 and three Ju87s damaged. By AA one Me110 and eight other aircraft confirmed, also four damaged. There are probably others which did not reach their base but cannot be checked. One Hurricane and one pilot lost after first shooting down one Ju87 included above. For this blitz every serviceable Hurricane and every available pilot was put up and they achieved results against extremely heavy odds. The only answer to this kind of thing is obviously more fighters and these must somehow be provided if the air defence of Malta is to be maintained.

The signal almost certainly related to the massive raid that the Germans launched on 5 March, when upwards of sixty bombers, escorted by Me109s, dropped bombs across the island. At least two German aircraft, a Ju88 and a Ju87, were definitely shot down. Two days before Carmel Camilleri, a Maltese police constable, was awarded the George Medal for his actions that had taken place on 4 November 1940. The gallantry award read:

In the early morning of 4 November 1940, a Royal Air Force aircraft crashed on a house at Qormi, and the front portion of the machine fell into a 40 ft shaft at the bottom of a deep quarry beyond the house. Moans were heard coming from the shaft, from which flames were spouting, and an injured airman was observed supporting himself under the vertical edge of the shaft. A wire rope was lowered which the airman grasped, but after being drawn up a few feet he could not maintain his hold and fell back into the shaft. PC Camilleri, who had been one of the first on the scene, immediately volunteered to go down for him, in spite of the flames from the burning aircraft and in disregard of danger from the possible explosion of heavy calibre bombs, and was lowered into the shaft. The rope slipped and he fell to the bottom, fortunately without serious injury. A third rope was lowered to which PC Camilleri tied the injured airman who was then hauled up. The rope was again lowered for Camilleri, who was brought up with no injuries beyond slight burns.

On 6 March, whilst German bombers carried out a number of attacks, and enemy fighters struck flying boat bases, five Hurricanes, led by a pair of Wellingtons, arrived from Egypt as reinforcements for the island. The following day Sergeant Jessop was attacked by an Me109 on his first flight around the island. He was picked up by HSL107. Me109s also made strafing attacks at St Paul's Bay, hitting a Sunderland flying boat. Sergeant Alan Jones, firing a Vickers machine gun, tried to beat the fighters off, but was shot and killed.

Me110s returned once again to shoot up St Paul's Bay on 10 March. They hit the same Sunderland, this time setting it on fire. The crew could not get the blaze under control and the flying boat was towed into Mistra Bay, where it eventually sank. At night large numbers of German aircraft dropped bombs and at least one was shot down by anti-aircraft fire. The Germans targeted Sliema on 11 March, killing a number of civilians and on 15 March German bombers hit the airfield once more. A mine exploded in the main harbour, killing three and wounding ten others. There were also bombing casualties in Gozo.

On 18 March half a dozen Hurricanes, led by a Wellington, arrived from Libya to replace casualties that had been inflicted on the fighter squadrons in the past few weeks. There was a brief lull in operations until 22 March, when ten Ju88s, escorted by a number of Me109s, raided the island in the afternoon. It was a particularly bad day for the RAF, as five Hurricanes were shot down, four of which hit the sea, all four pilots were drowned. There were further night attacks and reports at the same time suggested that up to twelve enemy aircraft had been claimed by anti-aircraft fire.

On 23 March a convoy reached Malta from Haifa, bringing supplies and reinforcements into the Grand Harbour. It proved to be a tempting target for the *Luftwaffe*. An air raid developed at 13.35, when thirty Ju87s, escorted by twenty Me109s, attacked the ships. Fourteen Hurricanes were sent up to intercept. They managed to shoot down nine dive bombers, anti-aircraft fire claimed another four. The cargo ships were the *City of Lincoln*, *City of Manchester*, *Clan Ferguson* and

Perthshire. Three of them were slightly damaged in the air-raid attack, as were a cruiser and destroyer that were escorting them. The Germans tried again to sink some of the convoy ships in the Grand Harbour on Monday 24 March when there was an evening attack by Ju88s with accompanying Me109s.

On the night of 25 March a Sunderland flying boat left Cairo bound for Malta. Onboard was the Foreign Secretary, Anthony Eden, the Chief of the Imperial General Staff, General Sir John Dill, the Chief of Radar Development, Robert Watson Watt, Admiral Lyster of the Fleet Air Arm and two American senior servicemen. They were making the journey from Egypt via Malta and Gibraltar to England. One of the crew members recalled the flight:

> We had taken off from the Nile at Cairo in late afternoon sun-shine and as darkness closed in we received the first message from Air HQ Malta, which warned of bad weather conditions and advised caution on landing there. This was soon followed by a second message stating sea conditions as very bad, also ten-tenths cloud cover over the island. From a fuel situation we were passed the point of no return, so we could only go on; it was Malta or nowhere. AHQ Malta had decided to beam one searchlight vertically to assist our approach. Our navigator was on top form and after a flight of about 900 miles he was spot on, almost straight ahead a patch of illuminated cloud layer indicated the searchlight position. Our very experienced captain brought the aircraft down through the cloud cover and made a good approach run. The very bad conditions prevailing in Marsaxlokk Bay made it impossible to use the normal flare path of marker buoys, so two launches with searchlights were positioned to guide us in. Our landing lights revealed a frothing, heaving sea beneath, as we hurtled in through the darkness for the touch down. There was an almighty bounce, then a series of smaller ones and finally that sturdy hull settled down into the angry sea. After finding a buoy, mooring up and with engines shut down, hearing the howling wind and the crashing waves made us all realise what a terrific landing the pilot had pulled off. Then he later admitted to us that after the first bounce 'it was in the lap of the Gods'. Our passengers seemed unperturbed and Sir Anthony made a little joke about the landing; they were then

taken ashore by launch. Our captain and VIPs came back on-board the next evening and much activity ensued. Sir Anthony and his secretaries were drafting important letters and signals, which were then taken ashore for onward transmission.

Throughout March there had been 105 air-raid alerts and 402 bombs had been dropped on the island. The pressure was still intense and the German aircraft were as active as ever.

On 3 April an Italian SM79 bomber, escorted by a pair of CR42 fighters, attempted a machine gun attack on HSL107 on patrol near Linosa. The Italians later claimed that they had sunk the boat, but she was in fact undamaged. On the same day a flight of twelve Hurricanes was flown from the aircraft carrier HMS *Ark Royal* in Operation Winch. These were newer, Mark IIAs, which it was hoped would be more than a match for the Me109s. They were also piloted by men that had had experience during the battle of Britain. The aircraft were brought in led by Skuas in two flights of six each. The aircraft had been in Gibraltar on 1 April and one of the pilots later described his experiences between 1 and 3 April when they finally landed safely in Malta:

> 1st April. At Gibraltar. We left the *Argus* and went about the *Ark* after lunch. She is the most enormous ship and carries about 160 officers and 1,600 men. Also five squadrons of aircraft. We were supposed to sail at 17.00 hours, but it was postponed. We are not allowed to go ashore, so a party started in the ward room.
>
> 2nd April. At sea. Woke up to find everything vibrating like the devil, with the ship doing 24 knots. We have HMS *Renown* and *Sheffield* and five destroyers with us. Had a long talk from the Commander (Flying) with all the other pilots on deck procedure for flying off, and then we were shown our proposed course after we take off. In addition to the Skuas who are leading us, we are picking up a Sunderland flying boat after about 100 miles which will lead us the rest of the way. Had a run over my aircraft for R/T test and ran over engine. Everything Ok.
>
> 3rd April. The arrival. Was called at 04.00 and got out of bed with a real effort. Had breakfast about half an hour later. All the knives and forks were leaping about the table because we had increased speed to 28 knots. We eventually took off at about 06.20 and everything went according to plan. The

only snag was that X made a bad take-off and punctured one of the auxiliary tanks and broke off his tail wheel. He was naturally scared stiff of using up all his remaining petrol and making a bad landing. However, all went well. He landed at the first airfield he saw, which was Takali, where we are now stationed. Most unfortunately Y crashed on landing. He came in too fast and had to swing to avoid something at the end of his run. The undercarriage collapsed. It is really sickening to have an aircraft, which is worth its weight in gold out here, broken through damned bad handling.

The island saw the return trip of Sir Anthony Eden and the other VIPs on 7 April. Instead of flying straight onto Gibraltar they had headed for Greece first then back to Malta before their onward flight to England via Gibraltar.

The new Hurricane arrivals had the chance to engage the Germans and Italians on 11 April when a dozen Macchi 200s, six CR42s and a number of Me109s covered a German reconnaissance mission over the island. Several Hurricanes were scrambled. A pair of them got on the tail of the Me110 reconnaissance aircraft and managed to shoot it down into the sea some 20 miles to the north of Gozo. Unfortunately both of the Hurricanes were then intercepted by Me109s and shot down. During the night Ju87s dropped bombs across the island, causing a number of civilian casualties.

It was Easter Sunday on 13 April 1941 and it marked Malta's 500th air alert. There were four raids that day. Flight Officer Mason, of 261 Squadron and his wingman attacked four Me109s out of the sun. Mason managed to shoot one of the Me109s down, but in turn he was shot down by the remaining three. Mason was badly injured but he managed to coax his Hurricane down to sea level and prepared to ditch. He already had been hit in the wrist and palm, as well as his elbow and he had splinters in his left leg and his skull. When his Hurricane hit the water Mason was thrown forward and broke his nose on the windscreen. Mason was 4 miles out from the shore, so he began to swim until he was picked up by HSL107.

There were continuous raids from 14 to 22 April. The Italians tended to attack during the day, whilst the Germans concentrated on night attacks. On 22 April Ju88s and HE111s used flares to identify their targets and a number of bombs and mines were dropped, particularly around Valletta, causing substantial damage.

The following day Canadian pilot Henry Huger was shot down to the south-east of Hal Far by Me109s escorting a German reconnaissance aircraft. Huger managed to bale out and came down in the sea. Air Sea Rescue was ordered not to put to sea, as it was feared that the Germans would take advantage of the situation and shoot them up. It is believed that Huger drowned, as his body was never found.

On 27 April another twenty-three Hurricanes arrived via HMS *Ark Royal*. Originally they had planned to launch twenty-four in Operation Dunlop, but only twenty-three reached the island safely. The Hurricanes were led in, in three flights, by a Fulmar, with three Marylands and a Sunderland from Malta also assisting. Also on this day the remaining Wellington bombers operating from the island left Luqa airfield, bound for Egypt. They were to make room for the first half a dozen Blenheims from No. 21 Squadron of No. 2 Group, Bomber Command. The Blenheims were flown in from England via Gibraltar. The RAF believed that the Blenheims would give Malta a greater advantage, as the Wellingtons were only used at night. The Blenheims could now be used for coastal operations and anti-shipping attacks during the day.

The newly arrived Hurricanes were to give the half a dozen Ju88s a nasty surprise, when the German aircraft launched an evening raid on Valletta on 29 April. No less than seventeen Hurricanes were scrambled. One of them was shot down near Ghajntuffieha.

The Grand Harbour and Valletta suffered heavy raids the following day. The first wave of German aircraft that evening dropped mines and bombs. They were swiftly followed by a second wave of raiders. St John's Co-Cathedral was heavily damaged, as was the museum. The Greek Orthodox Church was destroyed. The Exchange, two banks, St George's Overseas League Club and numerous shops and other businesses were also heavily damaged and Kingsway main gate was blocked by rubble.

Throughout the month of April there had been ninety-one air raid alerts, of which fifty-eight had developed into proper raids and 651 tons of bombs had been dropped on the island. There had been a slight change in enemy tactics and night raids were becoming more commonplace. However time was running out for the *Luftwaffe*: after weeks of constant attack on Malta, the German squadrons would soon be transferred from Sicily to the Balkans. Here they would replace other squadrons that were moving east for Germany's impending invasion of Russia.

Sergeant Ray Ottey was out on patrol on 2 May in his Hurricane. It is believed that he fell victim to oxygen starvation, passed out and then crashed into the sea: his body was not found. In Valletta on the same day service personnel undertook the hazardous task of trying to diffuse and remove unexploded bombs around the city. St Publius Church, the parish church of Floriana, was severely damaged on Sunday 4 May. The front door, all the windows and its organ were completely destroyed. The clock was stuck at twenty to ten, although bizarrely its bells continued chiming every quarter of an hour.

A major assault developed on 6 May. There were vicious dogfights over the island. Pilot officer Grey's Hurricane was shot down and he was wounded in his thigh. A pair of Hurricanes that had scrambled to intercept a Ju88 on a reconnaissance patrol collided with one another. One of the pilots died, but the other, Sergeant Walker, managed to bale out. There were extensive raids on 7 May by Me109s and HE111s and it is believed that a Dornier was shot down over the island. German aircraft were attracted to the Grand Harbour on 9 May when Ju87s launched dive bombing attacks on the *Amerika, Breconshire, Hoegh Hood, Settler, Svenor, Talabot* and *Thermopylae*. Malta's Hurricanes scattered the attacking force, pursuing them back towards their bases in Sicily and managing to shoot one down.

Bombs dropped in St Lucia Street and Kingsway in Valletta on 10 May and on the Sunday Me109s attacked Malta's seaplane bases, setting one aircraft on fire. More raids followed on the Monday and on the Tuesday against both Valletta and on the British airfields. Six Hurricanes left Malta to reinforce the British air force in Egypt. The pilots themselves were to return to Malta on the night of 21 May, onboard a Sunderland, when they would then fly more Hurricanes to Alexandria.

Whilst Me109s fought Hurricanes over Malta on 13 May, killing Pilot Officer Peter Thompson, hundreds of miles away in England a pair of Spitfire VBs, named *Malta* and *Ghawedx* (another name for the island of Gozo) were subjected to their maiden flights. The population of Malta, despite having been under siege from the Italians and the Germans, had generously provided sufficient money to their own Spitfire Fund to allow the presentation of two new Spitfires. The two new aircraft were at first sent to 8 Maintenance Unit at Little Rissington, Gloucestershire, between 14 and 16 May. On 18 May they were sent to No. 74 (Trinidad) Squadron, based in Gravesend, Kent. *Malta* was first flown by the squadron at 11.45 on 23 May 1941. It was piloted by Sergeant Dykes for a short, five-minute test flight. *Malta* (W3210) went on its first convoy patrol on 7 June at 05.00. On a sweep over France two days later Pilot Officer W J Sandman claimed a probable Me109. Invariably *Malta* was flown either by Sandman or Pilot Officer Krol.

Malta was to have a relatively short career, as on 27 June 1941 Sandman, of the Royal New Zealand Air Force, was reported missing. He had taken off at 20.50 and was flying a fighter sweep over North Eastern France. He encountered enemy aircraft in the vicinity of Amiens and Abbeville. *Malta* was one of three Spitfires of 74 Squadron to be shot down. Sandman baled out and became a prisoner of war. *Malta*, just forty-five days old, was destroyed when it hit the ground.

The second aircraft, the *Ghawdex*, had its first recorded flight on 24 May at 12.00 hours. On 16 June it was on a Blenheim escort operation, piloted by Sandman when he claimed a probable Me109. The aircraft's last flight with 74 Squadron was on 6 July. It was then transferred to 92 (East India) Squadron, operating out of Biggin Hill. The squadron moved to Gravesend and then to Digby in Lincolnshire. The squadron left for the Middle East in February 1942 and the *Ghawdex* (W3212) was transferred to 417 (City of Windsor) Squadron on 6 February. Although it was not involved in any offensive operations, it nearly came to grief when it was being flown from Digby to Colerne in Wiltshire. Sergeant Hazel reported a faulty fuel gauge and the aircraft ran out of fuel and he had to make a forced landing on Charmy Down, Somerset. Until February 1943 the aircraft remained in storage, until it was transferred for conversion to a Seafire 1B. Now as NX883 it entered service with 897 Squadron of the Fleet Air Arm. The aircraft was also to fly with 748 Squadron in Cornwall, 761 Squadron in Somerset and 759 Squadron, also in Somerset. In the spring of 1945 it was transferred to the escort carrier, HMS *Ravager*. Its movements after that are unknown.

In a letter to *The Maltese Times*, dated 15 January 1941, it was clear that many Maltese had hoped to see the aircraft in action over the islands:

> Some Maltese people are very anxious to know what has become of the money collected in Malta for the fighter planes, namely *Malta* and *Ghawdex*. They were supposed to arrive in Malta by the end of the year. Nothing has been heard about them lately. Will the government please note this serious matter that concerns every Maltese citizen.

Meanwhile, back in Valletta, the determination of the Maltese people to continue to live as normally as possible was amply illustrated by the fact that the Coliseum Theatre was ready to reopen and the Manoel Theatre was nearing completion of full repairs. Elsewhere, flower shops, cafes and other businesses reopened, albeit in improvised premises.

There were further civilian casualties on 15 May and on 20 May. On 20 May Lieutenant General Sir William Dobbie was appointed Governor and Commander in Chief of the island. He had been fulfilling the role as Acting Governor since May 1940.

Malta received some cheer on 21 May when Operation Splice got underway. The two aircraft carriers, HMS *Ark Royal* and HMS *Furious* were due to launch forty-eight Hurricanes. In fact due to delays forty-one took off, accompanied by five Fulmars. One pilot did not make a satisfactory take-off and had to ditch into the sea and became a prisoner of war.

Both the Germans and the British, however, had their attention temporarily elsewhere. At the beginning of May the 5th Destroyer Flotilla, commanded by Captain Louis Mountbatten, on HMS *Kelly*, had been operating from Malta. They had lost HMS *Jersey* to a magnetic mine in the entrance of the Grand Harbour. The flotilla left on 21 May, bound for the Greek island of Crete.

Having overwhelmed mainland Greece, British Commonwealth and Greek troops had been forced to evacuate Crete. The Germans had taken the decision to launch an airborne and seaborne invasion of the island. Initially, the German parachute troops had been earmarked for an airborne invasion of Malta, but instead they had dropped on Crete from 20 May 1941. The German air force had complete air superiority over the island, something despite their boasts that they could not claim about Malta. Although the campaign to seize Crete was ultimately successful, the German paratroops suffered enormous casualties and the supporting air fleet lost considerable numbers during the operation. This was to be one of the last major German operations in the Mediterranean for some months, as the German invasion of Russia had been earmarked for 22 June 1941.

The newly appointed governor sent a situation report on Malta to the Secretary of State for the Colonies on 23 May:

> The outstanding feature of the last month has been the frequent occurrences of night raids by about forty bombers dropping parachute flares and mines, as well as bombs. Damage both from mines and bombs has been widespread, but has been greatest in Valletta. St John's Cathedral has been damaged and the Law Courts and Banks destroyed. A mine fell on the Civil Hospital and the hundred patients who had not already been removed were carried out in the night without one casualty. There has also been extensive damage to

dwelling houses and shops. The main street and several others are blocked with great quantities of stone from destroyed buildings and it will take a long time to clear with our limited resources. The extensive damage to their principal city, which was founded immediately after the Great Siege of 1565 and has stood unchanged since the time of the Knights, has been a profound shock to Maltese sentiment and the damage of several large churches, including the Co-Cathedral of St John, has given deep offence. Added to that, but separate from it, is the material loss caused to a large number of individuals by the destruction of property and business which it has taken them many years to acquire. Nevertheless the reaction of the people is deserving of the highest praise. They have hardened in anger towards the enemy and are facing their own individual calamities with cheerfulness and fortitude. With the first light after the destruction of their homes and shops, they are busily engaged with hammers and boards, patching up damage where they can and rescuing their stock and possession from among the debris to make another start. As one of them recently said after the destruction of his home, 'we will endure anything, except the rule of these barbarians and savages'. The homeless are received by others, especially among the poorer classes with the most remarkable hospitality and people in the undamaged areas have been living for nearly a year with comparative cheerfulness, in conditions of close overcrowding and consequent discomfort. The great majority are, I am sure, quite unshaken in their belief in final victory and the prime minister's recent statement that 'Malta, with Egypt and Gibraltar, will be defended with the full strength of the Empire' meant very much to the people here.

In London, on 26 May, Air Vice Marshal Hugh Pughe Lloyd met with Air Chief Marshal Sir Charles Portal (Chief of the Air Staff). Lloyd had just accepted the post of Air Officer Commanding Malta. Portal told Lloyd:

Your main task at Malta is to sink Axis shipping sailing from Europe to Africa. You will be on the island for six months as a minimum and nine months as a maximum, as by that time you will be worn out.

In a matter of days Lloyd would be onboard a flying boat heading for Malta. In his own memoirs he said:

> The final course was then set for Malta, where we were fortunate to alight in Marsaxlokk Bay in one piece. The direction of alighting was towards the island and our pilot overshot three times and went round again, narrowly avoiding the high ground on each occasion. When we did alight the aircraft was swung so violently to miss a rock that all the passengers were thrown into a heap and battered in the process, all the crockery onboard was broken and a wing float torn off. Fortunately I was sitting next to the pilot and only bumped my nose. One hundred and forty five hours had elapsed between my conversation with Babington [Air Marshal Sir Philip] at the headquarters of Bomber Command.

This was to be a new and major departure for Malta in the Mediterranean air war. Henceforth the island would mount far more aggressive offensive actions against the Italians and Germans. By the end of May there had been seventy-five raids on the island. Only two days had been free of attacks and the Maltese people had had twenty-four nights of interrupted sleep. A total of 453 tons of bombs had been dropped on Malta, but British reconnaissance flights began to confirm that the *Luftwaffe* was leaving Sicily. The Germans had been partially successful: they had caused damage to the naval base and they had seriously damaged Malta's ability to send up sufficient fighter cover. They had not, however, prevented the Swordfish of the Fleet Air Arm and the RAF Wellingtons from striking at targets of opportunity. For a short period of time Malta would now just face the attentions of the Italian air force.

CHAPTER FIVE

THE SHADOW OVER ROMMEL

When Air Vice Marshal Sir Hugh Pughe Lloyd arrived in Malta he found himself facing just the Italian air force. For a short period, after a winter of sustained night raids and dive bombing attacks on the island, he could concentrate on building up an offensive striking force to harass the seaborne supply columns and the harbours that were supporting Rommel's efforts in North Africa. Tripoli would be the main target from Malta. Allied submarines could cover the routes to the east and west of Sicily and Lloyd's aircraft, the Blenheim bombers, could strike at night.

Soon after his arrival Lloyd decided to see for himself the extent of the facilities and the damage that had so far been inflicted on the island's bases. In his memoirs he recalled his reflections on Kalafrana:

> I then went off on a tour of the island. After driving for 6 miles along narrow roads and through picturesque villages, each with an enormous church, I came to Kalafrana, commanded by Group Captain Livock, which was the equipment and repair depot, the flying boat base and the headquarters of the Air Sea Rescue organisation. The station had been a peacetime establishment and I liked the look of it. The barracks, messes, recreation rooms, etc were very good but the big hangars, where the greater proportion of all technical work was done, were very tempting targets. Furthermore, most of the spares and equipment, consisting of thousands of items, were concentrated in another appetising target which was all the more attractive since the only engine repair shop was on the ground floor where, just outside, there were the only test benches on the island for running engines after overhaul or repair. A few bombs on Kalafrana in the middle of 1941 would have ruined any hope of Malta ever operating an air force.

Lloyd witnessed his first major raid by the Italians on 3 June. An SM79 was shot down by a Hurricane off Gozo and in the second raid of the afternoon a German Ju52 was also shot down. Later in the evening a

Hurricane pilot mistook a flare path in Kalafrana Bay for Hal Far airfield and nearly ditched into the sea.

On 6 June forty-three Hurricanes arrived in Operation Rocket from HMS *Ark Royal* and HMS *Furious*. The last major German attack on the island for the time being took place on the night of the following day, when there were raids by HE111s. From now on the air attacks on Malta eased off, as the task of subduing the island fell to the Italian air force.

On 9 June, four SM79s on a reconnaissance mission, escorted by Me109s, were intercepted by four Hurricanes of 249 Squadron. One of the SM79s was shot down.

Lloyd's intentions were to operate one or two squadrons of Welling-ton bombers, a squadron of Blenheims and two squadrons of aircraft from the Fleet Air Arm. There would need to be significant work carried out on the airfields and dispersal areas would need to be constructed. He also ordered anti-invasion measures to be taken, with runways being mined and landing places obstructed. It was also obvious that the Hurricane Mark Is, which had struggled against the Me109s, would be more than competent to deal with the Italian Macchi 200s. In any case, new Hurricane reinforcements were Mark IIs, which could out-perform the Italian fighters.

On 11 June a reconnaissance SM79, escorted by seventeen Macchi 200s, headed for the island. The Italians were intercepted some 15 miles off Valletta by seven Hurricanes. The reconnaissance aircraft itself was shot down, but so too was Flight Lieutenant Norman Burnett's Hurricane. A similar operation was launched by the Italians the follow-ing day. Again a single reconnaissance SM79, this time escorted by thirty Macchi 200s, was intercepted by eighteen Hurricanes belonging to 46 and 249 Squadrons. There were confused claims over the number of aircraft shot down that day and at least one Macchi was seen to crash into the sea. Pilot Officer Saunders of 249 Squadron was shot down, but he was picked up by HSL107. Later Pilot Officer Monroe of the same squadron also crashed into the sea, but he was not recovered. In the afternoon a Cant Z506B and a CR42 were despatched to find the pilot of the missing Macchi 200. The CR42 was shot down and later another Cant was shot down into the sea. The Italians claimed another Hurricane when a CR42 shot down Sergeant Walker over 40 miles to the north of Valletta.

More Hurricane reinforcements arrived on 14 June thanks to HMS *Ark Royal* and HMS *Victorious*. Operation Tracer involved forty-eight Hurricanes leaving the aircraft carriers in flights of twelve, led by four Hudsons. Unfortunately, not only did one Hurricane fail to take off, but also the Hudson crews, being new to the role, lost their way. As a result, two Hurricanes ran out of fuel over the sea and two more crashed on landing.

Whilst the island braced itself for continued air attacks and readied itself to begin launching major operations against Axis shipping, the Italians continued their raids against Malta. Raids were virtually a daily affair, albeit of lesser intensity than when the Germans had been present in Sicily. On 25 June an Italian SM79 reconnaissance flight was escorted by thirty-six Macchi 200s. A pair of the Italian aircraft was shot down when they were intercepted by nine Hurricanes.

Further reinforcements arrived on both 27 and 30 June. In the first, code named Railway One, twenty-one Hurricanes arrived via HMS *Ark Royal*. A twenty-second Hurricane went missing and had to ditch near the coast of Sicily, where the pilot was picked up by an Italian Cant and became a prisoner of war. Railway Two, on 30 June, saw thirty-five of forty-two Hurricanes arrive on Malta from HMS *Ark Royal* and HMS *Furious*. There were delays due to a Hurricane crash on HMS *Victorious*.

On the 27th the Italians launched another reconnaissance operation, with an SM79 escorted by twenty-two Macchi 200s. Nine Malta-based Hurricanes claimed two of the Italian fighters. The episode was repeated on the 30th, when in the early afternoon Hurricanes were involved in a dogfight with Macchi 200s, leading to one of the Italian fighters being shot down over the sea.

Lloyd was beginning to build up his offensive force. Wellingtons were using Malta for night raids and seventeen Blenheims had arrived on detachment from England. Meanwhile, Swordfish operating out of Malta had attacked shipping in Tripoli. Blenheims had been used to make attacks on Axis shipping. They had managed to sink two large ships and damage three others. British submarines, operating out of Malta, had sunk or damaged thirteen other enemy vessels.

Throughout the month 154 tons of bombs had been dropped on the island. Nineteen daylight bombing raids had been launched, in addition to the twenty-nine night operations launched by the Italians. The reason for the disparity in the number of night attacks compared to daylight raids was largely as a result of the clear nights. Brigadier C T Beckett, who commanded the Royal Artillery on the island, explained the situation:

> The conditions over Malta were unlike those anywhere in England, for not only were there airfields within the gun defended area, but it was usual for aircraft to arrive either from Egypt or Gibraltar nightly, for bomber flights to take

place almost nightly, or for the Fleet Air Arm to carry out strikes or reconnaissance. Night fighters were usually up, and the enemy was almost invariably present. The problems of dealing with all these factors (of which the most difficult were the arrival of strangers from Gibraltar inadequately briefed as to our plans, and the return of damaged bombers from Sicily, who were not always able or willing to comply with the rules) necessitated very clear cut instructions to the guns and search-lights, as well as to the air defences, if we were all to give of our best in support. Simplicity was essential, since personnel changed very rapidly, and any extended period of inactivity almost always meant beginning the work all over again, educating the pilots and the fighter controllers in the details of control.

There needed to be significant collaboration, particularly between the Malta Night Fighter Unit and the guns operation room and the search-lights. Together the army and the Royal Air Force devised a plan which effectively split the island into two parts: the line ran through Valletta. When a raid approached a Hurricane was sent to patrol each area. The pilot was kept informed by radio of the speed, course and height of the raiders. They were not ordered to intercept (as was the case in daylight raids). The pilots instead had to put themselves either side of the raiders when they were 15 miles out from the island. They would then move towards the raiders, as they set their course for their main objective. The result was that the raiders would be illuminated by the searchlights. Beyond the raiders would be a pair of Hurricanes, converging on the enemy. By adopting this approach the vast majority of raiders were picked up by the searchlights and this significantly increased the anti-aircraft units' chances of knocking them out of the sky. The Royal Artillery acted as the eyes on the ground for the Hurricanes that would then be sent in to intercept.

On 4 July a single Cant 1007bis appeared in the morning on a reconnaissance flight. It was accompanied by thirty-eight Macchi 200s. The Cant suffered a technical problem and turned away from the island, but the fighters continued on. Four Hurricanes belonging to 185 Squadron scrambled to intercept and managed to shoot down one of them 10 miles north of the Grand Harbour. One of the Hurricanes, belonging to No. 126 Squadron, which had taken off from Safi at dawn, failed to return. Sergeant Hackston was believed to have come down into the sea by accident.

The Italians, however, did manage to press home an attack on that Friday, causing a number of civilian casualties at Hamrun. Three children were killed in the same location the following day. On 7 July there were more civilian casualties, this time at Paola and on the Tuesday a Fiat BR20, illuminated by searchlights, was shot down by anti-aircraft fire. Hurricanes also managed to scare off a formation of Macchi 200s.

The Italians hit Kalafrana on the night of 9 July. Initially an SM79 was picked up by searchlights and promptly shot down by a Hurricane. Nonetheless the Italians managed to drop about twenty bombs on the Kalafrana base. They managed to cause a little damage to two store buildings, but destroyed a local farm.

The Italians launched a major attack on Friday 11 July when at least forty Macchi 200s appeared in the afternoon. Hurricanes scrambled to intercept and some of the Macchis peeled off to make strafing attacks on Luqa airfield. The Hurricanes were later to claim three enemy aircraft. There were more civilian casualties the following day and on 15 July two mines were exploded during minesweeping operations outside the Grand Harbour. There were more reconnaissance flights and nuisance raids on the next two days, but the arrival of a significant seaborne force on 25 July would attract far greater Italian attention.

The cargo ships, *City of Pretoria*, *Deucalion*, *Durham*, *Melbourne Star*, *Sidney Star* and *Port Chalmers* arrived from Scotland via Gibraltar on 25 July. They were escorted by a battleship, a battle cruiser, four cruisers, seventeen destroyers and a mine layer. The passage had not been without incident: HMS *Manchester* and HMS *Firedrake* (a cruiser and a destroyer respectively) had been damaged on 23 July in attacks and on the following day *Sidney Star* had been damaged. Operation Substance, as it was known, managed to bring in 65,000 tons of supplies to the island. As part of the coordinated effort, HMS *Ark Royal* launched seven Swordfish as reinforcements for Malta. The target-rich environment of the Grand Harbour was too good an opportunity for the Italians to pass up. Forty Macchi 200s and a Cant approached the island, to be intercepted by twenty-two Hurricanes. A pair of Macchi 200s, as well as a Cant, were shot down.

The Italians were not finished with the force that had arrived in the Grand Harbour. On Saturday 26 July the naval authorities released a communiqué:

> Italian light forces consisting of E-boats of various sizes, attempted to breach the defences of Malta at about dawn on 26 July. As has been customary throughout this war all

the defences, many of which are manned by local units of this fortress island of Malta, were ready and waiting for any form of attack. At about 4.30 am 26 July, the searchlights were switched on and the battle began during which a large explosion was heard in the vicinity of the breakwater viaduct near St Elmo. For a few minutes the illuminated area off the entrance of the Grand Harbour was crisscrossed by a devastating fire which was visible to the naked eye. The tracer bullets were a regular Brocks' benefit. The firing soon ceased but it was obvious from the explosion in the illuminated area that the guns had found their targets and many of the enemy boats had been sunk and that the attack had failed. As daylight approached it was easier to see those of the enemy who had escaped the attack and soon accounted for the remainder. It is very difficult to ascertain which boats fell to the shore defences, and which to the air, but there seems no reason to believe that a single boat escaped back to Sicily. Several prisoners were taken. Thus ended in complete disaster the enemy's first attempt to break through the defences of Malta.

The attack had actually been launched by the Italian navy X-MAS flotilla. They had been intent on destroying shipping in the Grand Harbour and to carry out an attack on the submarine base on Manoel Island. Involved in the attack was the despatch vessel, *Diana*, a pair of motor torpedo boats, a carrier for two baby submarines, a command boat and nine explosive boats.

Italian fighters had taken off at first light to cover surviving units retreating back towards Sicily. Hurricanes were already swarming around the retreating Italians. A Hurricane was shot down 30 miles to the north of Malta. Pilot Officer Winton of 185 Squadron baled out and swam towards a stationary battalion motor-torpedo boat. He climbed aboard and found eight dead Italian crewmen. Winton returned to Malta in some style, with a captured Italian ensign.

By all accounts it was a major attack and a shock to both the defenders and the Italians. As one eye witness reported:

The shock of an explosion and the sound of gunfire immediately after the sounding of the signal of all clear at the end of an early alert, sent hundreds of people in Valletta, Sliema and Floriana rushing, not to public rock shelters, but to bastions and shore fronts. In the hazy mist of the hour before dawn, these spectators were treated to an unforgettable spectacle of Malta's shore defences in action. When I got there, jostled, and jostling many others who had spent the last few hours in shelter, the show was on. And what a show! The foreshore of the forts guarding the Grand Harbour was illuminated in a ghostly manner, the morning mist wreathing and swirling through a floodlit expanse, while overhead the stars still shone bright though the sky was paling in the east. Through the mist, from the massive walls, that had kept watch and ward for centuries, belched flame. From three directions, came lightening streaks of flame, that were tracer bullets. All concentrated on one point and where they converged was a microscopic spot of rushing wave as an e-boat was attempting to sneak through Malta's defences to attack the harbours of Valletta.

Despite the attack by the Italian navy, the Italian air force itself was showing itself to be disinclined to attack the island. Lloyd and his construction teams had feverishly developed the island's air facilities. They built new airfields, taxi tracks, radar stations, dispersal facilities and operations rooms. One of the major problems in providing sufficient aircraft dispersal space was that every square inch of the island, which was largely poor soil, was needed to grow crops. The stone-walled roads were stripped to create the Safi strip that linked Luqa and Hal Far airfields. Malta was beginning to strike out against enemy ports and shipping and it was beginning to worry the Germans in particular. Admiral Raeder, commanding German naval forces in the Mediterranean, sent a report to Hitler:

> German shipments to North Africa are suffering heavy losses
> of ships, material and personnel as a result of enemy air attacks
> by bombs and torpedoes and through submarine attacks.

Between 1 June and 31 October 1941 upwards of 22,000 tons of German and Italian shipping was lost due to naval and air operations. Submarines in the main accounted for 94,000 tons and around 115,000 tons by aircraft of the Fleet Air Arm or Royal Air Force. Three-quarters of Italy's shipping was employed on the African supply routes. Around 90 per cent of all of the lost shipping was south-bound, meaning Rommel was losing out on the supplies coming to him, rather than the Allies sinking empty vessels heading north. Around three-quarters of the 115,000 tons sunk by Allied aircraft was the work of Malta-based squadrons.

Singled out for particular praise by Lloyd were the crews of the Blenheims:

> Under such conditions the attacks required incalculable courage, determination and leadership on the part of our young men.

The Blenheims carried four 250 lb bombs with an eleven seconds delay. This meant that they had to be released virtually at mast height, so that all four bombs would land squarely on the target. The Italians and the Germans reacted by arming the ships and providing escorts, which meant that the low flying attacks were even more dangerous. It was almost impossible to swoop down on an enemy vessel without being seen several miles out. The Blenheims would come in low, amongst sheets of fire and water and press home their attack.

The Italian response to the X-MAS attack was entirely different, as was to be expected:

> The presence of the convoy was detected on Friday. Immediately the Italian navy decided to attack with these tiny but powerful craft on which the designers have worked in silence for many years – one of the most precious secrets of the Italian war machine. The men chosen for this attack knew that retreat was impossible – they must be either killed or taken prisoner. None flinched before this task, despite the formidable nature of the British defences. The violation of Malta will go down in history as one of the remarkable exploits of this war.

Overall, throughout July there had been forty-nine night bomber raids and eight daylight attacks. The night raids were spread over twenty nights and around 183 tons of bombs had been dropped on the island by the end of the month.

August and September saw a positive drop in Italian air activity. Malta-based Blenheims engaged in dozens of low-level attacks. They tended to operate in groups of two to ten. It was remarkable that so many attacks could be launched, as no more than two squadrons of Blenheims were ever available at any one time. Ultimately, as the year wore on, the Blenheim attacks were less and less successful, largely due to the increased escort strength of the enemy convoys. As a result, the Blenheims would turn their attention to enemy transport on land, attacking airfields and trucks.

The Hal Far based Swordfish of the Fleet Air Arm were no less busy. They laid innumerable mines and attacked enemy shipping with torpedoes. Although accurate figures are not available, it is believed that they alone sank 110,000 tons of enemy shipping between May and November 1941 and damaged another 130,000 tons.

Reinforcements were continually arriving on Malta and on 2 August, a day after Malta had experienced its 800th alert, Operation Style brought 100 RAF personnel to work at Kalafrana and 200 to operate from Luqa. One of the new arrivals was Aircraftsman Second Class Wireless Operator Mechanic, William Jackson. He would serve on HSL107. Jackson described the facilities at Kalafrana:

> There was one other significant feature about the barrack blocks, a feature we would very much appreciate in future months. Running parallel to the outer wall and about half the length of each block was a concrete domed structure about 6 ft wide. This was the solid concrete top of an air raid shelter, which had been dug into the solid limestone below it to a depth of 15 to 20 ft. I found out when things got a little bit hectic that in an emergency I could dive out of the window, do a forward roll over the concrete and then sprint round to the shelter entrance while the whistle of a bomb was still loud in my ears. This was to happen often when enemy fighter bombers flew in low over the sea to carry out a sneak attack but for many days after my arrival we were only subjected to an occasional high level attack by a lone Italian bomber.

The majority of August saw sporadic Italian attacks, with almost daily raids but mercifully limited casualties. On 22 August Lloyd received a telegram from the Secretary of State for Air, Sir Archibald Sinclair:

> Heartiest congratulations to you and all ranks of squadrons operating under your command on the magnificent success of air operations from Malta. The brilliant defence of the island by Hurricanes, the audacious attacks of Beaufighters on enemy airbases, the steady and deadly slogging of the Wellingtons at the enemy's ports; the daring and dextrous reconnaissances of the Marylands, culminating in the tremendous onslaughts of Blenheims and Fleet Air Arm Swordfish on Axis shipping in the Mediterranean are watched with immense admiration

by your comrades in the RAF and by our fellow countrymen at home. You are draining the enemy's strength in the Mediterranean. Good luck to you and good hunting.

There were more sporadic attacks throughout the remainder of August.

A Maltese citizen, Joseph Gauci, was rewarded for his sterling wartime work by being awarded the British Empire Medal. He was an Admiralty diver and was called to examine the hull of a damaged ship. He knew that the enemy bombers would return at any minute, but still chose to carry out his mission, in the certain knowledge that had the enemy reappeared then his crew would find it impossible to bring him back up to the surface. He also willingly faced the risk of an enemy bomb exploding underwater. Nonetheless he examined the hull and the ship was later able to sail out of the harbour.

The number of alerts throughout August had dropped to the lowest level since December 1940; just eighteen night bomber raids had been launched and seven day time attacks. The tonnage of enemy bombs dropped on the island had also fallen to ninety-two.

In mid-August Flight Lieutenant J Buckley and Flight Lieutenant O W Knight, both New Zealanders, had attacked a 9,000 ton Italian transport off the island of Lampedusa. Around the supply ship, which had run ashore, was an Italian destroyer, a number of torpedo boats and other vessels, which were attempting to salvage the deck cargo of motor vehicles. Buckley and Knight's Blenheims came in low and flew into the face of heavy anti-aircraft fire, which was stiffened by anti-aircraft guns that had been placed on the cliffs overhead. A bullet shattered Buckley's windscreen and hit him in the hand. A second bullet went straight through his navigator's map case and exploded on his Very pistol. Pieces of the pistol were blown back into his legs. Nonetheless his bombs hit the Italian transport and set her on fire. The Italian vessel burned for eight days, as her primary cargo was oil. Knight also fearlessly pressed home his attack, sinking a 700 ton schooner lying alongside the transport.

The Wellingtons were also hard at work. They struck at Naples, Benghazi, Tripoli and Taranto. In order to support the North African Offensive Crusader, they attacked enemy airfields at Berka, Benina and other targets in Tripoli. The Maltese-based Wellingtons, in the last six months of 1941, flew over 1,000 sorties. As Lloyd later recounted:

It was an incredible achievement. The crews never asked for a rest but continued to go out night after night despite the weather. In the autumn heavy rains played havoc with the taxi tracks and dispersal points at Luqa and it became impossible to move aircraft at night so that on their return the Wellingtons had to remain on the airfield until it was light enough to taxi away; this was an added strain on the pilots.

On 4 September a large formation of Macchi 200s was intercepted by Hurricanes. There was a vicious dogfight, during which up to six Italian aircraft were shot down. Amongst them was Carlos Romagnoli who was born in Naples in 1905 and was a veteran pilot who had shot down nine enemy aircraft in his Fiat CE32 during the Spanish Civil War. He was something of a legend in Italy. However he was part of the group of Macchi 200s that was intercepted by the Hurricanes around 10 miles from Malta. It is unclear as to who precisely shot Romagnoli down, but undoubtedly it was a pilot from either 126 or 185 Squadron. Romagnoli had already shot down three Hurricanes between December 1940 and July 1941, one of which had been over Malta.

There were further dogfights over Malta on Sunday 7 September, but on the night of 8 to 9 September the Italians reverted to night attacks. Five Italian crewed Ju87s dive bombed Valletta. A BR20M struck at Hal Far and nine Cant Z1007bis were intercepted *en route* to the island. A pair of Hurricanes was guided in by the searchlights and one of the bombers was shot down to the east of the island. During the day HMS *Ark Royal*, in Operation Status One, delivered fourteen more Hurricanes. A few days later, on 13 September, she and HMS *Furious*, in Operation Status Two successfully delivered forty-five out of forty-six more Hurricanes.

In the meantime, 10 and 12 September saw additional night attacks. The British claimed a pair of BR20Ms on the 12th. There was now a brief lull in the attacks, as the Italians shifted their attention to a convoy, Operation Halberd, which was due to arrive in Malta on 28 September, via Gibraltar.

Cargo ships *Ajax*, *Breconshire*, *City of Calcutta*, *City of Lincoln*, *Clan Ferguson*, *Clan Macdonald*, *Dunedin Star*, *Imperial Star* and *Rowallan Castle* were being escorted by an aircraft carrier, three battleships, five cruisers and eighteen destroyers. The Italians launched their attacks on the convoy at dawn on 27 September. The first attack came from torpedo bombers that managed to break through the destroyer screen and anti-aircraft fire to attack battleship HMS *Nelson*, the convoy's flagship, and she was hit. After the damage to HMS *Nelson* the three battleships turned and headed back towards Gibraltar, escorted by half of the destroyers. The remaining escorts would have to see the cargo ships into Malta. The Italian fleet showed no inclination to engage with even the reduced escort, but there was still danger from mines, the Italian air force and submarines. On the same day that HMS *Nelson* was badly damaged one of the cargo ships, *Imperial Star*, was also sunk.

George Crockett was part of a contingent of Royal Air Force servicemen onboard the cruiser, HMS *Kenya*. He recalls the last leg of the journey:

> It was while I was looking round in the light of this new day, Sunday 28 September that I noticed in the line of ships astern of us a gap that *Imperial Star* had filled the previous evening. During the night's attacks only one torpedo had been effective and *Imperial Star* had stopped that one, rudder and propeller blown away; too close to enemy territory to make towing a feasible proposition, she had to be sunk by gunfire from one of our own destroyers. With her went my lovely new high-speed launch. Tired, unshaven and hungry, life seemed very black at that moment.

Onboard the *Imperial Star* was HSL148 and Crockett would have been one of the crewmen.

On 29 September Maltese-based Hurricanes of 185 Squadron struck the airfield of Comiso on the southern coast of Sicily. Here they encountered for the first time Macchi 202s. They had the same Daimler Benz engine as the new Me109F. One of the Hurricanes, flown by Pilot Officer Lintern, was shot down to the north of Gozo. He managed to bale out but he was never found. A Swordfish sent to find him was also shot down by a Macchi 202.

Throughout September there had been thirty-one air raid alerts and seventy-eight tons of bombs had been dropped on Malta. The arrival of the Macchi 202 was an ominous sign. From the first encounter it was obvious that they were capable of out performing the Hurricanes.

The first day of October saw seven Macchi 202s launch a sortie over the island. The Hurricanes came off worse when eight of them from 185 Squadron were pounced on by the Macchis to the north-east of the island. Squadron Leader Peter Boy Mould was shot down and killed. 185 Squadron lost another Hurricane to the new Macchis on 4 October when Pilot Officer Veitch failed to return after he and seven other Hurricane pilots attempted to intercept the Italian aircraft.

The RAF Air Sea Rescue effort, despite the loss of a new high speed launch when the *Imperial Star* was lost, was given a considerable boost at the beginning of October. HSLs 128 and 129, new whaleback high speed launches, could now considerably improve the chances of pilots that had ditched into the seas around the island. They were slightly shorter than HSL107, but wider and more streamlined. The RAF feverishly worked on the launches to get them to full readiness. It was now possible to set up a second station at St Paul's Bay.

There were sporadic attacks on 5 and 8 October and on 14 October five Hurricanes of the Malta Night Fighter Unit intercepted six Macchi 202s that had launched a strafing attack on Luqa airfield just before dawn. All five of the Malta Night Fighter Unit Hurricanes were aloft, to be followed by three Hurricanes, each from 185 and 249 Squadrons. One of the aircraft shot down was being flown by Pilot Officer David Barnwell. He was just nineteen years old and the last surviving son of Captain Frank Barnwell, who had designed the Blenheim and Beaufort light bombers. George Crockett, onboard HSL128, was one of those sent out to try to find him:

> Shortly before dawn that morning young Barnwell had intercepted a flight of Italian aircraft, making a hit and run raid on the island's airfields and as is usual with modern aircraft, the drama that followed was swift and deadly. His voice was heard over the radio telephone at Fighter Control ... "Tally ho! Tally ho!" He had sighted the enemy and the hunt was on, then "Got one! Got one!" The successful completion of a job he had been trained to do – the same end to combats which had already earned him a Distinguished Flying Cross. But within the next couple of minutes something had gone very wrong and then his voice was heard again: "Baling, baling, engine cut and baling out. I am coming down in the sea." Then silence.

It is unclear whether Barnwell actually managed to bale out in time. He may well have been too low to risk using his parachute. The likelihood was that he lost consciousness when his aircraft hit the water and did not get out before his Hurricane sank.

Operation Callboy from HMS *Ark Royal* delivered eleven Albacores and a single Swordfish on 18 October. One other Swordfish was lost *en route* to Malta. There were a number of raids through 17 and 18 October and on 22 October, in the afternoon, Luqa was attacked on two occasions by fourteen Macchi 202s. Once again the Macchis got the better of the nine Hurricanes of 249 Squadron, which were scrambled to intercept. The Macchis pounced on them while they were still climbing over St Paul's islands. Sergeant Owen was forced to bale out, but he was picked up. There was a further night raid on 31 October and an enemy Cant Z1007bis was shot down.

Although the arrival of the Macchi 202s was an ominous sign, there had been just fifty-eight air raid alerts during October and ninety-six tons of bombs had been dropped. A similar pattern began in November.

In the early hours of 1 November four BR20M bombers approached Malta. One was intercepted and shot down at 11,000 ft. It was Malta's turn the following day, with twenty-two Wellingtons of 40 and 104 Squadrons striking an enemy air depot near Tripoli. It was being used by the Germans to repair air frames and engines. The attack caused enormous damage and loss of ammunition and petrol and the pilots could still see the fires when they were 100 miles away.

The Italians launched heavy raids over the weekend of 8 to 10 November but again on 12 November Hurricane fighter bombers struck against the enemy, this time an airfield at Gela in Sicily. The operation involved Hurricanes from 126 and 249 Squadron which strafed and bombed the airfield. A Macchi 202, scrambled from Comiso, shot down the Hurricane flown by Sergeant Simpson. On the same day HMS *Ark Royal* and HMS *Argus*, in Operation Perpetual One ferried in thirty-four Hurricanes and a Swordfish. They were due to deliver additional aircraft in Perpetual Two, but this operation never took place due to the loss of HMS *Ark Royal*. This was to be the last aircraft reinforcement for Malta for the year and it was also the last time that Hurricanes were ferried into the island.

The Royal Navy, in cooperation with the RAF, had managed to deliver an enormous number of aircraft between 1940 and 1941. The aircraft carriers had delivered eleven Albacores, nineteen Swordfish and 328 Hurricanes. Five of the Hurricanes had crashed on landing and 150 of the Hurricanes that had been delivered to Malta were then flown on to North Africa.

Also due that day were the cargo ships *Empire Pelican* and *Empire Defender*. They had left Gibraltar on 11 and 12 November respectively. Operation Astrologer was unfortunately a disaster, as Italian torpedo bombers had managed to sink both vessels.

Three Wellingtons were inbound to Malta on 15 November when they were attacked by five CR42s around 90 miles west of Kalafrana. One of the Wellingtons was shot down. On 17 November there was another ominous change in the enemy's strategies for the Mediterranean. The Germans had made the decision to reinforce the *Luftwaffe* in the

Long range Hawker Hurricane.

Hurricane - "Another victim of the blitz".

Hurricane wreckage at Tal Kali.

Mosquito at Luqa.

Hudson, Malta 1942.

Bristol Bombay at Luqa airfield.

Swordfish wreckage.

Malta based Blenheim
attacking Axis shipping.

Beaufighters at Luqa.

Beaufighter wreckage at Luqa being cannibalised.

Beaufighter, Luqa 1942.

Kittyhawk at Luqa, 1943.

Walrus at Luqa, 1943.

Short Sunderland on fire, Kalifrana Bay.

Wellington crash site on Malta.

Wellington crashes after raid on Sicily.

A downed Me109 being cleared and stripped.

'Faith', having been dismantled for storage is restored.

Operations Room 'Plotter' Valletta.

Grand Harbour Bofors crew.

Anti-aircraft position, probably at Marsa 1942.

Radar listening equipment at Quara Tower.

Siggiewi 2 AA gun position.

Unexploded German
Bomb.

'Whacker' Coxon with
unexploded mine.

1943, lancer position, Malta.

Unexpected fall of snow on Malta.

Air raid at Siggiewi.

More bombs falling at Siggiewi.

A welcome break from the raids and the bombing for Royal Artillery men.

Oil tanker on fire. Grand Harbour 1942.

Supply convoy under attack.

Mediterranean and Field Marshal Kesselring had become Commander-in-Chief of the Southern Theatre. It would be at his direction that Malta would be nearly brought to her knees in the following year.

For now, however, Malta was relatively secure. It was receiving regular supply columns and for the time being its air defences were holding out against the Italian threat. Governor Dobbie delivered a speech to the Council of Government on 25 November:

> For nearly eighteen months Malta has been at the forefront of the battle and has stood firm against the attacks of the enemy. The steadfastness of the garrison and the fortitude of the people have won the admiration of the whole free world. Never in her history, neither under the Knights, nor when Napoleon's forces were driven out, has the star of Malta shone more brightly. We have maintained ourselves up to now, and, with God's help, we shall continue to do so. Here in the centre of the Mediterranean, Malta remains a target for the enemy bombers and a thorn daily more venomous, in the enemy's side. We have known heavy bombing raids and returned them with interest. Malta has had 972 air raids, of which 350 have been bombing raids. A total of 344 people have been killed and 685 injured seriously enough to be detained in hospital, 2,552 houses have been destroyed or seriously damaged. We have a place in the struggle and a share of responsibility for the course of events. The burden of this responsibility is heavy, but, with the help of God we shall know how to bear it until victory is won.

By the end of November 1941 bombers operating out of Malta were striking targets in Sicily, the Italian mainland and all along the North African coast. Some operations were relatively modest, but others delivered up to 30 tons of bombs in a single operation. German and Italian transport was not safe all along the coastal roads of North Africa, as Maltese-based aircraft launched strafing attacks. The Italians had also increased their air operations throughout November and brought the total weight of bombs dropped on the island up to 219 tons.

Whilst bomb disposal experts dealt with unexploded bombs lying in the wreckage of Malta's Opera House at the beginning of December, the island's offensive continued to gather pace. In the first two or three days of December a destroyer was sunk, a tanker with 11,000 tons of petrol, a large merchant ship and at least nine petrol lorries on the North

African coast. The Germans, in particular, were becoming increasingly determined to deal with Malta once and for all. On 5 December the *Luftwaffe Fliegerkorps* II moved to Messina in Sicily from their former base in Russia. Their task would be to subdue the island and to destroy its offensive capabilities.

Meanwhile, however, the main threat was still the Italians. Air raids continued throughout December, becoming more intense towards the end of the month. Four Ju88s and twenty Me109s and Macchi 202s launched a raid in the late morning of 21 December. Eighteen Hurricanes were scrambled to intercept. Sergeant Hayes of 185 Squadron was shot down, as were two Macchi 202s. A mixed force of enemy fighter bombers and fighters attacked the Grand Harbour the following day. One Hurricane was shot down in the ensuing fight. Maltese-based anti-aircraft batteries shot down a Ju88, a Blenheim was lost from 18 Squadron when it failed to return from a reconnaissance mission. Another Blenheim was lost belonging to 107 Squadron, flown by Sergeant Henley. The Blenheim crashed into the sea after raiding the coast of North Africa.

The Blenheims and the Wellingtons maintained their attacks and throughout the whole period Sunderland flying boats were carrying out transport missions, ferrying personnel and providing sea reconnaissance.

New Zealander Flight Lieutenant Hughes, pilot of a Sunderland, was involved in a bizarre situation towards the end of December 1941. He left Aboukir in Egypt shortly before midnight, heading towards Malta laden with supplies. Also onboard the Sunderland was Pilot Officer Easton and his crew. Their Wellington had crashed in North Africa and they were returning to their squadron in Malta. The Sunderland hugged the North African coastline, but 50 miles north-east of Benghazi they were intercepted by a pair of Me110 fighter bombers. The Sunderland managed to shoot down one of the Me110s and the other peeled away, but not before two of the crew's gunners had been wounded and a passenger killed in the Sunderland. The Sunderland itself had suffered damage to the two starboard engines and the aircraft was beginning to lose height. Hughes managed to turn the aircraft into the wind and safely landed on the water. The sea tore off the starboard wingtip float, so the crew had to put their weight along the port wing to stop it from capsizing. The Sunderland began moving stern first, helped by a strong north-east wind, towards land. The Sunderland then struck a reef and two hours later was still stuck firmly on the reef and beginning to break up. There were twenty men onboard and only one serviceable dinghy. Two at a time they slid down the wing and into the sea.

By midday the crew were safely on land on a rocky beach about 100 miles to the east of Benghazi. The men were exhausted and unarmed. Suddenly they saw Italian soldiers. Hughes stepped forward to offer their surrender, but instead the Italian raised his rifle above his head and threw it onto the ground. A large group of eighty Italians then arrived and this time the British were told that they were now prisoners of war. A stretcher was made for the wounded man and together with the Italians they began to march away from the beach. The Italians were scared of Arab raiders and would not allow fires to be lit when the party stopped to camp for the night. In due course the party was reinforced by another 100 Italians, led by a major. The major told Hughes that they would march towards Benghazi. Unbeknown to the Italians, there were Indian troops just 15 miles away. The group continued to march towards Benghazi and soon the British lines were reached and Hughes was able to hand over 150 Italian prisoners, most of who were delighted that their war was over.

Meanwhile, in Sicily, Kesselring was building up his air force, ready to suppress Malta. He had upwards of 250 long range bombers and reconnaissance aircraft and nearly 200 fighters. Lloyd's forces on Malta had around sixty serviceable bombers and seventy fighters. Lloyd could only dream of the prospect of receiving more fighter reinforcements and he would have to wait another three months before he would see his first Spitfires.

In the last week of December Malta faced its most stern test so far. Kesselring aimed to eliminate the RAF first and concentrated on the fighter airfields at Hal Far and Takali, the bomber airfield at Luqa and Kalafrana flying boat base.

Shortly after 10.00 hours on 24 December Ju88s dive bombed the Grand Harbour and, in response, seventeen Hurricanes were scrambled. Two of the Ju88s were shot down and at least one Hurricane was lost. Further attacks were made by Ju88s at Hal Far after dusk. On the 27th three Ju88s and twenty Me109s headed towards Kalafrana. A Ju88 was shot down, as was a Hurricane and at night the Malta Night Fighter Unit and the anti-aircraft batteries engaged more Ju88s, shooting down at least one of them.

The raids continued through 28 and 29 December with more Ju88s and fighter escorts. Another Hurricane was lost, flown by Flight Sergeant Owen on the 28th. The heaviest action was seen on 29 December. Sixteen Hurricanes scrambled to deal with thirty-six Sicily based German aircraft but, unfortunately, two Hurricanes collided in mid-air. Twenty-four more raiders attacked in the afternoon and were intercepted by eighteen Hurricanes and at least one Me109 was shot down. The Germans were also attacking a motor schooner off Gozo. Two of the four Hurricanes scrambled to investigate were lost. Luqa airfield was attacked by twelve Me109s and bombers. They managed to destroy fifteen RAF aircraft on the ground.

Bombers struck against Luqa, Takali, Hal Far, Kalafrana and the Grand Harbour just before midday on 30 December when one of the Ju88s was shot down. This was to be the last air action of the year, although Ju88s did carry out strafing attacks on Hal Far and Takali on 31 December without being intercepted.

The month and indeed the year had produced a crescendo of raids. There had been 168 air raid alerts during the month and 559 tons of bombs dropped. In the latter part of the month enemy raids had seen up to seventy enemy aircraft in any one attack. Malta's offensive actions had not been severely disrupted until the Germans began to strike with increased ferocity. Wellingtons had hit Naples, Tripoli, Benghazi, Taranto and Patras in Greece. Enemy shipping had been hit in Benghazi and mines laid. In the six months ending December 1941 the Luqa-based Wellingtons alone had flown over 1,000 sorties.

The worst, however, was yet to come. A true siege of annihilation awaited the scant air defenders of Malta.

CHAPTER SIX

BLUDGEON

The German attack on HMS *Illustrious* in 1941 had been opportunist but now Kesselring aimed systematically to destroy Malta as a weapon. In many respects Kesselring's plans to deal with Malta were very similar to the strategies adopted by the *Luftwaffe* during the battle of Britain. Effectively a number of bludgeoning blows delivered by overwhelming numbers of aircraft would seek to sweep the skies of the RAF and to shatter the airfields and defences. Kesselring had the distinct advantage of almost limitless replacements, although he accepted that he would suffer enormous losses in his goal. He would first aim at the airfields and the fighters then he would strike at the dockyards and harbours and finally his air force would concentrate on the barracks, communications and stores. Kesselring's attacks would certainly blunt Malta's offensive capabilities. They would also come perilously close to destroying them for good.

Also lurking in the background were invasion plans for Malta. The Italians had created an invasion plan codenamed *Operazione* C3 sometime before which required barges to move 40,000 Italian troops. The plan also suggested that upwards of 500 combat aircraft would be needed first to suppress the defenders of the island and then to cover the landings. Crucially, the plan also required the support of the Italian navy, which had so far shown great reluctance to expose itself to the Mediterranean fleet. The Italians, rather optimistically, believed that the whole operation could be achieved in a timescale of just 48 hours. This was an important consideration, as it took into account the time that it would take Cunningham's Mediterranean Fleet to sail from Alexandria to make any impression or contribution to the defence of the island.

The Italians planned to land troops at Mellieha Bay and St Paul's Bay and to launch diversionary attacks near Marsaxlokk. The Italians could not rely on paratroops as the Germans had in their successful but bloody conquest of Crete in 1941. The Italians lacked sufficient numbers of parachutists, they had no gliders and the eighty or so transport aircraft they had were needed in North Africa. The Italians carried out some exercises using motorised barges, but no real action had been taken to build landing craft. The Italians knew that the barges that the Germans had used in the invasion of Crete were handled very roughly by the Mediterranean Fleet and had proved to be incredibly vulnerable. Even so, had the Italians had their own landing craft success was still far from certain in the unpredictable waters around Malta. Whilst the Italians postured and made aggressive comment about invading the island, in truth they had made little planning to carry it through.

As for the Germans, had they not suffered such massive casualties on Crete when they had deployed their airborne forces the prospect of invading Malta by air would have been a far less daunting endeavour. As it was, other events, notably the Russian invasion, had taken precedence and after the huge losses on Crete Hitler had forbidden a full scale paratrooper assault ever again.

The Germans had invariably been single-minded in their strategies, yet in the Mediterranean they seemed torn. On the one hand Malta maintained itself as a constant danger to shipping, supply and troop movement along parts of the North African mainland. Equally, it was striking at will against Sicily and the Italian mainland. On the other hand, the Germans seemed hell bent on driving along the North African coast and seizing Egypt and the Suez Canal. The glory and the strategic advantage of achieving these goals always seemed to outweigh the advantage of occupying Malta. This was despite the fact that Rommel in particular was certain that complete mastery of North Africa could only be achieved once Malta was under German control.

Kesselring had become Commander-in-Chief of Southern Operations in late 1941. He had a number of impelling and contradictory objectives. On the one hand he needed to ensure continued success in North Africa, or at least to ensure stability. On the other he realised that Italian efforts in all Mediterranean areas of operation were embarrassing or disappointing at best. It did not take Kesselring very long to realise that he needed to take Malta. It seems apparent from Count Galeazzo Ciano, Mussolini's Foreign Minister, that the Italians were unaware of the precise German plans until at least April 1942. Ciano wrote in his diary that month:

> The Duce informs me that Marshal Kesselring on his return from Germany brought Hitler's approval for the landing operation on Malta. It appears that the island has been really damaged by aerial bombardments. This does not however alter the fact that the coastal defences are still intact. Therefore in

the opinion of some naval experts, the undertaking is still dangerous and in any case would be expensive.

Nonetheless, Ciano ordered Field Marshal Ugo Cavallero, the Italian Chief of Staff, to put together a plan, which Ciano noted in his diary:

> Cavallero outlines our programme for carrying on the war in the Mediterranean. At the end of the month [May 1942], Rommel will attack Libya with the aim of defeating the British forces. If he can he will take Tobruk and will go as far as the old boundaries; if not, he will limit himself to forestalling an attack by the enemy by striking first. Then all the forces will be concentrated for an attack on Malta. The Germans are sending a parachute division commanded by General Student and are furnishing us with technical material for the assault. It will take place in July or August at the latest. Afterwards it will no longer be possible because of the weather. Cavallero declares: 'I know that it is a difficult undertaking and that it will cost us many casualties, and I know too that I am staking my head on this undertaking. If we take Malta, Libya will be safe.' Cavallero does not conceal the fact that he hopes to derive a great deal of personal glory from this operation, but I believe he will never acquire it.

The Italian air force, however, was not as convinced as either Kesselring or Cavallero. For one thing the anti-aircraft defences remained intact and there was still the lurking shadow of the Royal Navy. Ciano wrote:

> The landing of paratroops would be very difficult; a great part of the planes are likely to be shot down before they can deposit their human cargo. The same must be said for landings by sea. Again it must be remembered that two days of minor aerial bombardment by us only serve to strengthen resistance. In these last attacks we, as well as the Germans, have lost many feathers. Even Fougier [Commander of the Italian Air Force] is anxious about a landing operation and the German General Lorzer did not conceal his open disagreement. The supporters of the operation are Kesselring and Cavallero, the latter going through his usual tricks to put the responsibility on the shoulders of others.

The Italian air force itself was certainly unsure of the possible success of any attempt to occupy the islands. One Italian pilot, Franco Pagliano, noted in his own book that neither he nor any of his fellow pilots expected to survive more than seven sorties over Malta. Be that as it may, by June 1942 Kesselring planned to have his forces ready for an invasion of Malta. Two things were needed: first the bludgeoning attacks had to work and second Rommel had to take Tobruk.

The bludgeon was certainly impressive. In the first three weeks of January Kesselring threw 950 raiders against Malta. Meanwhile, Rommel's forces were retreating and the 8th Army was forging forward in the desert to relieve Tobruk.

There were torrential rains, winter gales, electrical storms and low cloud cover in early January 1942. The fighter airfields at Takali and Hal Far became waterlogged and the fighters had to be transferred to Luqa. Even here strong crosswinds prevented the use of the airfield and on many days the Wellingtons were grounded.

The 8th Army continued to advance in Egypt. In Malta the Germans managed to maintain an average of 150 sorties a week throughout the month of January. On 3 January twenty-two Hurricanes of 126, 185 and 249 Squadrons scrambled to intercept Ju88s escorted by Me109s. A German bomber and a fighter were shot down and Sergeant Westcott was accidentally shot down by British anti-aircraft fire.

Thirty German aircraft approached Luqa in the early hours of 4 January. Anti-aircraft gunners shot one Ju88 into the sea. Blenheims, meanwhile, attacked Castel Vetrano airfield on Sicily. The ten Blenheims happened on some seventy-five Ju52s and S82s, all transport aircraft. The Blenheims came in as low as 20 ft and destroyed thirty-five and damaged several more. There were no British losses. The following night Wellingtons hit the same target, destroying another fourteen and illuminating the sky when they blew up a petrol dump.

Between the end of December 1941 and 20 January 1942 Fleet Air Arm Swordfish and Albacores, RAF Beaufighters, Beauforts and Mary-lands launched fifty-two sorties against Tripoli. The fighters were no less active and between dawn and midday on 19 January, ninety-three Hurricane sorties were launched from Luqa airfield. This was in response to the imminent arrival of a convoy, which had left Alexandria bound for Malta on 16 January. The cargo ships, *Ajax*, *Thermopylae*, *Clan Ferguson* and the *City of Calcutta* were being harassed by German bombers. The *Thermopylae* was sunk on 19 January and as the convoy approached Malta seventy-two German aircraft swarmed in to attack the three remaining vessels and targets on the island itself. The remaining ships reached Malta safely and their precious cargoes were unloaded. An Albacore was shot down that day, as was a Ju88, which had been chasing a Wellington that was returning to Malta.

There was an outbound convoy on 25 January, which attracted the attention of several German aircraft. Despite four Hurricanes being shot down over Kalafrana, the naval store ship, *Breconshire*, braved continuous attacks from Ju88s and Me109s to reach Malta on 27 January. In covering the final approach of the ship Flight Lieutenant Kemp's Hurricane was shot down and he spent 24 hours paddling towards Malta in his dinghy before he was found by HSL128.

By the end of the month the Germans had dropped 669 tons of bombs onto Malta. Incendiary bombs had landed on Kalafrana and in one raid alone, on 2 January; twenty-five people had been killed, with one family suffering nine casualties. It was becoming increasingly more difficult to beat off the seemingly inexhaustible supply of German aircraft. The weather had certainly saved the island from the worst that the Germans could throw at them. All Kesselring could hope for was improved flying conditions, in order to remain on schedule for his outline proposals for invasion.

By February the 8th Army was back in retreat and Malta had become even more isolated than ever before. The Germans had counter-attacked in North Africa on 21 January and from that date to 24 February they launched 1,960 bomber sorties against Malta. It was to have a drastic impact on both the defensive and offensive capability of the island.

The British were acutely aware that the Germans intended to invade once they had neutralised the island. Yet with reverses in North Africa, Malta was starving due to shortage of supplies. On 27 February Lord Cranborne, the Secretary of State for the Colonies, wrote to Winston Churchill:

> This is hardly the place to discuss the consequences likely to follow the loss of Malta, not least of which would be the surrender of 300,000 most loyal British subjects, who would then be verging on starvation, to the mercy of the enemy. I feel it is my duty to emphasise that unless supplies can be substantially replenished within the next two months, the fortress will be within measurable distance of falling into enemy hands.

The Germans were taking the prospect of the Maltese invasion incredibly seriously. The German navy was in full support and Hitler had even given the invasion plan a codename: Operation Hercules. Yet Malta had not yet been subdued. A heavy raid on Kalafrana on 2 February destroyed a Sunderland on the slipway. Hal Far was hit the following day and 100 incendiaries were dropped on Kalafrana. RAF bombers and Fleet Air Arm torpedo bombers were still launching attacks on enemy shipping and land targets in North Africa.

On 4 February Blenheims struck shipping in Palermo harbour. Six Blenheims had set out but only two returned. A Ju88 was shot down over Kalafrana and there was a serious dogfight between Hurricanes and Me109s in the late afternoon. At least two Hurricanes were lost.

George Crockett wrote:

> Wednesday, 4 February 1942 – my thirty-sixth birthday – and the *Luftwaffe* seem determined to put on a really spectacular show. The air raids came in fast and furious and when I listened to the operations room repeater system I could hear how the island's airfields were catching the full weight of the bombing and strafing. Our few Hurricanes gave what fight they could but they made little impression on the Ju88 bombers, even when they succeeded in getting within range – and always they had to keep one eye over their shoulders for the new German Me109 fighters which outclassed them for speed and fire power. Feeling anxious at the obvious vicious-ness of the raids, I slipped down to our underground control room several times during the morning.

There was a heavy air raid on the morning of 6 February and anti-aircraft fire managed to down a Ju88 and an Me109. That night the RAF struck at Sirte airfield in North Africa, whilst Fleet Air Arm torpedo bombers attacked axis shipping. They managed to torpedo two merchant ships, one of 8,000 tons and the other of 3,000 tons. Three Blenheims returning from a sortie to the North African coast were bounced by Me109s and shot down. A Hurricane was also lost late in the afternoon.

The intensity of the bombing raids was still increasing. Hurricanes chased half a dozen Ju88s on their return trip to Sicily on 11 February, managing to shoot down one. Three inbound Beaufighters were shot down in the early hours of the morning on 12 February and later that morning a Ju88 was shot down as it approached the Grand Harbour, escorted by Me109s. Flight Lieutenant Allen was shot down and lost in the ensuing dogfight.

A much needed convoy left Alexandria the same day. *Clan Campbell*, *Clan Chattan* and *Rowallan Castle* were escorted by three cruisers and sixteen destroyers. *Clan Campbell* was forced to head back for Alexandria on 13 February after it had been damaged and the two remaining cargo ships were both sunk on 14 February.

Numerous Maltese citizens were killed from the heavy raids on 12 February. There was intense enemy air activity on 14 February and all day long on Sunday 15 February there were air raid alerts. There were four daylight raids that day. Luqa airfield was bombed by seven Ju88s: one was shot down by anti-aircraft fire. In the second raid the Germans shot down a Beaufighter and in the third an Me109 crashed into the sea after it was shot down after delivering an attack. In the evening, a Maryland that had been on a reconnaissance sortie was on its way back to the island. Hurricanes were sent out to cover its return, but instead they were attacked by Me109s that were escorting incoming Ju88s. Pilot Officer Lowe was shot down and killed in his Hurricane. The Maryland had been suffering from engine problems and as it came in to land four Me109s attacked it. Two Me109s were hit and peeled off and as the Maryland approached Luqa airfield two more 109s came in. The Maryland was hit but managed to ditch just outside Kalafrana Bay. Hurricanes arrived and drove the Me109s away and anti-aircraft fire kept a determined German fighter pilot from shooting up the still floating Maryland. Later that night another Maryland, coming back from Egypt after repairs, was attacked and shot down, probably by the same Messerschmitt that had attempted to destroy the first Maryland.

The 15 February was the first clear day of February and this allowed Kesselring to launch over 120 Ju88s and fifty Me109s against Luqa airfield. The Hurricanes could only just outpace the Ju88s and their machine guns made little impression on the German aircraft's armour plating. The losses were mounting, primarily due to the fact that the Hurricane could not compete in speed or fire power with the German Me109s. As a result, Luqa airfield, with its predominant clay limestone and earth runway, was heavily cratered, yet the RAF struggled successfully to keep the airfield in action, constantly having to disarm unexploded bombs. Steadily the defence works were built up, including anti-blast aircraft pens. The army supplied 3,000 men to help with the work.

An intended reinforcement of aircraft, due on 17 February failed to arrive due to poor weather conditions. A pair of Wellingtons was shot down by Ju88 night fighters and German anti-aircraft guns claimed another over Sicily. Yet another Wellington was lost when it had to force land in North Africa and a Hudson crashed off the Sicilian coast.

Towards the end of February the weather began to improve and Malta possessed just twenty-one serviceable Hurricanes. The majority of the 990 tons of bombs that the Germans dropped on Malta during the month fell on the three airfields and the Grand Harbour. Every air combat seemed to end with the loss of at least one Hurricane. Three Ju88s and escorting Me109s were intercepted by eight Hurricanes in the morning of 22 February. Squadron Leader Chaffe, who was the new commanding officer of 185 Squadron, was shot down. A bombing raid damaged five newly arrived Wellingtons at Luqa. On the following day Messerschmitts again attacked intercepting Hurricanes aiming to beat off some Ju88s. Later a Ju88 was shot down by anti-aircraft fire and in a third raid an Me109 was also shot down.

During the afternoon of 24 February an American pilot officer, Don Tedford, flying a Hurricane was shot down after a tussle between Hurricanes and Me109s. On the 27th Ju88s and fighter escorts attacked the Grand Harbour in the afternoon. A second enemy force was approaching from St Paul's Bay and a Hurricane managed to shoot down the Ju88. The most significant single loss of life had been at the Regent Cinema in Valletta on 15 February. Bombs had struck the cinema, killing fifty servicemen and twenty-four civilians.

March opened with a dogfight that claimed two Hurricanes at midday. The Grand Harbour was targeted, leading to the deaths of several civilians. Kalafrana was targeted the next day. Two Swordfish due to reach Malta that evening failed to arrive. Luqa and Kalafrana were bombed during the night by Ju88s and on this occasion anti-aircraft guns shot one of the raiders down. The Wellingtons were active that night: sixteen dropped twenty-six tons of bombs on enemy shipping in Palermo Harbour. Two cargo ships were sunk and a third was set on fire. The Wellingtons also hit an oil dump, a shipyard and a seaplane base.

On 4 March the Air Minister, Sir Archibald Sinclair, explained to the House of Commons that 175,000 tons of enemy shipping had been sunk in the previous six months. As importantly, Lloyd sent a signal the following day urgently requesting Spitfires. They would arrive very soon.

Meanwhile, Hurricanes had to contend with five Ju88s and ten Me109s to the north of the Grand Harbour on 5 March and yet another Hurricane was lost. Luqa was bombed by Ju88s and a number of Wellington bombers were destroyed on the ground.

At Gibraltar Spitfires were being assembled and loaded aboard the aircraft carrier, HMS *Eagle*. On 7 March as part of Operation Spotter, fifteen Spitfires took off from the aircraft carrier for a 700 mile flight. The Spitfires were covered by Hurricanes as they landed at Takali airfield. At long last Spitfires, which were to become part of 249 Squadron, were in Malta. They were to be the first Spitfires to be based overseas.

Amongst the new pilots was Flight Lieutenant Philip Whaley Ellis Heppell. He would see his first action on 17 March when he and his section attacked some Me109s. Heppell shot down one of the enemy aircraft, which was to be the 100th kill credited to 249 Squadron. Heppell himself was shot down on 8 April, but not before he had destroyed a Ju88 close to the Grand Harbour. His aircraft crashed in Sliema cemetery and he parachuted into a bomb hole. In all probability his aircraft was actually hit by ground based anti-aircraft fire. Heppell was to spend some time in hospital, but returned to active duty in December 1942. He joined 1435 Squadron based at Luqa and in his new role as Flight Commander he would lead low-level sweeps over Sicily. By April 1943 Heppell had become a squadron leader and took command of 229 Squadron whose principal role was again against ground targets. In one of the encounters he was wounded after a dogfight with an FW190. As a result his active career over Malta came to an end; he was returned to England on 10 May and admitted to hospital. Heppell would go on to take command of 229, 129 and 118 Squadrons. With 118 Squadron he played an active role in Operation Market Garden in 1944. His operational career came to an end in March 1945 and by then he had won a Distinguished Flying Cross and the French Croix de Guerre with three palms. He left the RAF in April 1946.

The Malta Night Fighter Unit was reinforced on 8 March with the arrival of four Beaufighter night fighters and three Blenheims. The Beaufighters would take over responsibility for night defence from the Hurricanes. That night Italian bombers attacked the airfields, accompanied by Ju88s. One of the newly arrived Beaufighters claimed the first kill when it shot down one of the Ju88s. A pair of Wellingtons belonging to No. 37 Squadron, operating out of Luqa collided with one another whilst taking off. The aircraft caught fire and the mines that they had onboard exploded. From that point on Malta had virtually lost its Wellington strike force. Despite heavy enemy air raids, including one at midday on 9 March, when eighteen Ju88s and twenty-six Me109s attacked Luqa, Safi and Hal Far, Hurricanes were still used to intercept. A Hurricane shot down a Ju88 and earlier the Hurricanes had covered the arrival of more Blenheims. Anti-aircraft units also claimed another

Ju88, which crashed near Hal Far. Fleet Air Arm Swordfish sunk an enemy merchant ship that was being escorted by three Italian destroyers. One of the pilots coaxed his aircraft to within 30 feet of the sea to launch his torpedoes.

The Germans attacked Malta on the evening of 12 March with nine Ju88s. A Beaufighter and three Hurricanes were scrambled, the former shooting down one of the enemy raiders.

The Spitfires were almost ready to be thrown into battle. As Major R T Gilchrist, commanding one of the anti-aircraft batteries, said:

> Spitfires began to make a welcome appearance in the air, they were hopelessly outnumbered by enemy fighters. Perhaps the most heroic sight throughout a heroic year was to see about half a dozen of these fighters in the air taking on all comers. They were frequently shot down, but seldom without first having scored a success against their opponents.

At 08.00 on 14 March a reconnaissance Ju88 shadowed by a pair of Me109s came under fire from anti-aircraft guns on the island. The Ju88 was damaged, as was one of the Messerschmitt, which promptly collided with the other. One of the pilots managed to bale out whilst the other, still in his aircraft, crashed into the sea. A couple of hours later more Me109s buzzed around, hunting for the two missing pilots. Four Spitfires scrambled and engaged the Me109s, now over Gozo and the Spitfires claimed their first kill. The Germans returned in the afternoon with twenty-nine Me109s, escorting a DO24 flying boat. Lieutenant Seiz (the pilot of the first downed Messerschmitt) and Adolf Jennerich (the pilot that had been shot down by the Spitfire) were both picked up by the flying boat.

There were more dogfights on Sunday 15 March and on the following day, to bring heart to the citizens of Valletta, Spitfires came in low and performed stunts over the city. There were more heavy raids on 17 March, with numerous civilian casualties.

The Gozo ferryboat, *Royal Lady*, was attacked by three Me109s covered by four others as it docked at Marfa with over 200 passengers onboard on 18 March. The damage caused to the *Royal Lady* forced her to be laid up for ten days but luckily only one civilian and two soldiers had been wounded. A Maryland was shot down in the afternoon some 6 miles out and in the evening Hal Far and Luqa came under attack. Spitfires and Hurricanes were scrambled. A Spitfire was shot down, as was an Me109. Two Hurricanes were also lost: both of the aircraft crashed into the sea. Later there were reports that a Ju88 had crashed after receiving damage during an attack.

At 08.05, at 10,000 ft, four Spitfires provided cover for Hurricanes intercepting Me109s on 20 March. The Messerschmitts were approaching from the south, over Filfa. The Spitfires peeled off and made for the Me109s and Pilot Officer R W Buck McNair, a Canadian, described the action:

> We got our scramble call and soared up to 10,000 ft. We were just turning down into the sun, when Daddy [Flying Officer Daddo-Langlois] called on the R/T that there were 109s at six o'clock – behind and above. We had time to turn around and break into them and I screamed round to the right and found I had turned too quickly and the Huns were still some distance away. I eased up a bit on my turn, for if I had continued it, I would have put my belly to a 109, so I straightened up and he would have to turn his belly to me. He did and I let off a great squirt at him. The 109 went into a spiral dive and looking round and finding no other Huns about, I went down after it, having no trouble in following. I waited my chance to fire again and got a good burst into it, I saw hits on the starboard wing, pieces came off but he still didn't take any evasive action, just continued with the spiral dive. Down to 3,000 ft I started clobbering the 109 all over. I emptied my cannon and continued with the machine guns. Oil and glycol from its cooling system poured out. The white glycol looked beautiful streaming out into the clear air; it was a really lovely day. Looking round there was still nobody behind me. The German now pulled up over the roofs of Valletta, reached the sea and crashed into it.

The body of the German pilot was recovered on the shores of Sicily seven weeks later.

Several waves of Ju88s of between fifty and seventy-five aircraft each time struck Malta on Saturday 21 March. Predominantly they were coming in, in close formations and making for the airfields. There were enormous civilian casualties, predominantly in Mosta. There were mass bombing raids against Takali airfield on Monday 23 March. It seemed that the intensity of the bombing attacks was increasing. The Maltese defenders claimed seventeen enemy planes shot down and at least ten others damaged. The Germans were also attracted to the island by the arrival of another convoy.

Clan Campbell, Pampas, Talabot and *Breconshire* arrived along with an escort of seventeen destroyers and five cruisers. They had left Alexandria on 20 March. The previous day three of the destroyers, HMS *Lively,* HMS *Havoc* and HMS *Kingston* had been damaged, as had the cruiser HMS *Cleopatra.* A day after the convoy had left Alexandria HMS *Eagle* in Operation Picket had delivered nine more Spitfires to Malta. These Spitfires were already aloft, contributing to the heavy price that the Germans paid for their continued attacks.

The Germans were not content to see the convoy being unloaded without attempting to destroy the supplies. There were large scale and determined attacks on the Grand Harbour on 24 March. In fact this day saw the beginning of an intensive operation against the harbour defences and up to 12 April, 2,159 bomber sorties were launched against the Grand Harbour. The Germans delivered 1,870 tons of bombs which caused enormous damage. On 24 March alone the *Talabot* unloaded 497 tons of supplies and a further 310 tons from the *Pampas.* The *Breconshire* had been hit by three bombs on 23 March and her engine room had been flooded. She was drifting inshore, close to Zonqor Point but on 25 March she was brought into Marsaxlokk Bay. Meanwhile, in the afternoon, thirty Ju88s, twenty-five Ju87s and twelve Me109s attempted to sink the *Pampas* and the *Talabot* in the Grand Harbour. Six Spitfires and eight Hurricanes were scrambled to intercept.

At midday on 26 March, twenty-four Ju88s and twenty Ju87s attacked the *Talabot* and *Pampas*. The *Talabot* was set on fire and sank: she still had a considerable amount of cargo onboard. The *Pampas* was also set on fire and sank. The first wave of bombers was tackled by seven Hurricanes and the second wave by four Spitfires. At least one Ju88 was shot down.

Buck McNair recalled the combat:

> Bud Connell was leading, Junior Tayleur his number two with Paul Brennan as my wing man. We came across a bunch of Huns diving and bombing and it was then a case of each man picking a target. I selected one, decided it was going too fast and that I couldn't catch it. I saw another and went full out at it. Brennan was above me and had a go too and he thought he'd hit it then he saw another Spit going for it – me – so pulled off to give cover. I was 800 yards behind the 88 and could scarcely gain on it. He nipped into cloud 1,000 ft thick.

I followed on course and when I came out he was still ahead of me. If he'd had any sense he would have turned and foxed me but he just tried to outrun me. The Spit didn't have that much speed advantage over a fleeing Ju88.

The Germans returned the same evening, targeting Kalafrana. Twenty-four Ju88s and eighteen Ju87s were escorted by a number of Me109s. One Ju88 managed to hit the *Breconshire*. This was around 17.30 and four Spitfires and six Hurricanes were scrambled to intercept. For a brief time the *Breconshire* was on fire, but this was quickly brought under control.

Content with the damage that they had done in the Grand Harbour, the Germans spent the remaining days of the month concentrating on the airfields. This gave the Royal Navy a chance to deal with the damaged ships and the wreckage around the dockyards. HMS *Penelope*, that had been holed by air attacks on 26 March was brought into the Malta dry docks. The shrapnel holes were plugged with wood, which would earn her the nickname HMS *Pepper Pot*. She eventually managed to get back to Gibraltar on 10 April, having survived repeated air attacks after she had left Malta on 8 April

HMS *Eagle* delivered seven Spitfires to Malta. These had been the ones that had had their flight cancelled in Operation Picket on 21 March. On 31 March the Germans switched back attacks to the dockyards, hoping to disrupt repair work being carried out. HMS *Penelope* had been the target and she would continue to act as a magnet for enemy aircraft until she finally sailed on the evening of 8 April.

Throughout the month working parties from both the army and the air force had ensured that the three airfields remained as operational as possible. The army had managed to lay 27 miles of dispersal runways. They had built fourteen large bomber pens, 170 fighter pens, seventy reconnaissance aircraft pens and thirty-one naval aircraft pens, all in the space of three months. The month had been extremely trying, with 2,208 tons of bombs dropped on the island.

But there was worse to come and April would be dubbed by the defenders of Malta as 'the cruellest month'.

CHAPTER SEVEN
FIGHTING FOR ITS LIFE

During the month of April 1942, 6,728 tons of bombs were dropped on the island of Malta. On average 170 enemy bombers raided Malta in three waves every day. Fighter defences were down to an absolute minimum: on a good day the RAF could muster ten fighters, on a bad one just four. The dockyard area was devastated, with around half of all of the bombs landing in this area. The submarine flotilla was forced to leave the island, but amazingly and largely due to the rock shelters, only around 300 civilians were killed during the month. The majority of the bombs fell on selected targets. The dockyard area received 1,556 tons, Luqa airfield 805 tons, Takali 841 tons, Hal Far 750 and Kalafrana 196. Another 980 tons was scattered at various points around the island.

During April alone 10,000 buildings were destroyed or badly damaged, Valletta's streets were blocked by masonry, the palaces of the Knights of St John were wrecked, the Opera House was demolished, and the Palace of the Grand Masters, the museum and the university all received severe damage. Although the headquarters of *The Times of Malta* had been hit on 31 March the paper was on the news stands the following day. There were just three days of respite during the month, when poor weather kept the Germans at bay. In all, the total length of the raids during the month came to 12 days, 10 hours and 20 minutes, bearing in mind that each raid lasted around an hour.

One of the Hurricane squadrons had been re-equipped with Spitfires in March and another would be re-equipped in the second week of April. But many of the Spitfires had actually been lost on the ground, so once again the front-line fighter in April was the Hurricane, sometimes engaging the enemy at odds of over ten to one. Servicemen and civilians alike lived in a twilight nightmare world throughout the month, as a corporal in the Royal Air Force recalled:

> During dinner the Hun started again. This time he dropped quite a number of bombs on Luqa village. A direct hit was scored on a shelter. It appeared that water was seeping into the shelter, drowning the people trapped there. The army and RAF squads were attempting to get through to them. After tea

another raid – bombs all over the place. As I am writing, the six pm news from Blighty can be heard in the sergeants' mess. It makes me just a little homesick. Back home I can picture the family having tea – Thursday evening – I wonder whether Dad has any inspections tonight. And my thoughts fly to Joan – she is probably making tea now for Jack and her Dad. How I wish I could be there. But this war can't last forever. The camp all clear has sounded. I wonder how much peace we shall get now. The place seems much the same after a raid, when the smoke dust has cleared – at least from a distance – as I look over the valley to Rabat on the hill, or slightly to the left to Takali then follow on to B'Kara, Hamrun and the harbour.

The corporal was certainly not exaggerating. At around 15.00 on 1 April a wave of German bombers flattened the Convent at Sliema, hitting an adjacent parish church and two chapels. The parish priest was hearing confessions and three women and a ten year old girl were buried in the masonry; only one of the women survived. Spitfires managed to shoot down an Me109 and more Me109s covering a flying boat, hunting for the pilot, were also engaged by the Spitfires and two more German aircraft were lost. A pair of Ju88s was shot down then fourteen Ju87s approaching Kalafrana and Hal Far were brought under fire by anti-aircraft units. One Ju88 was shot down and it crashed on Delimara Point.

Sergeant Hesselyn of No. 249 Squadron had had an extremely busy April fool's Day. He had engaged Me109s in his Spitfire and managed to shoot down one of them that was covering the German flying boat. It was his first kill, but his joy was short-lived, as a cannon shell went straight through his port wing. He gave chase to the Me109, but he exhausted his ammunition when he was about 40 miles out to sea and returned to refit. Just an hour and a half later he was involved in seeing off twenty Me109s, covering the large force of Stukas heading for Kalafrana and Hal Far. He fired a two second burst at one of the Stukas, which exploded and dived into the sea. As Hesselyn prepared to land he was attacked by an Me109. He retracted his undercarriage, opened the throttle and turned steeply. The Me109 overshot him and climbed away. Hesselyn would live to fight another day and in fact on 21 April he would have his best ever day, claiming a Stuka and a Messerschmitt destroyed and two other Messerschmitts damaged.

A mixed force of fifty Ju88s and Ju87s, with Me109 escorts, approached Malta at 09.30 on 2 April. Four Spitfires and two Hurricanes were scrambled to intercept. Two of the four Spitfires were shot down. Later the Germans attacked Kalafrana for the loss of a Ju88. A pair of Me109s strafed the cargo ship *Franco*, as she was making her way from the Grand Harbour to Gozo. Then another ten Me109s joined the attack. Amazingly the ship made it to Mgarr Harbour at 19.30: only one of her crewmen had been wounded and the ship itself had suffered only minor damage. The cargo had taken the bulk of the hits. Kalafrana was hit once again that night by Ju88s.

On 4 April the Secretary of the State for the Colonies wrote to the Governor of Malta:

> I have been watching with admiration the stout-hearted resistance of all in Malta – service personnel and civilian alike – to the fierce and constant air raids of the enemy in recent weeks. In the active defence of the island the RAF have been ably supported by the Royal Malta Artillery, and it therefore gives me special pleasure, in recognition of their skill and resolution, to assume the Colonelcy-in-Chief of the regiment. Please convey my best wishes to all ranks of my new regiment, and assure them of the added pride with which I shall follow their future activities.

The situation on Malta was, however, becoming bleaker by the day. On the same day as the despatch more attacks were made on Luqa, Hal Far, Takali and Valletta. Easter Sunday, 5 April, saw no respite, with heavy, widespread raids causing a number of civilian casualties. The 6 April, if anything, was even worse, with a major German attack on the dock-yards and airfields. Again there were large numbers of civilian casualties.

The following day Malta witnessed its 2,000th alert. Up to this point the longest alert had lasted nearly 12 hours and as if to celebrate this milestone, Malta suffered seventeen alerts in 24 hours. The Royal Opera House was hit and badly damaged. The first raids of the day, however, concentrated on the Grand Harbour and Kalafrana when upwards of eighty German bombers and forty-five Me109s took part. On this occasion Malta was not able to scramble any fighters, as none were serviceable. Even a Gozo fishing boat attracted the attention of a pair of Me109s. It was attacked at 10.00 hours: all six crewmen were injured and one died later in the day. The *Royal Lady*, still berthed at Mgarr, on Gozo, was attacked by six Me109s and once again she was rendered unseaworthy. Another Me109 attacked a Maltese fishing boat, killing a father and son. The biggest raid, however, had ruined the Opera House. It is believed that up to 100 German bombers had made this evening attack.

Malta was getting towards breaking point and the German attacks were systematically achieving their longer-term objectives of not only knocking out the defensive fighter cover, but also freely striking against both tactical and strategic targets. The RAF managed to scrape together a handful of fighters to be put up against an afternoon raid on 8 April. They faced a dozen Ju88s and twenty Me109s. One Ju88 was shot down, but the Swordfish hangar at Kalafrana was hit, destroying a Swordfish float plane and a Walrus.

The airfields were hit again on 9 April. Sixteen Ju87s, forty Ju88s and a similar number of Me109s struck Luqa. The air raid shelter took a direct hit, killing twenty-three civilians, eight of whom were from the same family. A second raid in the afternoon comprised sixty Ju88s and twelve Ju87s. Ten Hurricanes and two Spitfires were scrambled and one of the Hurricanes, flown by Sergeant Pauley of 229 Squadron, was shot down. Various targets were hit on Friday 10 April, including a civilian vessel in which eight people were wounded.

The *Royal Lady* was the point of attack on the following day, when four German aircraft strafed Mgarr Harbour. The island was visited by Air Marshal Sir Arthur Tedder, Air Officer Commanding Middle East, and he was able to see with his own eyes the damage that had been inflicted on the airfields and the perilous state of the air defences. Tedder would also witness eighty bombers involved in the first raid on 12 April when an Italian BR20 bomber was shot down.

By the middle of April fighter defences were at their weakest. On average around six aircraft were serviceable: four would be used to engage the enemy and two would be reserved for airfield defence. The system needed the four striking aircraft to get aloft as soon as news was received of incoming hostiles. The fighters would then try to gain height as rapidly as possible. The two air defence aircraft would be sent up at the last moment in order to conserve fuel. They would then fly to a point some 20 or 30 miles south of the island, ready to move in to intercept raiders attacking a particular airfield. The Germans soon were wise to the tactic and would fly towards the airfields as the striking force returned to refuel and rearm. The only thing that could save the incoming aircraft would be the airfield defence fighters.

The situation had reached such a state that Ju88 crewmen were no longer frightened to fly over the island in daylight without fighter escorts.

They were certain that the air battle for the island had been won. On average these pilots were making three sorties a day for four days a week.

It was British ingenuity that continued to keep the handful of fighters aloft, as Group Captain A B Woodhall, who was in charge of the operations room explained:

> On one occasion all our fighter aircraft were grounded in order to try to increase serviceability. The Hun bombers came over in force with quite a large fighter escort. It happened that there were several fighter pilots with me in the operations room, one of whom was a Canadian with an unmistakable voice. I put him at the microphone at a standby radio set and proceeded to give him dummy orders. He replied just as if he was flying his fighter. This, we suspected, caused a cry of '*Achtung! Spitfeuer!*' to go over the German radio. In any case, two 109s enthusiastically shot each other down without any British aircraft being airborne. The knowledge that the Germans intercepted our orders stood us in good stead. We claimed that Pilot Officer 'Humgufery' shot down the two Huns.

With the drastic reduction in the number of fighter aircraft, much of the defence of the island fell to the anti-aircraft crews. During the course of April they accounted for 102 enemy aircraft, with thirty being claimed for the week ending 8 April alone. Understandably, the anti-aircraft units also expended the highest amount of ammunition that week. On average every heavy anti-aircraft gun was firing sixty-nine rounds per day. The Bofors guns firing around fifty-six rounds each day. Even the Germans admitted in a radio broadcast that the anti-aircraft units were a force to be reckoned with:

> Malta's anti-aircraft artillery must be counted among Tommy's very best, and plays the greatest part in the defence of the island.

On the ground the Royal Artillery had obviously a very different view of the air raids compared to the fighter pilots engaged in aerial duels above them. One of the Royal Artillery staff officers described his view of the action:

> The dust after any air raid is terrific; but in Malta, where the soil is so light and the stones so soft, the cloud of dust that

rises is as thick as any smokescreen and makes the work of the gunners trying to see their targets doubly difficult. Sometimes an hour later one could see the dust cloud in a compact mass miles out above the sea, driven along with the wind. The weight of these attacks was particularly severe on the gun positions surrounding the airfields. At first, the enemy made the actual airfield itself his main objective. Gun positions suffered from badly aimed bombs and from those released too early or too late, but very soon his main objective became the fringes of the airfield where the aircraft were lying. Combined with this, he made deliberate attacks on the anti-aircraft positions. These suffered severely as they could not be moved out too far lest the airfield runways became bereft of protection, particularly by the light anti-aircraft guns.

As a result of the growing reliance on the anti-aircraft guns, compounded by the fact that the fighters were grounded for eleven days during April, there was a major shortage of ammunition. Crews were instructed to fire just fifteen rounds per gun per day. In order to maximise what little air defence there was, both fighters and anti-aircraft guns, Takali was created into a sanctuary for aircraft. The Bofors guns positioned around Takali did not have to restrict themselves and the fighters were instructed to make for Takali, so that the anti-aircraft guns around the airfield would be able to protect them as they made their approach. The gunners were both British and Maltese, fighting alongside one another. Twice daily ammunition expenditure was checked and reports were made. Communicating the ammunition expenditure was not always an easy task, as field telephones were in short supply and communication cables often severed or destroyed. One of the battery commanders was forced on at least two occasions to swim across a creek in the harbour in order to deliver his ammunition expenditure report.

It was not just communication cables that were being damaged or destroyed during this period. The main cables took seventy-eight direct hits during the siege itself; half of the hits taking place in April 1942. This meant that on numerous occasions there was no electricity, gas or water. Bombs dropped on water reservoirs meant that Valletta did not have mains water for four or five weeks. The only major horror that was absent in the air raids on Malta was fire, as most of the buildings were constructed of stone.

The priority for anti-aircraft defences and for the fighters was the bombers, as these were the enemy aircraft that would doing the bulk of the damage. More Spitfires were desperately needed. In the previous month, on 27 March, Group Captain Bouchier, Deputy Director of Fighter Operations, pleaded for more experienced Spitfire squadrons to be despatched to the island:

> Our fighter pilots place no great premium on life. Their greatest desire is to fight on and with their squadron or wing for as long as they can. *Esprit de corps* is terrific. Their confidence in themselves and their squadrons is born of good teamwork and flying together. Fighter squadron pilots do not only fly together, they play together, drink together, eat together, talk together. They become very attached to each other and their leaders. It is a greater sadness to them than most people appreciate to be constantly uprooted in penny numbers from what to them is everything on earth – their squadron and their friends.

Aside from the necessary reinforcements for air defences, Dobbie had other concerns and in April he signalled the War Office, expressing them:

> It is obvious that the very worst must happen if we cannot replenish our vital needs.

The bread ration was down to 10.5 oz a day, there was very little oil, coal or ammunition, sugar was in short supply, the victory kitchens were able to supply the Maltese with a hot meal each day, but this was barely above a starvation diet. Dietary problems were leading to diseases and Dobbie was concerned that this would undermine the strength and resolve to continue the struggle. He could order improvements to the defences by reinforcing the shorelines, building underground tunnels and other improvisations. What he could not do was to feed the people and the prospect of starving women and children haunted him.

The editor of *The Times of Malta*, Mabel Strickland, sent Lord Louis Mountbatten a telegram on 21 April. In it she implied that Dobbie needed to be replaced. She suggested that he had failed to coordinate the activities of the armed services. Churchill and the War Cabinet were informed and the Chiefs of Staff from the Middle East Defence Committee agreed that Dobbie had probably lost control of the situation and that he did need to be replaced. They recognised Dobbie as being courageous, but nonetheless both Churchill and the War Cabinet made the decision to replace him with General Lord Gort VC. Churchill also ensured that Gort would have the broadest possible range of power and authority. The new governor would become the Commander-in-Chief and Supreme Commander in Malta. Churchill was also acutely aware of the fact that the German bombing offensive was just a preliminary to invasion. He knew that Spitfires had to be despatched to Malta, but launching a handful of Spitfires at maximum range from an aircraft carrier, in the hope that they would reach the island intact, was not an option. Churchill turned to Roosevelt to find a solution. It would take a little time to organise, but the Americans were amenable and a Spitfire relief force would soon be on its way.

Meanwhile the heavy blitz over Malta continued. On 14 April Pilot Officer Kelly of 249 Squadron was shot down by Me109s. He was forced to bale out at just 800 ft, 3 miles west of Hal Far. His parachute failed to open properly and he hit the water, becoming entangled in the parachute lines and losing his dinghy. A pair of Spitfires went out to find him and circled round. Luckily Kelly was a strong swimmer and HSL128 picked him up at 11.40. Later that day Beauforts were attacked by Me109s as they returned to Malta. Five Hurricanes were scrambled to protect the Beauforts. One of the Beauforts was shot down as it skimmed towards the island, virtually at sea level.

Hesselyn recalled an afternoon in mid-April during the height of the attacks on the airfields. The pilots, on their way to dispersal had to jump into a crater at Takali as bombs fell around them. The German aircraft screamed overhead and the pilots raced to get into their machines before the next attack. Getting into the fighters, they had seconds before they were ordered to lift off to intercept another attack:

> We scrambled at three o'clock, climbing south of the island getting to 26,000 feet with the sun behind us. Wood called up and said: 'Hello Mac. There's a big plot building up but it's taking time to come south. Keep your present angels and save your gravy. I will tell you when to come in.' We stooged around until he gave us the word. Then we sailed in. Suddenly, glancing behind, I saw four 109s coming down on me. Three of them overshot. The fourth made his turn too wide and I got inside him. I was slightly below when I attacked from 200 yards, firing perhaps 20 ft ahead of him in the hope that his aircraft and my bullets would arrive at that spot simultaneously: they did. I kept on firing as I was determined to

make certain of him. He caught fire. Black smoke poured out, he rolled on his back and went into a vertical dive and straight into the drink. As he crashed it struck me suddenly that there might be something on my tail. In my excitement I had forgotten to look but luckily none of the other 109s had dived down on me. Wood now reported that the 88s were diving on Takali, and I pulled up to 10,000 feet. The next instant the 88s were diving past my nose and the other boys were coming down from above to attack them. I picked out one and went for him and as I pressed my gun button his rear gunner opened fire. I had fired for about a second when my port cannon packed up. Luckily I was travelling fast. This prevented my aircraft from slewing from the recoil of my starboard cannon as I was able to correct with rudder. I concentrated on the 88's starboard motor and wing root and could see my shells hitting. Bits were flying off him and flames began spreading as he continued in his dive; he was well ablaze when he crashed. Returning to land I had my first experience of being beaten up in the circuit. A great pall of smoke and dust from the bombing was hanging over Takali. I made a couple of dummy runs over the airfield and could see that the landing path was well cratered. Just then I sighted six 109s above at 5,000 feet, waiting to pounce. The other boys were kicking about the circuit waiting to try and get in. I beetled up Imtafa valley, skipped round some windmills at the top and swung down a valley on the other side. Again and again the 109s dived down from above and attacked me. Again and again I thanked my stars that the 'Spit' was such a manoeuvrable aircraft. Each time I was attacked I turned violently and their shells and bullets whipped past behind me. It was a nerve-racking business. With all the violent turning and twisting I began to feel very sick. My neck ached from constantly twisting from side to side, looking back and from holding it up while doing tight turns against the extra gravity force. Eventually Mac said that we were to go in and he would cover us. I started a normal circuit about 300 ft above the airfield, put my wheels and flaps down, did weaving approach and, as my wheels touched ground felt a sigh of relief. I taxied to my pen, forgetting to put up my flaps. All I could do when I got there was to lie back in the cockpit and gasp for breath. The ground crew had to help me out of my aircraft and, dazed and dizzy, I groped my way along the wing out of my pen. I met Laddie as I was wandering over to dispersal. Both our tunics were soaked with perspiration. We looked up to see how Mac was getting on. He was making his approach about 50 ft up when suddenly two 109s darted out of the sun. Their shooting, however, was poor and whipping up his wheels Mac turned sharply into them. The 109s overshot him, carried on and beat up the aerodrome. Mac made a quick dart, put down his wheels and managed to get in. He landed with two gallons of petrol – at the pace we were using it, sufficient fuel for only another two minutes in the air. I had had five gallons; the others about the same.

On 15 April 1942 King George VI sent a message to Dobbie:

> To honour her brave people I award the George Cross to the Island Fortress of Malta, to bear witness to a heroism and a devotion that will be long famous in history.

The award, second only to the Victoria Cross, had normally only ever been awarded to individuals. Accepting the award on behalf of the island, Dobbie replied:

> By God's help Malta will not weaken but will endure until victory is won.

The George Cross was the highest gallantry award for civilians. In January 1941 the award was created at the insistence of Winston Churchill, who believed that a new medal was needed to recognise the acts of bravery performed by civilians. The Cross can still be seen at Fort St Elmo in Valletta and it still appears on the Maltese flag.

The 18th saw twenty-five Ju87s attack Kalafrana at 09.30. Twelve Ju88s hit the base at 11.30 and at 17.30 fourteen Ju87s and twelve Ju88s arrived. The hangars were hit and four RAF servicemen and two dock-yard policemen were killed, with a number of others injured. There were a number of civilian casualties due to attacks by Ju88s, particularly around the Grand Harbour.

Help was, however, on its way, in the shape of forty-six Spitfires that were flown in from the American aircraft carrier, USS *Wasp*, in Operation Calendar. Originally fifty Spitfires were to be sent out, but forty-seven began the journey and just one failed to reach the island.

The USS *Wasp* had left Scapa Flow on 9 April heading for the Clyde, where it loaded Spitfires of 603 Squadron on 13 April. *Wasp* left for its perilous journey via the Straits of Gibraltar on 14 April: protecting it was Force W of the British Home Fleet, including HMS *Renown*. At 04.00 on 20 April the USS *Wasp's* own Grumman Wildcat Fighters were launched to give top cover for the force, whilst the Spitfires were brought up from the hangar deck. One by one they lifted off from the aircraft carrier, bound for Malta. The launch took place to the south of Sardinia. This was to be the first of a number of deliveries made by USS *Wasp*.

Once the launch of the Spitfires had been completed the *Wasp* and her escorts turned back towards England. The American vessel would provide a vital link in the reinforcement chain until she was hurried back to the United States for refitting and repairs and posted to the Pacific.

Within 20 minutes of the Spitfires landing at Takali airfield they were dive bombed by up to ninety German aircraft. The service personnel worked all night amongst burning aircraft and fuel bowsers and by morning it was clear that just twenty-seven aircraft had survived the attack and only seventeen were air worthy. Over a hundred fighters were laid up on the airfields awaiting repair. Spares were at a premium and aircraft had to be cannibalised in order to ensure that any of them remained in service.

Amongst all of this was the constant arrival of aircraft that were bound for Egypt. During March and April alone 300 were landed, refuelled and despatched via Malta to Egypt. This was despite the fact that there were constant night attacks by the German air force and the airfields had to be repaired so that the transit aircraft could land and take off.

At dawn on 21 April half a dozen Wellingtons of 148 Squadron arrived at Luqa from Egypt. They were carrying additional aircrew and ground crew. The bombers had been detailed to operate out of Safi. At 07.00 the Grand Harbour, docks, Luqa and Takali came under attack from thirty-seven Ju88s and thirty-four Me109s. In response, five Hurricanes and ten Spitfires were scrambled at around 08.30 and an Me109 was shot down, as was a Spitfire, flown by Pilot Officer Brooker. Squadron Leader Bisdee was also shot down over Hal Far at midday. An evening raid by German aircraft destroyed five Wellingtons and damaged two of the new Wellington arrivals. Nonetheless a Wellington took off with pilots during the night to collect some replacement Hurricanes and ferry them back to Malta.

At 09.15 on 22 April four Spitfires chased a Ju88 reconnaissance aircraft towards Sicily. They managed to shoot it down 10 miles to the south of the island. A Hurricane had been lost over the Grand Harbour, when it had tried to finish off a stricken Ju88 that had been hit by anti-aircraft fire. Instead it was the Hurricane itself that was hit by friendly fire.

A dozen Hurricanes and Spitfires were scrambled to meet a large raid against the Maltese airfields and the dockyards on 23 April. The raiders consisted of forty-four Ju88s and fifteen Ju87s, escorted by Me109s. A single Ju88 was shot down off Kalafrana. The same targets were hit the following day by thirty Ju88s and twenty Me109s. The *Royal Lady* came under attack once again at 07.00.

Despite the arrival of the Spitfires the defenders were still fighting an uphill battle. One New Zealand Spitfire pilot wrote:

> We were also feeling the strain, not only of the continuous air fighting but also of the bombing and the general living conditions of Malta. Our barrage was also falling away. The gunners were growing tired and many of the gun barrels were becoming worn. All of us were getting less sleep for the enemy bombers were coming over in greater numbers at night when the moon was favourable. They were pressing home these attacks with more determination than previously and were coming down much lower. We had insufficient night fighters to hold them all back. With the lengthening days, we were doing longer periods of readiness and the night bombing prevented us from obtaining proper sleep. We were becoming irritable and on edge.

Air Vice Marshal Sir Hugh Lloyd mirrored the concerns:

> Conditions had become extremely difficult. The poor quality of food had not been noticed at first, then suddenly it began to take effect. In March it had been clear enough that in April most belts had to be taken in by two holes and in May by another hole. Our diet was a slice and a half of bread with jam for breakfast, bully beef for lunch with one slice of bread, and except for an additional slice of bread it was the same fare for dinner. There was sugar but margarine appeared only every two or three days; even drinking water, lighting and heating were all rationed. And things which had been taken

for granted closed down. The making of beer required coal so none had been made for months. Officers and men slept in shelters, in caverns and dugouts in quarries. Three hundred slept in one underground cabin as tight as sardines in a tin and two hundred slept in a disused tunnel. None had any comfort or warmth. Soon, too, we should want hundreds of tons of fuel and ammunition.

Dobbie did his best to bolster morale and broadcast to the island:

> The safety and well being of this fortress rests under God on four supports. They are the three fighting services and the civil population. Each one of these is essential to the well being of the others, and each one depends on the other three and cannot do without them.

The same night the Italians broadcast to the island:

> This is but one more preposterous deception by the British government. Had not our unfortunate Maltese brethren been under the heel of British domination which is being forced on them under the threat of guns and bayonets, we have no doubt as to how the Maltese would behave.

Malta soldiered on despite daily civilian casualties, aircraft losses, food shortages and dwindling supplies. March to May 1942 was the most vital time for the Allies to reinforce Egypt. Malta had played its part in two major ways: firstly the defences of the island had taken second place and secondly, between November 1941 and July 1942, 750 aircraft had passed through the island. None were earmarked for Malta: all would be needed by Montgomery and the 8th Army in Egypt. Salvation would not necessarily be found by continuing to replace the dwindling resources on the island. Instead, hope would come from the 8th Army in its intended drive west along the North African coast.

Malta suffered 283 air raids during April alone, 300 civilians had been killed, 4,272 buildings destroyed or badly damaged. No building was safe, be it a home, a church or a government building. Even thirty-four elderly women and two nuns had lost their lives when an old people's home at Hamrun had been hit. Over 6,000 tons of bombs had been dropped on the island and numerous vessels had been lost.

Yet hanging over the island was an even greater peril: the imminent danger of invasion. If the enemy believed for one moment that the island's resolve to resist had been swept away then landings would be inevitable. The British, acutely aware of the dangers, sent out photo reconnaissance sorties to discover preparations for invasion. It was obvious that large quantities of stores and ammunition would be required and if the Germans were to use airborne troops then their gliders would be based somewhere close. Three airstrips were discovered on Sicily and a close watch was maintained on troop movement, aircraft reinforcement and the movement of men and materials by road.

Kesselring, however, may have had a significant change of mind. Supplies were beginning to get through in greater quantities to Rommel in North Africa. Malta's strike power had been neutralised, perhaps the invasion of Malta was no longer necessary?

Over the course of the month the Germans had employed over 400 aircraft against the island and 300 of these had either been destroyed or badly damaged. The continued preoccupation with Malta, particularly in the using up of bombs and aircraft fuel, could only ultimately be detrimental to the effort in North Africa. In any case, commitments elsewhere would mean that the Germans could no longer afford to throw such huge resources at the island. Mercifully, this would mean a period of respite.

CHAPTER EIGHT

TRIUMPH

The lull in the attacks on Malta proved to be a much needed respite for the defenders. But it was also a major mistake by the Germans and Italians. Had Kesselring chosen to strike at this point, either in late April or early May, then it would have been an almost foregone conclusion that the attack would have been successful.

On 1 May Hitler and Mussolini met to discuss the invasion plans of Malta. Hitler was adamant that precedence should be given to the effort in North Africa, rather than the invasion of the island and that at the earliest the island should be occupied in mid-July. The Germans in particular were convinced that Malta as an offensive arm of the Allied effort was neutralized. As a result, forty-five fighters and forty-five bombers were transferred to North Africa. Additional air assets, including bombers and fighters, were posted to the Russian front.

Originally the plan had been for Rommel to strike in North Africa as far as the Egyptian frontier. There he would wait until Malta had been invaded and captured. Now Rommel was convinced that the priority should be Alexandria and that the chance to conquer Egypt had to be exploited. The postponement would prove more costly to the Germans and the Italians than they could possibly imagine.

Back in England there had been a desperate call for experienced pilots to volunteer to fight in the Mediterranean, over Malta. No. 603 Squadron (City of Edinburgh) was preparing to board USS *Wasp*, which was docked at Glasgow. Once the Spitfires and their crew members were onboard the aircraft carrier sailed to Scapa Flow and set sail for Malta on 3 May. She was escorted by a pair of American destroyers, USS *Lang* and USS *Skerrett*. The British part of the escort contingent included the battle cruiser HMS *Renown*, the cruiser HMS *Charybdis* and the destroyers HMS *Echo* and HMS *Intrepid*.

One of the Spitfire crew members was Robert 'Barney' Barnfather, formerly of 234 Squadron. By the end of April 1942 he had 200 flying hours experience, of which 100 was in Spitfires. The pilots of 603 Squadron were amazed to discover that US ships were teetotal. Officers were housed in two-man cabins, most of which had air conditioning. The Spitfires were safely housed on the hangar floor, with their wheels kept in place by wooden blocks. The Spitfires' wingtips were lashed to the decks by ropes and cables. Others were suspended from the roof girders.

On 5 May, while *en route*, the pilots received confirmation that they were indeed heading for Malta. None of them really knew what to expect but they were aware that provisions on the island were limited and this led to some panic buying from the ships' stores. In order to avoid being spotted slipping into the Mediterranean the fleet would pass through the Straits of Gibraltar at night and the pilots were told that they would be launched from a position off Algiers.

The Spitfire V, with an additional 400 litres of fuel in drop tanks, had a range of 950 miles. If the drop tanks were jettisoned once they were empty the range increased to 1,050 miles. The pilots were told that they would be 660 miles from Malta when they were launched, so this gave them a margin for error. This did make the Spitfire extremely heavy to lift off from the aircraft carrier. As a result, two of the four cannons were left unloaded and the other two were only given sixty rounds each. Despite the panic buying, the pilots were also told that they should only take their own personal kit. Any additional belongings would be flown into Malta at a later date by courier aircraft.

The Spitfires would need to rev up to 3,000 rpm, release their brakes and select emergency boost override. After take-off they would form up in four formations. The Spitfires would follow the coasts of Algeria and Tunisia to Cap Bon then turn south-east to skirt the enemy-held island of Pantelleria and then strike east for Malta. It was proposed that the Spitfires would launch before midday in the hope that they would reach the island before dark. They were also told that the aircraft had to be absolutely ready for combat, as it was likely that they would be pressed into immediate action once they arrived.

On the night of 7 May the convoy was joined by HMS *Eagle* and her own escorts. Onboard she had a further seventeen Spitfires. Additional engines, medical supplies and stores were onboard another newcomer, the mine layer, HMS *Welshman*. Bizarrely, the *Welshman* was to be disguised as the French destroyer, *Leopard*, by having plywood bulkheads fitted to the superstructure.

There was a final briefing for the Spitfire pilots on the morning of 8 May. They were told that the first dozen Spitfires would be brought up to the flight deck in the afternoon and the suspended Spitfires in the hangar would be lowered. At first light the following morning USS *Wasp* would turn into the wind and Grumman Wildcats would be sent aloft to provide air cover. The pilots manning the last of the Spitfires in the hangars would be brought up as soon as the flight deck was clear. They would need to have their engines running.

Pilots that had already operated in Malta had been sent back to Gibraltar to help guide in the new Spitfires. Squadron Leader Stan Grant of 249 Squadron would lead the first sixteen new Spitfires onto the island. The pilots woke early, had breakfast and prepared for their departure. There were final checks by ground crews and one by one the Spitfires lifted off. Only one failed to lift off and another found that they had a faulty drop tank.

The first sixteen Spitfires reached a cruising altitude of 10,000 ft then, to conserve fuel they throttled back to just over 2,000 rpm. The aircraft followed the Algerian coastline and then headed towards Pantelleria. Grant told the flight and Malta that they were half an hour from Takali. Already Spitfires were covering the airfield. As Hesselyn recalled:

Oddly enough, on this crucial day the Ju88s had omitted their usual early morning raid and did not come over, nor did any Me109s. Between nine and ten, four boys were scrambled – the rest of us knew they had gone up to cover the arrival of the new Spitfires. Everyone was happy and excited, keyed up with expectation. In a few minutes, the new boys started coming in over Imtarfa Hill. At the same time, the 109s arrived over Malta. The first bunch of Spits landed and I led an aircraft into my pen. The waiting ground crew pounced on it eagerly and began to rearm and refuel it. Its pilot, Pilot Officer Barnfather, an Englishman climbed out of his cockpit and I handed him his written instructions. More Spits were coming over the hill and arrived in the circuit at the same time as a number of 109s. One of my erks, a big wild looking fellow who had not shaven for three days, kept changing tools every few minutes. One minute he would have a rifle in his hands and be taking pot shots at the 109s and the next he would grab a tool and be undoing a panel or some screws on the Spit. Barnfather and I watched the Spits circling. 'That one will get it in a minute', I remarked. It did. An Me109 blew a large piece out of the Spit's port side near the cockpit. The Spit made hurriedly for the aerodrome and after three attempts successfully force landed. By this time there was a terrific din going on. The ground defences were engaging heavily and there was a lot of cannon fire between opposing aircraft. On the aerodrome, newly-arrived Spits were being shepherded to their pens. They were refuelled and rearmed quickly, and pilots clambered into their cockpits ready to take off immediately the order came. Within ten minutes of landing many new Spits were going up again. It was a triumph of organisation.

On 10 May, the following day, HMS *Welshman* made it into Grand Harbour. Onboard were 100 RAF technicians, canned meat, powdered milk, anti-aircraft ammunition, aircraft engines and a host of other much needed supplies. No. 603 Squadron was ready at dawn and three pilots scrambled at 08.00 to intercept reconnaissance flights. There was no action, but just three hours later ten Ju88s and twenty Ju87s, accompanied by a host of Me109s, attacked the harbour. The anti-aircraft guns opened up and Spitfires of 603 Squadron joined the mêlée. Every time a German aircraft was shot down an enormous crowd cheered. The Spitfires were up again at 14.00, as more Ju88s and Me109s tried to hit the *Welshman*. Another raid, at 17.00, saw the arrival of Italian aircraft escorted by Me109s. At least one Italian aircraft was shot down and three more were damaged. Ju87s came in on the second wave of this attack.

Although Rome radio claimed that forty-seven Spitfires had been destroyed, only three in fact had been lost and two of those pilots had been recovered. HMS *Welshman* had already been unloaded by the end of the day.

On 11 May *The Times of Malta* ran a stirring story of the previous day's air battle. The title read 'Spitfires Slaughter Stukas':

> The last two days have seen a metamorphosis in the battle of Malta. After two days of the fiercest air combat that has ever taken place over the island the *Luftwaffe* has taken the most formidable beating since the Battle of Britain two and a half years ago. Teamwork has been the watchword during all these weary months of taking a pounding with very little else to do but to grin and bear it. For months on end the gunners have hurled steel and defiance at the enemy. They have been subjected to probably the most diabolical bombing the gunners have ever known, they have been ceaselessly machine gunned, they have suffered casualties but others have taken their places and never once have they faltered. The people of Malta owe them a debt which is incalculable.

The preparation for the new arrivals had been extensive. Wing Commander E J Gracie, who was leading the Spitfires that had arrived from the first delivery from USS *Wasp*, described the preparations:

> We went to our pilots and ground crews and administrative staffs and told them we were going to give them, we hoped, an organisation that would enable us to win the battle of Malta, which at that time we were in grave danger of losing. We then told them it would mean the hardest possible work under very difficult conditions, that we were going to enlist the aid of the army, both in men and materials, but that the battle was lost unless they all pulled their weight 100 per cent. The response was tremendous. Every man felt himself an important item in the battle and not merely an insignificant unit. So magnificently did the ground staffs work that our half hour service became an absolutely outside limit, and the official records show that six Spitfires of one squadron took off to engage the enemy within nine minutes of landing on the island. What a change in thirty-six hours! Within half an hour every serviceable Spitfire was in the air. I shall never forget the remark of one airman who, coming out of a slip trench, and seeing two or three squadrons in the air, said: 'Heavens, look at the fog!'

One of the incoming new pilots described his day:

> We took off from the *Wasp* at 06.45 hours. Landed at Takali at 10.30 hours. The formation leader flew too fast and got his navigation all to hell, so I left them 40 miles west of Bizerta, 5 miles off the North African coast, and set course for Malta, avoiding Pantellaria and Bizerta owing to fighters and flack being present there. I jettisoned the long-range tank 20 miles west of Bizerta and reached Malta with 20 gallons to spare in my main tank. Of the forty-seven machines that flew off the *Wasp*, one crash landed into the sea on take-off, one force landed back onto the deck as he had jettisoned his auxiliary tank in error, one landed in Algeria, one ran out of petrol between Pantellaria and Malta, one crashed on landing at Hal Far, and one crashed off Grand Harbour. On landing at Takali I immediately removed my kit, and the machine was rearmed and refuelled. I landed during a raid and four

109s tried to shoot me up. Soon after landing the airfield was bombed but without much damage being done. I was scrambled in a section of four soon after this raid, but we failed to intercept the next one, though we chased several 109s down on the deck. I ate lunch in the aircraft because I was 'at the ready' until dusk. After lunch we were heavily bombed again by eight Ju88s. Scrambled again the same section after tea – no luck again. One Spit was shot down coming into land and another one at the edge of the airfield. Score for the day, seven confirmed, seven probables and fourteen damaged for the loss of three Spits. The tempo of life here is just indescribable. The morale of all is magnificent – pilots, ground crews and army, but it is certainly tough. One lives here only to destroy the Hun and hold him at bay; everything else, living conditions, sleep, food, and all the ordinary standards of life have gone by the board. It all makes the Battle of Britain and fighter sweeps seem like child's play in comparison, but it is certainly history in the making, and nowhere is there aerial warfare to compare with this.

There was to be little respite for the newly arrived pilots and their machines. On his second day (10 May) one new pilot had an exhausting but triumphant day's work:

We climbed to 4,000 ft, and then the barrage was put up by the harbour defences and the cruiser. The CO dived down into it and I followed close on him. We flew three times to and fro in the barrage, trusting to luck to avoid the flack. Then I spotted a Ju87 climbing out at the fringe of the barrage and I turned and chased him. I gave him a one second burst of cannon and he broke off sharply to the left. At that moment another Ju87 came up in front of my nose and I turned into him and let him have it. His engine started to pour out black smoke and he started weaving. I kept the tit pushed hard, and after a further two or three second burst with the one cannon I had left, the other having jammed, he keeled over at 1,500 ft and went into the drink. I then spotted a 109 firing at me from behind and pulled the kite round to port, and after one and a half turns got on his tail. Before I could fire, another 109 cut across my bows from the port side and I turned straight on his tail and fired until my cannon stopped through lack of ammo. He was hit and his engine poured out black smoke, but I had to beat it as I was now defenceless and two more 109s were attacking me. I spiralled straight down to the sea at full throttle, and then weaved violently towards land with the two 109s still firing at me. I went under the fringe of the smoke screen to try to throw them off, but when I came out the other side I found them both sitting up top waiting for me. I therefore kept right down at zero feet and steep turned towards them, noticing the smoke from their gun ports as I did so. After about five minutes of this I managed to throw them off. I landed back at Takali and made out my report, claiming one 87 destroyed and one Me109 damaged.

The Germans had launched a major raid against the *Welshman* in the Grand Harbour and thirty-seven Spitfires and thirteen Hurricanes had been sent up to deal with them. The Germans also had to contend with a thicker than normal anti-aircraft barrage over the Grand Harbour. Pilot Officer Briggs of 601 Squadron was shot down and killed, Sergeant Dickson was hit by an anti-aircraft shell and his aircraft was blown in half. His seat straps snapped and he was thrown through the Perspex hood of the aircraft causing him to sustain a badly gashed leg. With amazing luck he managed to pull his ripcord and he fell into the sea a mile out from Marsamxett Harbour. He was later picked up and taken to an ambulance on top of a broken door, being used as a makeshift stretcher. That afternoon the Germans tried again to get the *Welshman*. Twenty-six Spitfires and six Hurricanes went aloft to deal with the seven Ju88s and thirty Me109s. At least one Me109 was shot down.

The Italians attacked in the evening, with twenty Macchi 202s and ten RE2001s, escorting five Cant Z1007bis. They were followed by twenty Ju87s and a swarm of Me109s. A 109 was shot down in the ensuing dogfight.

On that day alone there were 110 Spitfire sorties and fourteen Hurricane sorties, around fifteen enemy aircraft were shot down and the anti-aircraft gunners claimed another eight.

There was little in the way of respite on 12 May. Pilot Officer Mitchell of 603 Squadron was shot down during an early morning raid. A Ju88 was believed to have been responsible for the loss of Flight Sergeant Conway's Spitfire. Another Spitfire was lost, flown by Sergeant Graysmark. In the evening three SM84s and four Ju88s, escorted by Me109s and Macchi 202s, launched an attack at 17.30. One of the SM84s was shot down by a Spitfire.

There was a raid at Midday on 13 May comprising sixteen German bombers escorted by twenty-six Me109s. Spitfires were scrambled and the action was described by Hesselyn:

> I heard over the RT that something was doing over Kalafrana Bay and I beetled across there. I found a real mix up. Spits and 109s were everywhere at about 5,000 ft. As I arrived on the scene I saw a 109 diving on a Spit's tail. I went in at once, attacking him from the starboard quarter. I could see my shells striking his fuselage. He turned on his back. I turned on mine, firing all the time. He started to go down in a gentle dive and I kept firing to make sure of him. He crashed into the bay.

With every sortie, cannon or machine-gun shell the defenders of Malta gradually wrestled air superiority from the Germans and Italians. On the 14th three Ju88s and a number of Me109s tried to bomb Luqa and Takali. Twenty-eight Spitfires were scrambled to intercept. Sergeant Finlay was shot down.

Dobbie had been replaced by Viscount Gort on 7 May. Dobbie had prepared his last message to the people of Malta, which was broadcast on 8 May:

> I had very naturally desired to speak to you myself before leaving Malta, but for reasons of high security this was not possible – it was essential that the change of governor should be known to as few as possible until it was an accomplished fact. So I very reluctantly had to forego my desire and I am now speaking to you by proxy, who is reading to you what I wrote before my departure. I leave Malta with the greatest regret. I have been here for two eventful years, and I had hoped I would be able to see Malta through her present difficulties at any rate. But that was not to be. During my two years we have been through stirring times together, times I will never forget. I am glad I have had this experience because it has enabled me to get to know and appreciate the people of Malta. I have seen them facing experiences which were unfamiliar to them, and facing them with the determination and courage of veteran soldiers. I have seen them facing experiences which had become painfully familiar by the same courage and determination. I have marvelled at the way they

have accepted hardships and disasters with cheerfulness, and I consider that the people of Malta have rightly earned the admiration of the whole world, an admiration crystallised by the award of the George Cross to the island. And now Malta is still facing unprecedented difficulties with the same cheerful courage. I am sure that in God's good providence she will in due course emerge out of her difficulties into smoother water. Until then she will endure, and so ensure the final victory.

The new Governor Gort broadcast to Malta on Thursday 14 May:

People of Malta, I salute you – I admire you for your courage and endurance – I admire you for your cheerfulness – I admire you for your trust in almighty God and I admire the greatness of your faith. I am proud to come to live amongst you, to share your trials, to share your dangers, to share your privations, and I am proud to have the great honour of being sent here by His Majesty the King to do what I can to assist Malta forward to that great and glorious day when each and every one of us has fulfilled his or her duty and peace comes once more to this sorely tried but beautiful island.

A further reinforcement of Spitfires arrived on 18 May. Seventeen Spitfires safely arrived, but the six Albacores that were supposed to accompany them all had to turn back due to overheated engines. Around the shores of Malta the air battle continued. Pilot Officer Fowley was shot down off Hal Far and later a Hurricane piloted by Sergeant Pendlebury was shot down by Me109s. However, an Australian pilot, Sergeant Yarra, shot down an Me109 off Hal Far.

HSL128 sped out to pick up Fowley, but in fact picked up Jhonnes Lompa, but HSL128 was soon to come under attack from Me109s as the launch's log recounts:

At 11 am on 18 May 1942, we had a callout in HSL128 for a Spitfire pilot said to have baled out on a bearing of 160 degrees from Hal Far about 100 yards out. Sounded like a piece of cake, for even though enemy fighters were plentiful in the vicinity the position given was close to the island and we now had Spitfires on the job as well as Hurricanes. Getting on the given bearing we steamed 100, 200, 300 yards – still nothing seen – and kept on going, though enemy activity was getting more and more lively overhead. After we had steamed out about three miles one of the escorting Hurricanes was shot down a couple of miles ahead of us. It was while we were investigating this wreckage that Gerry got closest to us but even then the bullets only churned up the water over 100 ft away. As there was no survivor from this crash and still no sign of the original pilot for whom we had been called out, I decided to make for base, but, on our way back, we saw another fighter crash about 6 miles over to the westward and a parachute drifting down. We picked this pilot up within a few minutes of him hitting the water but it turned out to be a Hun – a cheery soul, who advised us to get back ashore before we were hurt. As we were then fairly well out I decided to run out and then come in on our original bearing from a distance of about 10 miles, as even the worst possible estimate of distance could hardly be over 10 miles. We actually found the Spitfire pilot in his dinghy about 9 miles from the land and the German pilot insisted upon shaking hands with him as he welcomed him aboard.

Throughout this operation Yarra stayed aloft, fending off attacks by Me109s on the Air Sea Rescue launch. He covered them for forty-five minutes, until HSL128 got back to Kalafrana. The following day Yarra visited Kalafrana and was thanked by the crew. Yarra was also awarded the Distinguished Flying Medal for his actions.

Pilot David Douglas-Hamilton described an encounter with Me109s on 15 May. The incident occurred just after 16.00 hours:

I drew blood for the second time on one of these fighter sweeps. We were stooging around at 25,000 ft for a consider-able time; it was very cold and I even got frostbite in a finger. We were bounced once by a pair of 109s but avoided them successfully. Eventually we were told to go down. Suddenly I saw a 109 sweeping down on my No. 2. It still came on, by this time at me, and we were approaching each other head on at great speed. I resolved not to give way before he did, and he evidently made the same resolution. We were going straight at each other, and as soon as I got my sights on him I opened fire, and kept firing. He opened fire a second afterwards. It all happened in a flash, but when he seemed about fifty yards away I gave a violent yank on the stick and broke away to the right. As I did so, his port wing broke off in the middle, and he shot past under me. I turned and looked back; his aeroplane did about five flick rolls to the left and broke up, then a parachute opened.

Enemy action tailed off towards the end of the month, but RAF aircraft were now once again able to strike against enemy targets. On the night of 25 May enemy shipping was attacked and on the following night high explosives and incendiaries were dropped on Messina in Sicily. After the reinforcements of Spitfires on 18 May local air superiority had definitely been won by the Allies. The Germans and Italians were reduced to smaller, daylight bombing raids and fighter sweeps. The majority of the action was now at night, which meant that the enemy bombing was far less accurate. The Beaufighters in the last three weeks of the month shot down twelve enemy bombers. Throughout the month there had been 247 air raid alerts and 628 tons of bombs dropped on the island.

The worst was, perhaps, now over. The Germans and Italians could not ensure air superiority over the island and, as a result, any invasion plans would have to be delayed. It was now time for Maltese-based aircraft to bring the war to the Italians and the Germans and strike against targets in an even greater intensity than ever before.

CHAPTER NINE
OUR TURN

One of the new arrivals in Malta in June 1942 was George Frederick Beurling, known as 'Screwball'. He was a non-conformist and destined to become a legend. He arrived in Malta and dubbed it a 'fighter-pilot's paradise'. Beurling joined 249 Squadron, which had originally been a Royal Naval Air Service Unit, which had been re-formed in May 1940. Beurling himself had qualified as a pilot at the age of fourteen. He had tried to join the Chinese air force and the Finns to fight against Soviet Russia. Eventually he joined the RAF.

Beurling was one of the new pilots that arrived in Malta on 9 June and he was to join the squadron commanded by Laddie Lucas. He already had a reputation as being an exceptional pilot. Beurling flew his first sortie the day after he arrived and within three days he had claimed his first damaged Me109. Like many of the pilots Beurling got off to a relatively slow start, but on 6 July he was one of eight Spitfires scrambled to meet a large formation of bombers and fighters crossing Gozo. Beurling promptly shot down a Macchi 202 and then a second. He then landed, refuelled, rearmed and took off again to shoot down an Me109 and a Cant 1007bis. On 27 July Beurling managed to shoot down a pair of Macchi 202s, two Me109s and damage two more. He was awarded the Distinguished Flying Medal and given a commission. By August his tally had reached sixteen. September and October brought his tally to twenty-six and a half. On October 14 Beurling was one of the pilots scrambled to deal with eight Ju88s and twenty-five Me109s. They engaged off the Gozo coastline. Beurling shot down one of the Ju88s and then an Me109. As he was doing this a burst of fire from a Ju88 cut across his cockpit, hitting him in the hands and the forearm. He put his Spitfire into a dive and tried to get back to Takali airfield. He was being chased by an Me109. Regardless of his injuries he turned his aircraft round and fired into the belly of the chasing enemy aircraft. A second Me109 punched holes in his Spitfire with its cannon. Shell splinters peppered Beurling's legs and heels. The Spitfire was out of control and he managed to bale out, parachute into the sea and then clamber aboard his dinghy. He had come down in St Paul's Bay. HSL128 pulled him out of the water. His only concern was not for his injuries, but for a

Bible that his mother had given him. He had carried it on every sortie and was terrified that it was lost and that he would lose its good luck. It was found and with that he fell unconscious. Beurling was taken to Mtarfa Military Hospital. He was awarded the Distinguished Service Order and was credited with twenty-seven kills over the island, making him the highest scoring pilot. Before the end of the war he was to claim another three. Sadly Beurling died in 1948, when he was delivering an aircraft to Israel.

There was no raid on 1 June. Nonetheless the squadrons still rotated their flights in readiness. One flight would cover from midday on one day and until midday on the following day. In quieter periods pilots could also look forward to one day off every fifth day, when one of the five squadrons was stood down. However, not everyone could enjoy a quiet period. The Air Sea Rescue launches picked up a Wellington crew 7 miles out and then 8 miles out the dead body of Canadian Pilot Officer McNaughton of 185 Squadron, a Spitfire pilot, was recovered.

By this stage in the air attacks on Malta upwards of 75 per cent of all of the houses in Valletta had been either destroyed or damaged. Similar percentages were applicable to Vittoriosa, Cospicua, Senglea, Floriana, Gzira, Kalkara, Kirkop, and Luqa. Across the island at least 50 per cent of the most populated districts had been devastated. The civilian population was reckoned to be somewhere in the region of 260,000. Since the war had begun one in seventy had become a casualty and one in 235 a fatality. Without the unique rock shelters on the island the tally would have been much higher.

At mid-morning of 2 June twenty Spitfires belonging to 185, 249 and 601 Squadrons were scrambled to meet three Italian SM84 bombers, covered by twenty-four RE2001s and thirty-two Macchi 202s. They were intercepted some 15 miles to the east of Kalafrana but Pilot Officer Halford was shot down.

On the following day, 3 June, in Operation Style, HMS *Eagle* was due to launch thirty-two new Spitfires. However, one of them crashed on take-off and four were lost *en route*. Spitfire pilots from the island were sent to guide the remainder safely onto the island. Meanwhile, offensive operations from the island continued as RAF bombers continued to strike at Sicily and Sardinia.

There was no major enemy action until Sunday 7 June, when a pair of German bombers, five Italian fighters and an Italian float plane were shot down. Unfortunately, shortly before noon on 8 June two Spitfires out of nine that were scrambled to intercept Me109s were shot down. Thankfully, though, more Spitfire reinforcements arrived on 9 June thanks to the aircraft carrier HMS *Eagle*. Operation Salient was due to deliver thirty-two Spitfires and all of them reached Malta, but one crashed on landing.

The second anniversary of the Italians entering the war occurred on 10 June. Since the start of those hostilities the island had been subjected to 492 day time bombing raids and 574 night attacks. This day was no different, as waves of enemy bombers once again came over the island. A Spitfire flown by Pilot Officer Innes of 601 Squadron plunged into the sea from a height of 25,000 ft. His aircraft broke up during the fall and Innes was lucky enough to be thrown out. His parachute also opened and he landed safely into the sea, to be picked up by HSL107.

A much needed supply convoy left Port Said on 11 June. It comprised the *City of Calcutta*, *Ajax*, *Potaro*, *Elizabeth Bakke*, *Aagtekira*, *City of Edinburgh*, *Bhutan*, *City of Pretoria*, *Rembrandt*, *City of Lincoln* and *Bulkoil*. It was escorted by a number of vessels, including eight cruisers, twenty-six destroyers, four corvettes, two minesweepers and a pair of rescue ships. Also accompanying the escort was a dummy battleship, HMS *Centurion*. It was to be an ill fated attempt. On 12 June *City of Calcutta* was damaged; two days later *Bhutan* and *Aagtekira* were sunk and the *Potaro* damaged. On 15 June HMS *Centurion* was damaged, as were three of the cruisers, HMS *Newcastle*, HMS *Birmingham* and HMS *Arethusa*. To compound matters the convoy also lost the destroyers, HMS *Hasty*, HMS *Airedale* and HMS *Nestor*. The following day brought no respite, with the loss of the cruiser, HMS *Hermione*. The convoy and its escorts had had enough and they headed for Alexandria.

Gort, amongst others, believed that the increases in food shortages were making life even more difficult than the bombing. Dobbie had announced the rationing of bread to ten and a half ounces per person per day. Back in April pasta, rice and tomato paste (the three staples of Maltese food) had also been rationed. Now, Gort, in the face of increased food shortages, had to make further cuts. Sugar and rice rations were cut, as were coffee, soap and kerosene. There was no fodder for animals, so cuts in livestock needed to be made. In fact there were very few livestock on the island: the horses were spared slaughter and the handful of goats would be needed to supply milk. The cows were kept and the chickens were needed purely for egg production. The island's remaining goats, sheep and pigs were all slaughtered.

Even more acute were the problems with water. The island's reservoirs had been emptied and in any case distribution pipes and pumping stations had all been badly damaged. What little supplies were arriving were the absolute basics: flour, oil, food, ammunition and spares for the aircraft.

Clothing was in severely short supply and people had to make do with patching what they had, often darning or using their curtains to make clothes. Parachute silk was often used and unused car tyres were pressed into service to replace worn out shoe soles. Once the all clear had been called Maltese citizens would queue for everything, from kerosene to bread and from water to coal. Furniture was being sacrificed in order to cook hot food, as there were only a few trees on the island. Homelessness was also an issue, although many city dwellers were cheerfully accepted by the villagers that still had a roof over their heads.

Insufficient food and poor living conditions brought disease: skin infections were common. For most people the lifeline was the Victory Kitchens. The idea behind them was straightforward enough: subscribers gave the kitchens part of their rations or paid sixpence and in return they would receive one hot meal a day, which could include meat and could be claimed either at midday or in the evening. Alternatively, a minestrone soup could be purchased for three pence. The number of subscribers and users of the kitchens increased as rationing tightened.

The average Maltese citizen was eating between 1,100 and 1,500 calories per day, about half of what they really needed. Servicemen were given priority, but even they were sick to death of corned beef in its innumerable incarnations, as stew, soup, beef hash or scraped onto a biscuit. There was a thriving black market: eggs and bread were available if you knew where to look for them. Farmers took to patrolling their land with rifles to prevent people from stealing fresh vegetables and in particular melons. On one occasion Sergeant Ken Griffiths, with the 32 Light Anti-Aircraft Regiment, who was nineteen when he arrived on Malta in July 1941, bought a black market egg sandwich for the equivalent of a week's wages. Griffiths was used to far less: three cups of tea spread out during the day, supplemented by two Number Nine biscuits and a tiny piece of bacon for breakfast, a small amount of corned beef for lunch and another piece of biscuit and jam for his tea. Like most of the servicemen and citizens he would go to bed hungry, spend the day hungry and wake up starving. Ensuring that what little food they had was not stolen by rodents became something of an obsession and sometimes people would go to extraordinary lengths to protect their food.

The promise of convoys always gave those on Malta hope. There was no fuel to transport the pilots backwards and forwards from the airfields and they would have to walk 2 miles each way. The result was that many of the men remained at Takali airfield all day, regardless of whether or not they were on duty. The pilots would sit around on rocks and use the wrecked wing of an aircraft as a table to play cards on. Luqa was no better: the underground headquarters was illuminated by a single light bulb. The pilots were never given any special treatment; there was no spare petrol to move fuel around, so everyone pitched in to carry the petrol by hand to each of the Spitfires dispersed around the airfield.

Mail rarely got through. Sometimes days would pass and at the worst times, weeks. Men began to wonder why their wives or sweethearts had never written but the truth was that they had. But there were many who did receive letters, only to discover that their wives had gone off with someone else, as many of the ground crew in particular had been stranded on Malta for nearly two years.

In Operation Harpoon a convoy consisting of the cargo ships *Troilus, Burdwan, Chant, Orari, Tanimbar* and the tanker, *Kentucky*, left the Clyde on 5 June, headed for Malta via Gibraltar. The cargo ships were escorted by two aircraft carriers, a battleship, four cruisers, seventeen destroyers, the minelayer, *Welshman*, and four minesweepers. It was to be another arduous journey. On 14 June the cruiser HMS *Liverpool* was damaged and the cargo ship *Tanimbar* was sunk. The following day the cruiser, HMS *Cairo* and the destroyer HMS *Partridge* were damaged. The cargo ships *Burdwan, Chant* and *Kentucky*, as well as the destroyer HMS *Bedouin* were sunk. There were more losses on 16 June as the convoy approached Malta. The cargo ship *Orari*, the destroyers HMS *Badsworth* and HMS *Matchless*, along with the minesweeper *Hebe*, were all hit by mines and the destroyer HMS *Kujawiak* was sunk. Nonetheless 15,000 tons of supplies were still delivered to the island.

The enemy was also in action against Malta's air defences that day. In the mid-morning a dozen or more Me109s made a fighter sweep and twenty Spitfires were put up to intercept them.

Despite the arrival of the convoy, very few supplies had actually got through. The comparative failure of Operation Vigorous and Operation Harpoon had made the supply situation even more perilous. Gort broadcast to the island on the night of 16 June:

> Some days ago, two convoys set out, one from the west and one from the east, to bring us the supplies which we need to restore our situation. The western convoy had to endure severe and prolonged attacks, and only two merchant ships survived the ordeal. The eastern convoy after suffering from prolonged and intense attacks by the *Luftwaffe* was ordered to turn back. I must break to you what the arrival of only two ships means to us. For some time past we have been short of

supplies and further privations lie ahead of us. Every effort will be made to replenish our stocks when a favourable opportunity presents itself. Meanwhile we must stand on our own resources and every one of us must do everything in his or her power to conserve our stocks and to ensure the best use is made of all the available resources that remain to us. Here on this island there stands on Mount Sceberras the image of Christ the King surrounded on all sides by bomb craters and demolished buildings. It remains, untouched and unscathed after the most intense and prolonged air bombardment in the history of the world. Trusting in Him, and guided by Him, we shall surely pass out of the darkness into the light.

Malta was not only prepared to continue to defend itself, but was also still capable of launching offensive operations. Beaufighters were out skimming along the North African coast, hunting for prey. German and Italian air raids were met with considerable force and tens of sorties by Spitfires were launched throughout 18 June. The enemy casualties were still mounting, and claims that day included three Me109s, five Ju88s, two BR20s, two Italian float planes, a Cant 506B and an RO43. There was further news on the growing danger of the dwindling food stocks on 20 June, when the Lieutenant Governor, Sir Edward Jackson, broadcast to the island:

If the enemy failed in his main purpose, he succeeded in part of it. He has delayed part of our much needed supplies. Greater privations than we have known hitherto lie ahead of us here. Fresh supplies will come to us. You have no fear of that. But we do not know when they will come. We got about 15,000 tons of stores in the two ships that arrived. It is a very small part of what we had hoped for. I have come here this evening to tell you plainly what our arrangements are. And I shall tell you the worst. Small quantities of vitally necessary supplies can reach us from time to time without all the difficulties and dangers that the running of a convoy involves. But though small additions to our stocks help us they cannot really change our situation. Our security depends more than on anything else on the time for which our bread will last. In examining our position we calculated first the time for which our bread could be made to last. That calculation gave us a certain date, I shall call it the target date. I cannot tell you what that date is but it is far enough off to give ample opportunity for fresh supplies to reach us before our present stocks run out. England will not forget us and her navy and air forces will see us through. The bread ration will remain as it is. Sugar will remain as it is except there can be no issue for the first period in July and the second period in August. Our stocks of edible oil are low. An issue can only be made once in every three periods. Soap and kerosene are two other necessities of which our stocks will not last, at their present rate of issue, as long as our stock of bread. We can only make one issue of soap in the second period of every month, beginning in July. Kerosene, in our present situation, is the most difficult problem we have to face. We can only issue the present ration once every two weeks instead of once a week. One issue of rice and coffee will be made in the first period of July. Tea will be issued during the second period of each month.

Night raids continued through 21 and 22 June. Incendiary bombs and high explosives were dropped on the airfields. Malta-based Swordfish launched attacks on enemy convoys on each day from 21 June to 23 June. The evening raid on 23 June consisted of three SM84s, escorted by twenty-seven Macchi 202s and eighteen RE2001s. Twelve Spitfires of 249 Squadron and eight of 603 Squadron were scrambled to intercept. A Macchi 202 was shot down to the west of Gozo and 603 Squadron's Flight Officer Mitchell's Spitfire was also lost.

The fuel situation had reached critical levels and on 26 June it was announced that weekend bus services would be indefinitely suspended and replaced by horse transport. Further raids continued over that weekend and several civilian casualties were inflicted on both the Friday and the Saturday.

Eight Me109s made a fighter sweep of the island on the morning of 29 June. Four Spitfires belonging to 603 Squadron were scrambled to deal with them, but Pilot Officer Barbour was shot down when he was targeted by a pair of Me109s. Later in the day Beaufighters operating from the island managed to shoot down two Ju88s. June had seen 172 air raid alerts and around 270 tons of bombs had been dropped on the island. Defensively, the island was holding its own, but civilians and servicemen alike were starving and it appeared that there was no immediate solution to the problem.

It was at this point, with Rommel's rapid advance and swift capture of Tobruk, that German and Italian plans changed. Although the opening days of July would spare Malta from the threat of invasion, it was once more to come under extremely heavy enemy air attack. Kesselring had managed to pull together around 500 aircraft and during the first fortnight of July they would fly 1,000 sorties against the island. As the raiders would discover, they would receive an extremely hot reception from the Spitfires and anti-aircraft batteries in the day and by Beaufighters at night. At the height of the attacks the Germans and Italians would lose six aircraft destroyed and nine damaged in one hour.

With Rommel so close to overrunning Egypt and pressing on to Alexandria, Kesselring was ordered to subdue Malta in order to ensure that Rommel's supply lines remained safeguarded. What now faced the raiders as they sought to fulfil Kesselring's orders was not a handful of hastily thrown together fighter units, but fully equipped Spitfire squadrons. The enemy raids would be continual, albeit on a smaller scale than the spring attacks. In the first ten days of July the enemy would lose over 100 aircraft. Losses were so high that one Ju88 squadron had to be stood down. By the middle of July losses to Ju88s meant that Kesselring had to cancel all dive bombing attacks.

Another key change during July was the replacement of Air Vice Marshal Lloyd on 14 July. He had nursed the air defences of Malta over some of the most difficult periods of the war. As he was preparing to leave Valletta a civilian presented him with a cigarette case bearing the letters MTAP. He pondered at what these initials could mean and was told they stood for 'Malta Thanks Air Protection'.

His successor was Air Vice Marshal Sir Keith Park. During the battle of Britain Park had commanded fighter squadrons and was experienced in fighting the *Luftwaffe*. On taking over Park said:

> The magnificent fighting by our fighter pilots at Malta in April and May has very rightly been generously acknowledged. The courage, endurance and fine work of the officers, NCOs and men on the ground has not, however, received full acknowledgement. During the blitz in the spring, the enemy was so vastly superior in strength that our day fighters were practically forced onto the defensive. Under these conditions it was inevitable that Royal Air Force personnel on the ground, and civilians, should undergo severe bombing daily, and I now pay tribute to the courageous manner in which they kept our airfields going in spite of the lack of protection from our fighters. Our day-fighter strength has during June and July been greatly increased, and the enemy's superiority in numbers has

long since dwindled. The time has now arrived for our Spitfire squadrons to put an end to the bombing of our airfields by daylight. We have the best fighter aircraft in the world, and our Spitfire pilots will again show their comrades on the ground that they are the best fighter pilots in the world.

Henceforth, the fighters would intercept enemy bombers before they crossed the coast. Aggressive tactics were ordered:

> All fighter formation leaders are warned that the enemy will probably reintroduce bomber formations whenever there is an important operation in the Malta area. Because our Spitfires, using the forward plan of interception, have recently stopped daylight raids, does not mean that only fighter sweeps are likely to be encountered over or near Malta in the near future. Any signs of defensive tactics by our fighters will encourage the enemy to reintroduce formations of bombers or fighter bombers. Therefore, the more aggressively our fighters are employed, the better will Malta be defended against daylight bombing.

The battle for the skies still had to be won. An evening raid occurred on 1 July aimed at Takali airfield. There were around thirty enemy aircraft involved and of the dozen Spitfires of 603 Squadron, which was scrambled to intercept the raiders, one was lost in the ensuing dogfight.

The Italians made an attempt to bomb Safi and Kalafrana on 2 July. Five Cant Z1007bis bombers with an escort of twenty-four Macchi 202s and fifteen RE2001s were intercepted by Spitfires. One Macchi and one Spitfire were lost. The Italians tried it again the following morning with three Cants escorted by thirty-six Macchi 202s. No. 126 Squadron's Spitfires were scrambled to meet them. One of the eight Spitfires was lost due to a propeller malfunction, rather than enemy fire.

Ten Spitfires engaged twenty-two Macchi 202s and three SM84s on the morning of 4 July. Lurking higher up were another seventeen Macchi 202s. The Spitfires concentrated on the bombers. One was shot down and crashed onto the island, a second was shot down into the sea and the third only just managed to make it back to Sicily.

The Cants were back on 6 July, escorted by fourteen RE2001s and twenty-four Macchi 202s. This time the Italians launched more Macchis ahead of the main force to clear the way for the bombers. The Spitfire pilots once again concentrated on the bombers first and made a head-on attack against them. The bombers were forced to jettison their bombs and flee. An unknown number of Macchi 202s were shot down. In the evening Me109s escorted three Ju88s to bomb Takali airfield. Twenty Spitfires from Squadrons 185, 249 and 603 intercepted. Two of the bombers were shot down, one crashing into the sea just off the Grand Harbour.

Twelve Ju88s with twenty-four Me109s and thirty Macchi 202s were intercepted by seventeen Spitfires of 185 and 249 Squadrons on 7 July. Two of the Spitfires, flown by Flight Lieutenant Raoul Daddo-Langlois and Flight Sergeant Bob Middlemiss, were late in getting off. They gained the same height as the enemy bombers and went straight in to attack the Ju88s. Suddenly Middlemiss saw an Me109 heading to cut him off. Middlemiss's aircraft was hit by the Me109 and Middlemiss later recalled:

> Suddenly my right hand left the stick with the impact of being shot in the right arm and back. Had I not been sitting back and looking over my left shoulder, I would have been a goner. The Spitfire was in a spin and smoking. I was unable to eject because of the centrifugal force but I managed to roll the aircraft over and fall out. I opened the parachute and drifted down, eventually landing in the water. I shed the parachute and pulled out my dinghy. The words went through my mind: 'slowly turn the tap of the CO_2 bottle'. To my dismay, as I frantically continued turning, I discovered that the bottle was empty. With my right arm useless, I had problems trying to attach the bellows pump to the dinghy; the chord attached to the dinghy kept getting in the way but I finally took out my knife and cut the chord, held the dinghy with my bad arm while I screwed in the pump and began the inflation. After a while there was enough air in the dinghy to allow me to climb in and begin paddling towards the island. I had been shot down on the eastern side of Malta but, unfortunately, the squadron was searching for me on the western side. Only when Australian Pilot Officer Paul Brennan and Sergeant de l'Ara flew out on patrol to protect some minesweepers was I spotted in the drink. They made one pass over me and then approached again. I thought of jumping into the sea in case they attacked the dinghy. However, they waggled their wings and I breathed again. Shortly afterwards, High Speed Launch 128 reached me and I was hauled aboard, wrapped in blankets

and given a shot of navy rum, which nearly made my eyes pop out. Later I saw the holes in my arm. The surgeon who operated on my back said I had missed death by about a quarter of an inch.

This was not to be the only loss on 7 July. Two Spitfires were shot down when they were in a dogfight with eighteen Me109s. One of the pilots, Sergeant de Nancrede, shot at a Ju88 and a German gunner onboard fired back and hit his engine. Later in the day five Cant Z1007bis, with thirty-five Macchi 202s and twelve RE2001s were intercepted by twenty-two Spitfires. Flight Sergeant Haggas was shot down. Sometime after 22.00 hours a pair of Beaufighters was scrambled to intercept three incoming enemy bombers. A Ju88 was shot down and it fell into the sea off the coast, near Mgarr.

Luqa was the target for the early morning raid on 8 July. Spitfires from three squadrons were scrambled to intercept seven Ju88s and a number of Me109s, as well as twenty-one Macchi 202s. No. 603 Squadron, led by Flight Lieutenant Sanders, pursued a Ju88 over Gozo. The Ju88 was hit but so was Sanders, which forced him to break off. He was then attacked by a pair of Me109s. The cooling system was badly hit and Sanders desperately looked for a safe place to ditch. He managed to ditch in Marsalforn Bay with the Spitfire hitting the water barely 100 yards from the shoreline. Sanders was fortunate enough that a Maltese family were out in a small rowing boat, fishing and he was almost immediately picked up. One of Sanders's other pilots, Pilot Officer King, was also lost when his Spitfire's wing hit the sea and crashed.

At around 20.00 hours half a dozen Ju88s and a number of Me109s made for Takali airfield on 9 July. Twenty-seven Spitfires were scrambled and they managed to shoot down two Ju88s for the loss of Flight Sergeant Ballantyne's Spitfire. A further Spitfire was lost the next day when Flight Sergeant Reynolds of 126 Squadron was shot down during the second enemy raid of the day.

Luqa seemed to be the main target for a raid consisting of eighteen Ju88s, Me109 fighter cover, ten Macchi 202s and six RE2001s on 13 July. In this early morning raid a number of raiders were reported to have been shot down or badly damaged. Sergeant Willie of 126 Squadron was also shot down; he managed to bale out 20 miles out to sea and was picked up.

Seven Ju88s raided Luqa on 14 July, the same day that Park, former Commander of No. 11 Group of Fighter Command during the Battle of Britain, arrived in Malta at dawn on a Sunderland. He had flown in from Egypt. The Ju88s were met by thirty Spitfires and one of the Ju88s was certainly shot down for the loss of a Spitfire.

On 15 July thirty-one new Spitfires arrived on the island in Operation Pinpoint. They had been launched from HMS *Eagle*. This was effectively the last day of Lloyd's command and from this point on Park would change the tactics and initiate his 'forward interception' plan.

Times had certainly changed and speaking of the vital months during which small numbers of Allied aircraft had prevented the Germans and Italians from gaining total air superiority, one of the Squadron Leaders said of Group Captain Woodhall, who was in charge of the control room:

> The boys had a fanatical, yes, fanatical faith in his controlling. It was a faith which gave them a completely unreasonable confidence when, one day in April, he had controlled three Spitfires and four Hurricanes against a Hun plot of 130 plus. And, remember, he it was who organised and conducted the fighter defence of the island before as well as after the Spits arrived.

The enemy tried their luck again in a mid-afternoon raid on 17 July, to be intercepted by twenty-four Spitfires. Five Ju88s, twenty Me109s and eighteen Macchi 202s were engaged. Several Me109s were claimed and at least two or three were definite kills. The 18th saw another afternoon raid, with sixteen Spitfires responding. Pilot Officer Chuck McLean was hit and it took McLean a minute to get out, by which time he had been badly burned. Nonetheless he managed to open his parachute and land four miles off Gozo. He was too injured and weak to try to inflate his dinghy and had it not been for the prompt action of one of his squadron, who circled him to bring in HSL107; he probably would not have survived. As it was he was in the water for just fifteen minutes.

Three Ju88s tried to cross the Maltese coast at 22.00 hours on 19 July. Two Beaufighters immediately intercepted and shot one of them down. At midday on the following day Flight Lieutenant Lambert was shot down. Luckily, although he was rendered unconscious, he was blown out of his cockpit and the parachute opened.

HMS *Eagle* made another delivery of Spitfires on 21 July, in Operation Insect. Twenty-eight of the thirty that took-off from *Eagle* managed to reach Malta. The forward interception plan was put into operation on 23 July. Henceforth radar would be used to assist flight controllers to direct Spitfire interceptions as far out from the island as possible. On the down side it would mean that dogfights would take place further out to sea, reducing the likelihood of ditched pilots being picked up. Nonetheless, the Air Sea Rescue launches picked up their 100th pilot on the same day, an Italian, whose Macchi 202 had been shot down by Spitfires 5 miles east of Kalafrana.

There were further combats during 27 to 28 July. On the second day a Spitfire was lost when eight Spitfires were attacked by twenty-seven Me109s that were protecting a reconnaissance aircraft. Later a Ju88 was shot down.

A bizarre incident took place on 29 July. As reported by the Air Ministry in 1944 in, *The Official Account of the RAF in Malta*, the episode had begun the previous day off Sapienza in southern Greece:

> The captain of the aircraft [a Beaufort] was Lieutenant E T Strever of Klerksdorp, South Africa; the rest of the crew were Pilot Officer (now Flying Officer) W M Dunsmore of Maghull, near Liverpool, Sergeant J A Wilkinson of Auckland, and Sergeant A R Brown of Timaru, both from New Zealand. After releasing his torpedo at a merchant vessel, and being badly shot up by flack, Strever realised that his aircraft was doomed. As it hit the sea, he went under, but somehow managed to clamber clear of the wreckage and join the crew in their dinghy. Ninety seconds later the aircraft sank. After paddling for some time towards the coast, they saw an Italian float plane [a Cant Z506B], which presently landed about 100 yards away. Strever swam over to it and was courteously received with a brandy and a cigarette; he then explained in pantomime what had happened. The rest of the crew were picked up, and the Cant float plane taxied to a nearby island [Preveza in Greece]. Here, after a hearty meal, they were given the run of the officers' mess for the rest of the day. In the evening they had another excellent meal with the Italian officers, who considerately gave up their rooms to the crew when bedtime arrived. The only sense of imprisonment was that the guards were posted in the passage and outside their windows. In the morning, after a breakfast of eggs and coffee specially provided for them, and having been photographed with their captors, the crew were taken aboard the Cant again, which then set off for Taranto. The Cant's crew consisted of a pilot, second pilot, engineer, wireless-operator-observer and a corporal acting as an armed escort. Wilkinson was the first

to see an opportunity of capturing the aircraft. Attracting the observer's attention, he hit him on the jaw and seized the escort's revolver. Passing this to Strever, he then used the corporal's body as a shield in approaching the first pilot. Strever followed, brandishing the escort's pistol, and held up the pilot before he could get at his own weapon. The Italian had put the aircraft's nose down as though to land, but at a menacing sign from Strever he changed his mind and pulled the stick back again. Meanwhile Dunsmore and Brown dealt with the rest of the crew and Strever took over the controls. The capture of the aircraft took only a few seconds, but Strever was now faced with the difficulty of having no maps or charts, and of not knowing the speed or capacity of the aircraft, nor how much petrol would be needed to reach Malta. He therefore set the second pilot free and put him at the controls. After making rough and ready calculations of his own, Strever decided that if they could not reach Malta they would come down in Sicily and trust to luck. The Italian steered the course set for him and Strever himself took the controls from time to time. At length they hit the toe of Italy, which enabled him to get some sort of fix, and he decided to chance the petrol situation and head for Malta. As they approached the island there began the most terrifying episode of the trip. While flying at deck level, three Spitfires attacked them. Brown spun the guns about to show the fighters that he was not going to fire, and Dunsmore took off his white vest and trailed it out of the cockpit as a sign of surrender. But still the Spitfires spat, and when one of the wings was hit by machine guns and cannons, Strever ordered the Italian to come down on the water. As they did so the engines stopped. They had run out of petrol.

The Cant had come down between Sliema and St Paul's Bay about 2 miles offshore. Initially it was towed in by HSL107 and then a seaplane tender took over to bring it into St Paul's Pier. The Air Sea Rescue men were amazed to see the Beaufort crew and their Italian prisoners. The war might have been over for the Italians, but it was not over for the Cant. The Italian insignia was over-painted with British roundels and it was pressed into service as a floatplane for the Air Sea Rescue. Strever personally supervised the Italians and felt that he had to return their hospitality in some way. Through a translator they agreed that there was nothing personal about what had happened and that they fully understood. In order to extend the fraternal spirit, Strever and the crew shared a bottle of wine with the Italians, which he had been hoarding to take with him on leave.

It was back to normal business on 30 July when at 08.00 twenty-three Spitfires were sent up to intercept an enemy fighter sweep consisting of twenty Me109s and six Macchi 202s. Above this fighter sweep were a further fifteen Macchi 202s and Me109s. A single Spitfire was shot down into St Paul's Bay and Sergeant Wood was killed.

The early afternoon of 31 July saw another large enemy fighter sweep across the island. Upwards of eighteen Me109s and Macchi 202s were engaged by sixteen Spitfires. The Spitfires were pounced on as they tried to gain height. One Spitfire was almost immediately shot down and then a second.

July had been a trying month but Malta was clearly regaining air superiority. There had been 188 air raid alerts and 667 tons of bombs had been dropped on the island. Despite this, in the period 26 May to 27 July, offensive sorties were up. Malta-based aircraft had launched 191, 102 of which were against enemy ports and bases. All the island could now hope for was an increase in the number of cargo vessels reaching the island intact.

CHAPTER TEN

STRIKE BASE

For months it seemed impossible for significant food supplies to be delivered to Malta. Nearly everything was rationed, from bread to petrol and from tea to ammunition. Malta desperately needed supplies.

Strategic bombing had been carried out to assist the convoy effort. The two convoys that had been due to arrive in June had both suffered after heavy attacks and only two ships had actually arrived in the Grand Harbour. On the two ships that did arrive there were Royal Air Force reinforcements. A Flight Lieutenant who was with them recorded the events of just one day, 15 June:

> 15th June 03.00. Took an hour's watch on deck, and saw the lights of Tunis. Flares dropped miles to the starboard. We had dodged the enemy. Alarm at 06.30. On going on deck saw shells splashing in sea around us. Warships of the Italian navy were attacking us. A heavy smoke screen was laid around the convoy while our AA ships and four destroyers left us to give battle. Italian units were chased away. We were left only with minesweepers as escort and were attacked by four or five planes of which one was brought down. A merchantman was hit but continued in convoy for five or ten minutes, when smoke came from her stern and she gradually dropped behind, sinking slowly. Probably all onboard saved, except those killed by bomb, understood actually to be seven. One plane was destroyed. The American oil tanker, which joined us at Gibraltar, then dropped out of convoy through engine trouble – later learned caused by near miss. Destroyer stood guard. We then sailed past two German airmen floating in the sea who had escaped from their wrecked aircraft. They shouted 'Hilfe' to us, as if we who had nearly lost our lives through them should risk them even further by stopping to save their lives. They were picked up by a warship. Stand down for breakfast at 09.00 hours.
>
> 09.30. Our escort returned, and then again attacked Italian units to the south. Laying a smoke screen, we turned north-west.

Understood later that our position seemed hopeless and we were making for a sandy beach in Tunisia, or at least to shelter in neutral waters until nightfall. Beaufighters and Spitfires now protecting convoy which was a hell of a relief.

10.30–11.00. Instructions cancelled and turned south again. Understood Italian navy beat it, though had they stayed they would have undoubtedly sunk every one of us. We were informed that a strong escort from Malta was expected but had not turned up. Later learnt that this was probably escort of convoy from east which had already turned back and never reached Malta. Feeling very unhappy, especially as there was nothing I could do about it. It is far better to be one of the men on the guns hitting back at the enemy than to be a helpless nobody just waiting for anything to happen.

11.00. Attacked by bombers. No direct hits, but another merchantman put out of action. Position of convoy now two sunk, two OK. After stand down, several alarms, but fortunately only Spitfires until 12.10.

13.15. Alarm and immediate attack by bombers which were chased away by Spitfires from Malta. Depth charges dropped at 14.05. Our warships firing at hostile surface craft. Travelling south-south-east at about 13 knots. False alarm at 14.15. It was a beautiful day, sea looking glorious with hardly a ripple. The only clouds were formed by dense smoke from burning oil. Alarm during afternoon. One bomber, but chased away by Spitfires.

18.30. Great feeling of relief as worst danger was past and we were now continuously escorted by Spitfires from Malta. Only fifty or sixty miles to go. The behaviour of the men onboard had been magnificent, perfect calm and no grumbling though they were all kept below and just did not know what on earth was happening. Our warships now returned, having chased the Italians away for good. At about 19.00 two or three Stuka dive bombers bombed *Troilus*, dropping bombs within ten yards of starboard. Came out of saloon and saw splash, and then blown back in again by another exploding bomb. It was terrifying, and knees started knocking together again after explosion. Could not hear engines and thought we too had had it but everything OK, as I was temporarily deafened. We had been attacked out of the sun dead behind us. The cruiser plus *Troilus* and *Orari* were all in direct line of sun. After raid we changed our positions.

22.40. Alarm but bombers chased away, now within a few miles of Malta and safety, but told it was too dark to enter harbour before dawn.

At the beginning of July the island of Malta had around 90 Spitfires. There were 4,000 RAF personnel both to fly them and service them. In addition the ground crews and pilots had to maintain the attacks that were being carried out by Wellingtons, Marylands, Baltimores, Beaufighters and Beauforts. July had seen a major change in the fortunes of the island, as in the first two weeks the RAF shot down over 100 enemy aircraft for the loss of twenty-five Spitfires. As a result, dive bombing was virtually abandoned by the Germans and instead they favoured high level bombing, from 16,000 ft.

The Ju87 pilots had been making vertical dives from around 15,000 ft and dropped their bombs at around 5,000 ft. When this height was reached the pilot pressed the bomb release and the aircraft automatically pulled out of its dive. This manoeuvre was often so violent that both of the crew members temporarily blacked out. This left the Ju87 defenceless.

The mainstay of the Middle East Night Bomber Force was still the twin-engine Wellington. It was effectively out of date as far as the mainland European theatre was concerned. The Royal Navy had already shown that the most effective way of destroying enemy merchant shipping was to use a torpedo, launched from a torpedo bomber. Beauforts, light naval forces and submarines could certainly cover the shipping lanes in daylight hours, but something was needed to make night attacks.

Trials were begun to see if the Wellington could be used as a torpedo bomber. Although it was slow and very vulnerable as a daylight aircraft, it had the distinct advantage of having a very long range, ideal for night operations.

The Allies deployed radar equipped Wellingtons, with parachute flares. They would patrol the shipping lanes in ten hour stints during the night. When an enemy vessel was spotted a sighting report was sent back to base. A strike force of torpedo Wellingtons was then launched. They could hone in on the target by position signals and direction finding radio. The search Wellingtons became known as 'Snoopingtons'. They would drop their parachute flares in an 'L' shape around the target convoy. This would effectively create a rectangle of light. The torpedo Wellingtons, or 'Torpingtons' attacked at sea level. The enemy merchant ships were silhouetted against the flares. The torpedoes were launched at around 70 ft above sea level. Usually pilots relied on their own judgement to work out the height. This did cause a number of accidents when pilots flew straight into the sea, but various forms of torpedo sights and radio altimeters were also used. The Squadrons Nos 38 and 221 were primarily based in Egypt but used Malta as an advanced base.

A typical operation took place on 17 September 1942. A sighting report was received at 22.00. Three merchant vessels and twelve destroyers had been spotted to the north-west of Tobruk. Ten aircraft of No. 38 Squadron were sent off as the striking force. Four of the aircraft carried a pair of 1,000 lb bombs and the other six had a pair of torpedoes. The attack went in at 22.50, led by Flight Sergeant Rusbatch. He released his pair of torpedoes against a 4,000 ton merchant vessel. The escorting destroyers were throwing up an intense anti-aircraft barrage. One of the last of the bombers to attack was flown by Sergeant Metcalf. He picked out a 3,000 ton merchant vessel. He saw two explosions as he peeled away. Once again his aircraft came under heavy anti-aircraft fire. Metcalf's aircraft had taken several hits: the main fuse box was blown off, the navigator was wounded in the leg and the wireless operator had wounds in both arms and his thigh. Metcalf set course for base and then concentrated on dealing with the wounded. The ordeal was not over, however, as once they got to their airfield they discovered that one of the wings was damaged and only one undercarriage wheel could be lowered, but luckily Metcalf managed to make a safe landing.

Although the day and night-time attacks by Allied air and naval forces were strangling Rommel and his Afrika Korps, there was still desperate shortages, which needed to be dealt with as soon as was possible. Planning had already begun for a major resupply effort, codenamed Operation Pedestal. Planning had begun in mid-July. The Admiralty, back in London, had begun the process of assembling the largest ever convoy for Malta. It would also be the most heavily escorted convoy of the war.

The Admiralty knew that speed was going to be the main problem and the hunt was on to find merchant ships that could maintain a reasonable speed and this was against the backdrop of enormous losses in merchant shipping across the North Atlantic and in the Mediterranean. Ideally, the merchant ships would have to be able to do 15 knots: twelve were eventually found and they were called to assemble either at Bristol, Glasgow or Liverpool. Each of the twelve convoy vessels was to be given the same basic load: fuel, food, ammunition, mechanical spares and medical supplies.

Supply convoy approaching the Malta coast.

Close shave for a Malta convoy under attack.

Troops awaiting the convoy. August 1942.

The *Melbourne Star* enters Grand Harbour, August 1942.

Unidentified ship entering Grand Harbour.

The award of the George Cross to the Island of Malta and its people. On 15th April 1942, King George VI awarded the George Cross to the then Governor, Sir William Dobie, on behalf of the people of Malta with the following words: "To honour her brave people, I award the George Cross to the Island Fortress of Malta, to bear witness to a heroism and devotion that will long be famous in history". On 13th September 1942, a special ceremony was held when the new Governor of Malta, Lord (Tiger) Gort handed the George Cross to the Chief Justice of Malta, Sir George Borg.

Street celebrations after the siege is lifted.

Stone quarriers at Fort Manoel.

Proud Maltese boy in RAF uniform, 1943.

Stait Street, Malta.

The Baracca Lift.

Horse drawn bus outside the Castile, 1942.

Mercanti, Market Strada, 1942.

"Spinola, a wartime view".

Shelters and dwellings at Cospicua.

St John's Church after the blitz.

Grand Harbour under attack 1942.

Zebra Street after dark.

German bombs bracket a Maltese village.

Aerial view of Malta taken by a German reconnaissance aircraft.

The Grand Harbour taken at height by a German reconnaissance aircraft, the German aircraft was later shot down and the photographs recovered.

Bomb damage after the blitz.

Night sky lit up with flak and searchlights as the defenders beat off another raid.

German reconnaissance aircraft view of the Grand Harbour; the film was later recovered from the wreckage of the aircraft.

Bombed out civilians of Valletta evacuating to the countryside with all their belongings.

Intensive bombing around the Grand Harbour as the Germans make their last attempts on the island.

Supplies on fire in Valletta, believed to be the work of an Axis spy on the island.

Taking cover during an attack.

The theory behind this was that even if most of the ships did not get through the island would receive a delivery of each of these vital supplies. The Admiralty also realised that the amount of fuel that could be carried on these twelve vessels was never going to be enough for Malta's needs.

The British merchant fleet did not have a tanker of a suitable size or speed. All the American tankers were needed for their own navy. The Ministry for War Transport contacted the British Merchant Shipping Mission in Washington to make enquiries as to whether an American merchant tanker could be borrowed. The United States Maritime Commission had already supplied two tankers. One of them, the *Kentucky*, had been lost during the June convoy effort. There was another, which was owned by Texaco and had been built in 1940; she was the *Ohio*.

As part of the Operation Pedestal effort there would also need to be additional Spitfires. Throughout the course of July the RAF in Malta had been losing Spitfires at a rate of around fifteen per week. There had been successful resupply missions in both June and July. Operation Pedestal proposed to use HMS *Furious* to deliver immediately thirty-eight more Spitfires and then return a week later to deliver another thirty-two. It would still take some time for the convoy to be assembled and begin its mission.

Meanwhile, there were still ferocious air battles over the island, claiming more lives, vital Spitfires and dwindling supplies. At 11.00 hours on 3 August, twenty-seven Me109s attempted to make a fighter sweep of the island. Twenty-three Spitfires of 185, 229 and 1435 Squadrons were scrambled. Sergeant Knox-Williams was shot down, but picked up by HSL107. Later three Beaufighters and HSL128 went out to find a Wellington that was due to arrive from Gibraltar. It had gone down 20 miles to the south of the island. Neither the aircraft nor crew were found.

There were more air battles over Malta on 5 and 6 August. Maltese Spitfires took another casualty on 9 August, when Sergeant Ritchie was shot down for the second time in less than two weeks. He was one of fifteen Spitfires that had been scrambled at 14.20 to intercept an enemy fighter sweep. The following day raiders made for Luqa airfield. It was a German attack consisting of Ju88s and Me109s. Spitfires from 185 and 1435 Squadrons were scrambled at 10.25 and they managed to shoot down an Me109. The badly wounded German pilot was later picked up. Just over an hour later, at 11.45, a pair of Spitfires of 126 Squadron on patrol saw a Ju88 heading north. The two Spitfires pursued the enemy aircraft. Pilot Officer Smith, who was behind the controls of one of the Spitfires, was shot down, but the Ju88 itself also failed to reach Sicily. Although this is conjecture, it is highly likely that the pair of them shot one another down.

Thirty-nine new Spitfires were due to be delivered thanks to HMS *Furious* in Operation Bellows on 11 August. Thirty-eight actually took off but one had to turn back and land on HMS *Indomitable*. The remaining thirty-seven landed safely on Malta.

Meanwhile the vessels making up the convoy for Operation Pedestal sailed past Gibraltar and into the Mediterranean on the night of 9 to 10 August. The convoy slowed as it reached Gibraltar, to allow the destroyers to enter Gibraltar for refuelling. The vessels had been spotted by pro-German Spaniards and it had also been spotted by an Italian spy in Spanish Morocco; he confirmed the position of the convoy. The convoy itself would now have to run the gauntlet of 650 enemy aircraft, half a dozen cruisers, nineteen E-boats, sixteen submarines and fifteen destroyers.

The first attack came in at 13.15 on 11 August. A German E-boat, stationed to the south of the Balearic Islands, hit the aircraft carrier, HMS *Eagle*, with four torpedoes. She keeled over and sank in minutes. From being hit to sinking beneath the waves, just eight minutes had elapsed and 163 of her crew went down with her. In the evening German and Italian aircraft found the convoy and launched a major attack. None of the ships were hit, but the enemy would have more opportunities as the convoy was getting closer and closer to their home bases.

By the morning of 12 August the convoy was to the south of Sardinia when numerous air attacks were launched. The merchant vessel *Deucalion* was struck by four bombs from a Ju88 at 13.00 hours. This was the second time she had made the voyage to Malta but this time she was disabled. HMS *Bramham* was sent to help her, picking up crewmen who had abandoned ship, believing that the merchantman was finished. Through persistence and a good deal of luck they managed to get her back underway at 8 knots, but she was now exposed, along with HMS *Bramham*, as they had fallen behind the rest of the convoy. The German aircraft returned to finish her off at 19.45. HMS *Bramham* did her best to keep a pair of Ju88s away. A little later, at 21.00, two Heinkel bombers appeared out of nowhere: they glided into combat with their engines turned off and hit the *Deucalion* with a pair of torpedoes. This time the merchantman was finished. HMS *Bramham* picked up all the survivors and as they sped off to rejoin the main convoy *Deucalion* exploded and sank beneath the water.

The rest of the convoy had not escaped the attention of the enemy aircraft. Dive bombers attacked the convoy ship *Waimarama* with Ju87s while other German bombers targeted HMS *Indomitable*. She took three hits and part of her deck collapsed. Now U-boats were closing in. The battle cruisers HMS *Cairo* and HMS *Nigeria* were both hit by torpedoes. The oil tanker *Ohio* was also hit by a torpedo. There was imminent danger that the cargo would explode. The captain ordered his men to stay onboard and to fight the fires. The engines were stopped and amazingly it was the hole caused by the torpedo that saved the ship. Seawater poured in and put the fires out.

In line with the plan, Force Z, which was the heavy escort, including the aircraft carriers, turned back towards Gibraltar. This left the convoy without any fighter cover and the protecting group, Force X, had already been badly smashed up by the German attacks. HMS *Nigeria*, the flagship, had to limp back to Gibraltar and HMS *Cairo* had to be abandoned and sunk. The new flagship was HMS *Ashanti*. They were still beyond the range of Malta's fighter protection and could only expect more attacks. There was wave after wave of German bombers arriving. The merchantmen did have anti-aircraft guns, so could add to the escort's attempts to beat the enemy off. The *Empire Hope* and *Clan Ferguson* were both sunk which meant that yet another two merchantmen were lost. The convoy was now past the worst in terms of submarine attacks and had now begun to approach Cape Bon but now they were attacked by enemy motor-torpedo boats. *Rochester Castle* was hit, but she continued to limp along at 13 knots. A fourth merchant ship, *Glenorchy*, was sunk and two torpedoes hit the cruiser HMS *Manchester*. The E-boats had managed to account for the *Glenorchy*, *Wairangi*, *Almeria Lykes* and *Santa Elisa*. HMS *Bramham* had once again tried to pick up as many of the stricken merchantmen's crew as possible.

The merchant ship *Dorset* was the next to be lost; she was so badly damaged that she had to be abandoned. The *Brisbane Star*, the seventh merchant ship, had been hit by a torpedo and was in danger of sinking. She headed for Vichy-controlled Tunisia and the French ordered her to enter port, which she ignored. She was intercepted by a French launch, but somehow the *Brisbane Star* managed to get out of the situation and she made her own way towards Malta.

The next merchant ship to receive the attention of the enemy was the *Waimarama* which took direct hits from a pair of Ju88s. Tinned petrol on the cargo deck burst into flames and she began to sink. The *Ohio* now received the attention of the Ju87s. HMS *Ashanti* tried to keep the dive bombers off and one of the Ju87s was hit and it skimmed onto the deck of the *Ohio*. Amazingly the tanker did not explode. It was a piece of bluff that saved the rest of the convoy. A Wellington had been sent up to track the Italian vessels closing in on the convoy. The Wellington was ordered to drop parachute flares every half an hour in order to convince the Italians that a major air attack was being planned against them. A second Wellington also joined in illuminating the enemy ships and some Albacores belonging to Fleet Air Arm were actually sent off to make an attack. The RAF knew that the Italians were listening to their radio traffic and from Malta the Italians heard controllers talking to Liberator bomber pilots. The Liberators did not exist, but just after 02.00 on 13 August the Italians fell for the ruse and turned away from the convoy to head back towards Italy. Mussolini had personally ordered his fleet home for fear of losing it. The Italians had demanded that the Germans give them air cover, but Kesselring had ignored them and said that all his available aircraft were needed to attack the convoy.

The merchantmen and the escorts continued to steam on towards Malta. Soon they would be within range of the Spitfires. At early light on 13 August Spitfires were sent out to find the convoy. They discovered it to be under attack by six Italian bombers, who were just beginning their bombing run. The Spitfires roared in, scattered the Italian bombers and shot one down and damaged a second. The convoy was in sight of Malta by the afternoon and an escort force had come out to meet them. The *Rochester Castle* was the first to reach the Grand Harbour at 18.25, followed by the *Port Chalmers* and *Melbourne Star*. The *Brisbane Star* managed to limp into Malta the following day. The rest of the convoy was still out to sea.

The most precious merchant ship was the *Ohio*. They had tried to tow her but this had failed and she was still under attack by enemy aircraft. By the afternoon of 13 August the *Ohio* had sixteen Spitfires protecting her at all times. As a result the enemy only managed to hit her once, but still she would not sink. By the evening the enemy had virtually given up their convoy attack and had switched their attention to the ships that were limping back to Gibraltar. HMS *Bramham* had picked up the survivors of the *Dorset* and could not find any sign of the *Manchester*. She now returned to help the *Ohio* in.

A dangerous and novel plan was brought together to get the *Ohio* into port. HMS *Braham* was tied to one side and HMS *Penn* to the other. Slowly the ships began to inch towards the Grand Harbour. It took them until 08.00 on 15 August finally to get into the Grand Harbour, by which time a band was waiting for them and the bastions of Valletta were heaving with crowds waving and cheering.

In all some 55,000 tons of supplies had been delivered. Nine of the fourteen merchantmen that had been sent out had been lost along with four Royal Navy vessels. But Malta now had sufficient fuel.

The arrival of the *Ohio* coincided with an important feast day on Malta – Santa Marija (Saint Mary). The arrival of the fuel and the food brought both real and symbolic hope to the islanders and defenders. It would not be the last but certainly one of the most dramatic. *The Times of Malta* wrote a feature on 15 August to celebrate the Feast of Santa Marija – the assumption of Our Lady into Heaven:

> Today is the Feast of St Mary, the celebration of the assumption of Our Lady into Heaven. It will be celebrated without any of the traditional manifestations of rejoicing, which accompanied Santa Marija, patroness of Malta, in pre-war days. Santa Marija is a day of thanksgiving to God through our Lady, for the mercies received and of prayer for added strength to resist the material powers of evil, and also a day of rededication to the cause which we are convinced is sacred and just.

On 17 August there was a half-hearted attempt by Ju88s to attack the Grand Harbour and HMS *Furious* launched thirty-one Spitfires in Operation Baritone. Originally thirty-two Spitfires were due to be delivered to Malta, but only thirty-one actually took off. One Spitfire crashed on take-off and two others had to abandon their flights due to defective undercarriages.

At around 12.00 Spitfires of 126 and 185 Squadrons were scrambled to deal with a fighter sweep of fifteen Me109s. Pilot Officer Stenborg led the first attack against the Me109s over Kalafrana. Stenborg shot down an Me109 but then his aircraft received severe damage: part of his starboard wing was shot off and smoke was pouring into the cockpit. He was flying at 27,000 ft and the aircraft was virtually out of control. His hood would not move and he had already dropped to 14,000 ft and was travelling at 400 mph. Stenborg managed to force the hood open and was thrown out of the aircraft. His parachute opened and he fell into the sea to the north-east of Delimara Point, where he was picked up.

On 20 August Maltese-based fighters began their first offensive fighter sweeps over Sicily. Eighteen Spitfires took part in the first operation, but failed to draw out any enemy fighters. The situation in North Africa was reaching a critical point. It was, therefore, imperative that the Maltese-based bombers strike at any Axis southbound convoys and prevent them from getting through. Convoys would be attacked either by the RAF or by Fleet Air Arm aircraft based at Hal Far.

The escort ships that survived Operation Pedestal (Force Z) were attacked on their return trip to Gibraltar. HMS *Barham* and HMS *Ashanti* which had made it all the way to Malta were headed back to England via Gibraltar. HMS *Ledbury* made it safely back to Gibraltar, but *Rochester Castle* would need several months of repair work before she could be used again. She was anchored in French Creek, near the *Melbourne Star*.

By the end of the month of August there were very few enemy aircraft chancing attacks on Malta. August had been a relatively quiet time for the fighter pilots and enemy raids had dropped to around fifty-seven for the whole month. In fact there had been 102 air alerts and only seventy-one tons of bombs had been dropped on the island.

On 27 August Spitfires were sent to attack enemy aircraft on Sicilian airfields. However, the Beaufort squadrons were kept extremely busy operating against enemy convoys, as a log kept by one of the Beaufort squadrons reveals:

17 August: six crews set out to prang one motor vessel and two destroyers south of Pantellaria. A successful operation, as the 6,000 ton MV was left well down in the water, with smoke pouring out of it. One observer, who was wounded, had to extinguish a fire in his navigator's bag.

21 August: nine Beauforts attacked a 10,000 ton tanker (with escort of five destroyers) near Corfu. Three hits claimed, and Beaufighters hit a destroyer with bombers. The tanker appeared to be stationary when last seen, and was emitting steam. Subsequent reconnaissance showed her beached, with a large patch of oil on the sea. Wellingtons tried unsuccessfully to ignite this oil with fire bombs. There was one crew lost but the Beaufighter escort destroyed one Ju52, two Piaggio 32s and two BR20s.

26 August: nine Beauforts attacked one MV of 6,000 tons escorted by one destroyer north of Benghazi. One torpedo broke ship's back, and subsequent hits set her ablaze from stem to stern. Escorting Beaufighter destroyed a Cant.

30 August: nine Beauforts attacked a 5,000 ton tanker and one destroyer southbound from Taranto. The CO's torpedo was seen to hit. A second hit caused the tanker to blow up and burn furiously. Superstructure was thrown high in the air.

One pilot's prize moustache was endangered when he performed a 'fly through fire' act at something like 250 ft. One
Cant 501 was seen flying above the ship. There followed an
example of mob violence of unequalled ferocity. All the escorting Beaufighters and almost all the Beauforts's air gunners
popped away at it until it was left minus a float. The bewildered
Cant crew must have had a very worried trip home.

6 September: four motor vessels with escort of eleven
destroyers, southbound from Taranto were attacked by twelve
Beauforts. The intense flack and fighter attacks prevented the
observation of results, but subsequent reconnaissance showed
that one MV of 10,000 tons was sunk and another MV of
6,000 tons beached. All the Beauforts were attacked by fighters.
Once again the Beaufighters saved the day with some damn
good work – thanks boys! They bagged three, confirmed. One
Beaufort was shot down by a Macchi 200.

This was indeed a critical period. Maltese-based aircraft launched 124
sorties against enemy vessels. Italian and German shipping now had to
try to get to Africa by moving along the Greek coastline and then through
the Corinth Canal, rather than try and face the prospect of ruinous
attacks by Malta-based aircraft off the west coast of the Peloponnese.
Every enemy supply vessel sent to the bottom of the Mediterranean
meant that Rommel was getting weaker, as Montgomery's 8th Army
grew at El Alamein, ready to launch a major offensive.

Nonetheless, through September, the enemy still tried its luck, albeit
less regularly, against Malta. On 5 September ten Me109s were intercepted over the Grand Harbour by a similar number of Spitfires of 185
and 249 Squadron. Two Me109s were damaged and a further Me109
was chased over Kalafrana, where it was shot down into the sea.

A typical attack on an enemy convoy took place on 6 September.
Thirteen Beauforts armed with torpedoes and a close escort of a dozen
Beaufighters took off to intercept four enemy merchant vessels and
eleven destroyers that were trying to get to Benghazi. Four other Beaufighters were flying top cover. The attacking force got to within 30 miles
of Cape Santa Maria di Leuca when it saw half a dozen Ju88s, Macchi
fighters and a DO24 flying boat flying cover for the enemy convoy.
There was a dogfight over the convoy, which saw the loss of a pair
of Beaufighters and a number of the Beauforts were damaged but the
enemy also lost several aircraft.

The Germans launched an offensive reconnaissance sortie over Malta, using Me109s flying at high altitude on 8 September. They managed to surprise and engage a group of Spitfires of 126 Squadron, claiming one of the Spitfires.

The tailing off of enemy bomb raids on Malta allowed the presentation of Malta's George Cross to take place on Sunday 13 September. It was attended by many dignitaries from the island and from the Allied military. The following day *The Times of Malta* wrote:

> Yesterday's ceremony of the presentation of the George Cross to the people of Malta by Viscount Gort on behalf of HM the King was one of austere and fitting simplicity, admirably carried out. Those who were privileged to be present were conscious of the stern chapter of the island's history through which we are all living, and His Majesty's award of the George Cross marked his kingly appreciation of the importance of Malta's resistance in the cause of free men.

The Germans were back on 17 September when fifteen Me109s were spotted over Zonqor Point. Eight Spitfires were scrambled to intercept. Another eight Me109s were seen 20 miles off the Grand Harbour. One Me109 was shot down. A little later Pilot Officer Farmer was shot down and he only just managed to get out of his Spitfire, even though his controls were shot to pieces. He baled out at 450 mph and the jerk of the parachute gave him a rupture, a dislocated shoulder and a broken arm.

By the end of the month Gort was pleased to announce that with the exception of aviation fuel and benzene, there were sufficient supplies to last until mid-December. Flour stocks would last until mid-December and, providing rationing remained in place, edible oils, preserved meat, sugar and other foodstuffs should last and would even allow for a small stock to be retained.

The renewed air superiority over the island had clearly been working. There were just fifty-seven air raid alerts over the month and just thirteen tons of bombs were dropped on the island.

By September Rommel's position had reached critical levels. Montgomery, on the other hand, was receiving tanks, other vehicles, aircraft, ammunition, fuel and personnel at a steady rate. Rommel's offensive capabilities had been severely blunted. He was lacking food and water. Nonetheless in September, 11,200 tons of fuel had been unloaded in

North Africa in addition to other supplies and ammunition. Not every ship could be stopped.

Kesselring was still acutely aware that Malta's existence still hung in the balance. He figured that having suffered a two-year siege, one more all out air attack could finish her off. Entering into negotiations with the Italian air force, Kesselring determined to deliver a final knockout blow. He was in the process of amassing 700 bombers and fighters. Kesselring thought that dealing with Malta once and for all could mean the difference between success or failure in North Africa. A new blitz was about to be launched and this time for the Germans and the Maltese defenders there could be no margin for error.

CHAPTER ELEVEN

ONE LAST GO

In a relatively short period of time Kesselring managed to amass a third of the entire *Luftwaffe* in the Mediterranean theatre and half of all bombers in the theatre in Sicily.

In the first battle of El Alamein (1 to 27 July 1942) Rommel's troops had tried to breach Allied defences, but the 8th Army had counter-attacked and Rommel had been forced to dig in. Under Auchinleck, the Allies had tried to dislodge Rommel's German and Italian troops, but the battle had ended in a stalemate. At least it had prevented Rommel from advancing on Alexandria. Auchinleck was replaced by Mont-gomery in August 1942. He would not be rushed into launching a decisive attack on Rommel. He would spend six weeks building up his forces until he had 1,100 tanks and 220,000 men ready to launch against Rommel's 559 tanks and 115,000 men. The second battle of El Alamein would not be launched until 23 October.

Nearly a fortnight earlier, on 11 October, the German air force began its renewed air assault on Malta, striking with fifty-eight bombers, escorted by fighter aircraft. In the first raid Spitfires managed to account for eight bombers and seven fighters. Over the course of the new German campaign Spitfires would destroy 132 enemy aircraft. The anti-aircraft guns would claim a further eight. In all, German and Italian losses would amount to 204 aircraft destroyed, or so badly damaged that they could not be salvaged. In return, the Germans destroyed thirty-one Allied aircraft. The Germans would lose this campaign, as it would cost them fifteen aircrews for every one RAF pilot killed.

Forward interception was to be the key and this tactic is one of the major reasons why so few enemy aircraft were claimed by anti-aircraft fire. Simply, fewer of them ever reached the island.

The stresses and strains of this period of the siege fell not only to the air and ground crews, but also to the unsung operators of radio location stations, as one described this period:

> It was fairly easy to estimate the *Luftwaffe*'s timetable for attacks. Always one could expect a raid a few moments after sitting down to what small amount of food there was. As

surely as the earth revolves, at precisely quarter past seven each morning, the first formation of his bombers could be discerned approaching from the east. I noticed also that the 'big stuff' was little used. No 1,000 pounders chained together this time – mostly anti-personnel and incendiaries. Even during the day one could watch the thin streamers of light high up in the sky, indicating another load of anti-personnel bombs leaving the plane. Then they would burst across one of the 'dromes like so many popcorns on a hot shovel. With nightfall there was no cessation of the attacks. Flares were continually in use – usually five, sometimes six. One bunch over Grand Harbour, another in the centre of the island, bathing it in soft mellow light and a pervading quietness before the next kite came in on his bombing run. Then once more came that Fifth of November effect – occasionally one of our own star shells, the weaving of numerous searchlights, incendiaries anywhere and everywhere, until it was time for bed and one had just to forget about it. There was the ironic angle, too – how often on one of those very rare visits to the cinema could one watch those pictures depicting celluloid people nonchalantly lighting a cigarette, only to grind it immediately into so many shreds of tobacco. And the groans from many throats as they thought of their own meagre ration and the rubbish they had smoked by necessity, if only to soothe tired nerves. Similar sounds would greet the placing of delicate dishes upon an already lavishly prepared table. This time, perhaps, they were prompted by a memory of bully beef and biscuits. The last daylight raid to reach the island was a formation of three Ju88s, all of which were shot down, the last one circling my station and eventually putting her nose down and diving straight for us. I ran, only to find everyone else running in the opposite direction, which is rather complicating. About a hundred feet from the deck she levelled out, crashing 500 yards away. I think it was the pilot's unlucky day for his 'chute never opened and I remember him flashing past my eyes to disappear in a cloud of dust fifty yards distant.

Throughout the worst period of the new offensive launched by the Germans, (11 to 19 October) there was around 250 raiders attacking each day. Despite this, none of the airfields was out of action for more than half an hour at a time and on only one occasion did British aircraft fail to make night attacks on enemy shipping. The German pilots had clearly been misinformed that the island had been virtually bombed into submission. They were to find the island stronger in October than it had ever been.

The Germans and the Italians felt the full weight of the attacks on their shipping. Gian Galeazzo Ciano, the Italian Foreign Minister, wrote in his famous diaries:

> Rommel is halted in Egypt because of lack of fuel. Three of our tankers have been sunk in two days.

Vice Admiral Weichold, the German Commander-in-Chief in the Mediterranean, recorded:

> The situation was becoming serious. At the front the soldiers of the *Afrika Korps* fought and conquered but far from the decisive areas of the land fighting, the British were systematically throttling the supplies of the German and Italian Panzer Army. In September shipping losses were again very high, with 23,000 tons sunk and over 9,000 tons damaged. [In October] practically every one of our convoys was spotted by the British air reconnaissance from Malta and successfully attacked. Of shipping proceeding to North Africa, 24,000 tons were lost and over 14,000 tons damaged – an enormous blow to the Italian transport fleet. Of the 32,000 tons of German cargo and 940 vehicles, only 19,000 tons and 580 vehicles reached North Africa. The loss of fuel was even greater; of almost 10,000 tons, only 3,300 tons reached Cyrenaica.

October began with enemy fighter sweeps, which were met by Spitfires and anti-aircraft fire. At the beginning of the month the raids seemed to be following the same pattern as September, with reduced enemy activity against and over the island. Repairs and preparations were underway and there was no slackening of night time attacks on enemy convoys. The relative calm was abruptly broken on Saturday 10 October, with Ju88s dropping bombs on Gozo.

Malta itself received considerable enemy attention as the new blitz opened on 11 October. Seven Ju88s escorted by four Me109s and twenty-five Macchi 202s approached the island. Nineteen Spitfires were launched and although there were numerous claims, many of which could not be substantiated, it is believed that in the attacks that Sunday the Germans lost seven bombers and five fighters and the Italians three of their Macchi 202s. There were also a number of enemy aircraft damaged.

The attacks intensified on 12 October with five major raids. In the first raid Squadron Leader Stephens was shot down by an Me109, but he was picked up by Air Sea Rescue. Squadron Leader Wicks was also shot down but unfortunately he was never found. The steady Spitfire losses continued, with Sergeant Winall of 185 Squadron shot down by Me109s. Sergeant Knox-Williams was also lost, but he was rescued, and in the fifth raid of the day Flight Sergeant Stevenson of 1435 Squadron was shot down.

Tuesday the 13th saw one of the biggest air battles over the island since May. Malta claimed twenty-two enemy aircraft destroyed and over forty damaged and Maltese defences claimed their 1,000th enemy aircraft destroyed during this day. On the fourth raid seven Ju88s escorted by forty-two Me109s and thirty Macchi 202s were initially intercepted by just eight Spitfires of 249 Squadron, to the north of Gozo. No. 249 Squadron was reinforced by another eight Spitfires from 229 Squadron and several enemy aircraft were shot down.

On Wednesday 14 October there were rumours that eighty-two enemy aircraft had been shot down within the last four days. If this was the case then certainly the enemy was not letting up in its attempts to subdue the island. There were four raids, the first saw forty enemy fighters escorting eight Ju88s. Twenty-nine Spitfires scrambled to intercept and Flight Sergeant Long was shot down about 12 miles out from Kalafrana. A second raid was intercepted 20 miles to the north of the Grand Harbour by eight Spitfires of 1435 Squadron. This time the raiders were seven Ju88s, forty-five Me109s and twenty-nine Macchi 202s. Two Spitfires were lost in this encounter. The same raiders were then intercepted by eight Spitfires of 229 Squadron. By this time the bombers were on their way back and another Spitfire was lost. In the third raid twenty-two Spitfires, including the aircraft flown by Beurling of 249 Squadron, were sent up to intercept seven Ju88s escorted by enemy fighters. There were at least twenty Me109s. It was in this encounter that Beurling was badly wounded and shot down off Kalafrana.

There were continued attacks on the island on 15 October. Six Ju88s tried to bomb Luqa in the morning and they were intercepted by twenty-six Spitfires from four squadrons and just one Spitfire, flown by Warrant Officer Farquharson (126 Squadron) was shot down. No. 249 Squadron lost Flight Sergeant Bryden in the second raid of the day. He had baled out into the sea after a dogfight with eight Ju88s and a number of Me109s. Bryden was later picked up in his partially inflated dinghy. He was cheerful; despite the fact he had a broken leg. Flight Lieutenant Rod Smith was forced to bale out after his Spitfire was hit by an Me109 when he was chasing a group of enemy fighters heading back to Sicily. He later recalled:

> For some reason I glanced down at my left wing and happened to see a small bullet hole in it just a few feet from me. I assumed I'd picked it up earlier, when we were sparring with the 109s high up, I then fired a few more rounds over the top of the 109 in front of me but he would not turn. I looked again at the bullet hole in my left wing and saw a second one about a foot from it. It took a long second for me to realise there must be a 109 behind. I broke violently to the left and upwards. In an instant things began to happen. Exploding balls of fire making sharp cracking bangs appeared on the left side of my engine. The aircraft shook as if poked from behind by long metal rods. The cockpit filled with the smell of cordite. The engine oil pressure dropped to nothing. The oil temperature shot upwards. But the engine kept going without missing a beat. Over my left shoulder I saw the yellow nose of a 109 about 100 yards behind me and closing in. Puffs of smoke were billowing from its guns and being blown back over it. It came so close it almost touched me as it passed behind. As soon as I was pointing back to Malta, I straightened out and climbed at full power. We had been told that if a Rolls Royce Merlin engine ever lost its oil pressure you should flog it, not nurse it. To my great relief I reached 600 ft then 1,000 ft. The engine kept delivering full power. I marvelled how it could do this with no oil pressure. I switched the RT over to emergency and called "Mayday! Mayday! Mayday!" the oral SOS. Immediately, the Malta controller responded. "Keep transmitting," he said, "we've got you!" Soon I was at 2,000 ft and Malta looked closer. To my wonderment and admiration the engine kept going till I reached 3,800 ft and was almost at the coast of Malta. By then, acrid smoke was pouring through the cockpit and the power was failing. I baled out and was rescued from the sea.

Smith was picked up by ST253 (a Seaplane Tender used by the RAF as an Air Sea Rescue launch) near the Sliema Point battery.

Four more raids were launched on 16 October, the first with eight Ju88s and a large number of enemy fighters. Spitfires intercepted them 15 miles out from Zonqor. At least two Spitfire pilots were lost at sea. Maltese fishermen picked up Sergeant Lundy near the Blue Grotto in the aftermath of the second raid. Flight Sergeant Carter was also lost and in the fourth raid a German bomber was shot down 5 miles out from Delimara Point. Air Vice Marshal Park, conscious of the casualties being caused to the Spitfire squadrons and their sterling defensive work despatched a message to each of the squadrons that evening:

> Grand work fighter-boys. Your magnificent fighting in the last few days is being watched not only in Malta but by the RAF on other fronts as well as by our Russian allies. Although heavily outnumbered last May, the Malta Spitfires came out on top and I am confident that you will win the second battle of Malta. Some of the enemy bomber squadrons have already shown they cannot take it. Keep it up and in a few days the other German bombers will throw in the sponge. Replacement pilots and Spitfires are on their way but there is still some stiff fighting to finish the job. Good luck to you and good shooting. Your [maintenance personnel] part in the present battle for Malta greatly appreciated but serviceability of Spitfires continues to fall. You can and must get it up again. Where you have worked hard you must work harder and faster. Give the fighter boys Spitfires and they will drive the Hun out of the sky.

There was a head on collision between a Spitfire and a Ju88 on 17 October 7 miles off Delimara Point and at midday a pair of Ju88s was shot down. Australian Flight Lieutenant Colin Parkinson DFC of 229 Squadron recorded in his diary:

> Malta pilots knocking them down like ninepins. I got two Ju probables. One Ju88 damaged, two BF109s destroyed, one BR20M damaged in this lot of the new blitz. Pilot Officer Nash shot down, baled out broken jaw. Sergeant Bryden baled out, broken leg. Sergeant Sandy baled out OK. Sergeant Miller baled out. This new blitz has relieved the monotony of the island for the time being. BF109 dive bombers have started. Ju88s don't like head-on attacks by Spitfires. They have been

turned back several times now. At least three, of six to nine, are shot down every time.

Attacks dropped off on 18 October but the daylight raids resumed on 20 October with the airfields being targeted. Torpedo attacks were made by the Maltese bombers that night, hitting a large tanker and another merchant vessel. Speaking in the House of Commons on Wednesday 21 October, Sir Archibald Sinclair, Secretary for Air, announced that up to 19 October there had been 1,660 bombing attacks on Malta, but that 1,069 enemy aircraft had been shot down.

In Cairo the Reuters correspondent, R F Rowland, wrote:

> Kesselring's eight day assault on Malta has failed in its main object – to improve the supply position of General Rommel's troops. The Axis is being hit in two ways. Their convoys are sought out and vitally important cargoes are being sunk at sea or in harbour.

Two waves of attacks came in on Friday 23 October, the first German and the second Italian, causing several civilian casualties. Fighter bombers raided on 25 October resulting in one Me109 and one Spitfire lost. Sergeant Nigel Park was shot down that day. Park probably crashed into the sea and went down with his aircraft. On 12 October he had made an attack on seven Ju88 bombers and he shot one of them down. Despite attacks from escorting Italian and German fighters, he turned and destroyed a second Ju88. He was back on patrol a few hours later that day, when he attacked and destroyed another bomber. On the 14th he destroyed an Me109 and damaged a Ju88. He wrote of that encounter:

> We were patrolling at 21,000 feet, 20 miles north-east of Grand Harbour, when we sighted nine Junkers 88 with a swarm of fighters heading south. We turned into the attack, Red 1 and myself going into the bombers. I got on one bomber's tail, but my guns had frozen so I broke away, and after shaking off two attacking Messerschmitt 109s, I dived away down to 10,000 feet. On hearing the Ground Controller broadcast the height and position of the bombers, I went east to Kalafrana Bay where the bombers were seen heading back to the north-east. I tried to intercept them, but was jumped by two Me 109s. I turned quickly to avoid, and

after a complete turn got on a Messerschmitt's tail. I closed in without opening fire to about 100 yards, when he turned I gave him a three-second burst from dead astern. He went into a steep dive straight into the sea.

Another high scoring Spitfire pilot was Flight Lieutenant Stenborg DFC, who recalled another dreadful experience during those times:

I was with an American sergeant flying at 31,000 feet. He saw Messerschmitts which I could not, so I told him to attack and I would follow, but as he went for six Huns, three more followed him up. I shot down one from his tail at point-blank range, but the next minute a great chunk flew off my starboard wing. I heard explosions and the plane shook everywhere and black smoke poured into the cockpit. I began diving out of control at 27,000 feet. I tried to get the hood off, but it would not budge. I tried all ways, while the Spitfire fell 14,000 feet at over 400 miles an hour, and the cockpit filled with smoke. I thought I had had it. It was a horrible feeling; I was expecting the plane to blow up at any moment. But fortunately the hood came off, and I suddenly found myself thrown out. I had seen a German pilot open his parachute at that speed and his harness was ripped off by the force of the sheer speed, so I waited for a while before pulling the ripcord in order to slow up, and then I pulled the cord and landed in the sea. I spent five minutes trying to get free from the parachute and get the dinghy working. That trip shook me to the teeth.

The first of two long-range Spitfires landed at Malta on 25 October, having flown direct from Gibraltar. They had an extra 29 gallon tank in the rear fuselage and a 170 gallon tank under their belly. These were to be followed by fourteen more Spitfires that would reach Malta during November and December.

Raiders attacked once again on 26 October. A total of thirty-five enemy aircraft were intercepted and at least one was shot down. A late morning raid saw another two Me109s fall to Maltese Spitfires and yet another during an afternoon raid.

HMS *Furious* ferried in twenty-nine of thirty-two Spitfires in Operation Train on 29 October. This was to be the last of the fighter reinforcements for the island. Events were progressing elsewhere, which would change the tactical and strategic importance of Malta. The second battle of El Alamein had been launched on 23 October and on 7 November Anglo-American forces would land in North-west Africa, in Operation Torch. The emphasis, as far as Malta was concerned, would be to make offensive attacks, as the German and Italian attempts to gain air superiority over Malta began to dwindle away.

October had seen extremely heavy enemy attacks with 154 air raid alerts during the month and 624 tons of bombs dropped on the island. Events were to overtake the battle for the island of Malta, with Montgomery breaking through at El Alamein in early November and forcing Rommel's *Afrika Korps* into permanent retreat. Kesselring had reluctantly called off the attack on Malta, as he later confessed: 'our losses were too high'. This was the last major air battle over Malta. The raiders would return, but in fewer numbers and less often.

There was a combined German and Italian raid on 3 November which caused more civilian casualties across the island. Pilot Officer Beurling managed to escape unhurt when the aircraft taking him home to Canada crashed near Gibraltar. On 4 November sixteen Beaufighters of 272 Squadron flew in from North Africa to Takali airfield. Six Wellingtons belonging to 104 Squadron reached Luqa airfield and they would become part of the offensive arm that would initially be used in French North-west Africa.

Raids were still underway against enemy airfields in Sicily, knocking out runways, dispersal areas and buildings. Meanwhile, long-range fighters attacked Tunisian airfields. Beaufighters of 227 Squadron intercepted a DO24 flying boat between Sicily and Tunisia and they then attacked an armada of thirty SM81s and sixteen Ju52s (troop carriers). The eight Beaufighters claimed four Ju52s and five probable, along with two SM81s and a probable with the loss of just one Beaufighter. On the following day, in the morning, Spitfires shot down an Italian bomber and more enemy transport aircraft were intercepted and shot down. Aircraft of the Fleet Air Arm sank a large tanker heading for Tripoli on 17 November.

The arrival of Operation Stoneage in Grand Harbour on 20 November (it had left Port Said on 16 November) effectively broke the Malta siege. The cargo ships, *Denbighshire*, *Bantum*, *Robin Locksley* and *Mormacmoon* had been escorted in by five cruisers and seventeen destroyers. Only the cruiser HMS *Arethusa* had been damaged *en route* (18 November). The convoy brought in 35,000 tons of supplies. Wing Commander Sandy Johnstone wrote of the arrival:

The Maltese went mad in a frenzied outburst of tears, laughter, and loud unrestrained cheering. Young boys and girls leapt and screamed, while their parents roared themselves hoarse as they watched the long awaited convoy gliding into safety. Old and young hugged and kissed each other; a few people just stood quietly, the tears of relief rolling unashamedly down their cheeks. Everywhere there were scenes of delirium. I have never seen such a heartfelt welcome being given to any force as was given to that small band of mariners who had opened up the sea route once again and given Malta the chance to breathe more easily.

The convoy had fought its way through despite bad weather and attacks from torpedo bombers. The convoy's success had been made possible by the 8th Army when they overran Matruba airfields in North Africa. This allowed the RAF to operate from Matruba and provide protection between Crete and Cyrenaica. The convoy was truly a united nations of relief. A pair of the merchant ships was American, another was British and a fourth was Dutch. Everyone waited for the inevitable German air assault on the ships as feverish preparations began to unload them. But the attack never came. Maltese-based Beaufighters and Spitfires had covered the last 135 miles of the convoy's voyage. This had been achieved despite the appalling weather and the fact that three Spitfires were lost during the operation.

However, rationing was far from over and there was still large numbers of enemy forces in North Africa and Sicily. But, hopefully, the worst was now over and Malta could look forward to better times, without the horror of enemy aircraft dispensing death and destruction from above.

Beaufighters were continuing to operate with increased successes: they attacked shipping with bombs, cannons and machine guns; they strafed airfields, shot up trains and transport columns. No enemy air convoys on their way in or out of Africa were safe. On the night of 7 November Wellingtons had struck at Cagliari airfield. The operation was planned as a diversion for the landings in Algeria. The Wellingtons would operate on every night for the rest of the year, with the exception of four in November and seven in December. Their principal targets were ports and airfields in Tunisia. Also, within their operational brief, were the airbases on Sicily and Sardinia. The targets on Sicily and Sardinia were close enough to allow the Wellingtons to make two sorties each night if the weather held. Between them the Wellingtons and the

Beaufighters did enormous damage to petrol dumps, airfields, ports, railways and storage areas. So effective were the attacks that a German airfield at El Aouina in Tunisia was out of action for several days in November due to the massive number of craters on the runways.

The Italians and Germans still tried to make their presence known in the last few days of November 1942. On 24 November an enemy fighter sweep over the island brought a violent reaction from anti-aircraft batteries. By the end of the month the enemy had managed to trigger thirty air-raid alerts but only twelve tons of bombs had been dropped on the island. There were three main reasons for this: first, the Spitfires were intercepting the enemy out to sea, breaking up their attacks before they could develop. Second, the offensive capabilities of the enemy squadrons had been severely curtailed due to the staggering losses they had suffered in air combat over the island in October. Third, the enemy air fleets were not even safe on their own airfields. They were attacked day and night and many aircraft were destroyed on the ground.

More convoys were due throughout December and on into the New Year. Their prospects of getting to Malta unscathed were far more promising than during the dark month of June 1942. With British and Commonwealth forces gradually conquering more and more of the North African coast, and Anglo-American forces overwhelming French North-west Africa, Malta had seen the worst of the war. But she would continue to be a vital pivot and base in the war that the Allies would now bring to Sicily and the Italian mainland.

CHAPTER TWELVE

PAUSE AND PLAUDITS

The final air raids on Malta would come on 26 February 1943, when the Italians tried to sneak a bomber over the island at daybreak. It did not make it. That evening a handful of enemy fighters tried a hit-and-run attack, but failed.

For the Maltese this was a landmark day. Throughout the siege nearly 1,600 civilians had been killed, over 1,800 seriously injured and nearly 1,900 wounded. The rationing had caused casualties too: infant mortality rates were incredibly high in 1942 when one baby in three would die. In fact 2,336 babies under the age of one died that year.

Of all the centres of population the dockyard town of Senglea had suffered the worst with 80 per cent of its buildings destroyed. Even the remaining 20 per cent was so badly damaged that they could not be lived in. Repairs were impossible as the streets were clogged with rubble.

Throughout the siege around 547 British aircraft had been lost in air combat. A further 160 had been destroyed whilst they were on the ground. Various estimates have been made of the enemy losses. In all probability 1,252 German and Italian aircraft had been shot down over the island. In addition there were 1,052 probable kills. In 1942 alone the RAF fighters had destroyed 773 enemy aircraft and possibly an additional 300, which could not be confirmed. Anti-aircraft guns had claimed over 180. In the same year the RAF had lost 195 fighter aircraft and 106 pilots. In 1942 alone the RAF and the Fleet Air Arm had hit eighty-three enemy ships with bombs or torpedoes and had damaged at least another fifty vessels.

The Royal Navy had returned to Malta by the end of 1942. It was now far safer to moor in the Grand Harbour. On 21 December Royal Navy destroyers sunk an enemy supply ship and on 16 January 1943 an Italian merchant ship was sent to the bottom. Between 19 and 20 January the Royal Navy sank an Italian water tanker and then sank eleven out of twelve enemy supply ships.

Compared to the previous months of 1942, December saw an enormous number of cargo vessels arriving at Malta. Sailing from Port Said on 1 December the cargo ships *Agwimonte*, *Suffolk*, *Glenartney*, *Alcoa Prospector* and the *Yorba Linda* arrived on 4 December. They delivered 55 tons of supplies. The cargo ships and the escort of three cruisers and ten destroyers suffered no losses *en route*. Another convoy sailed in on 10 December, having left Alexandria on 6 December; the cargo ships *American Packer* and *Ozarda* once again arrived safely. Beaufighters had gone out from Malta to escort the convoy in and they ran into three BV222 six-engine flying boats. During the encounter one of the flying boats was shot down, as was one of the Beaufighters. Another convoy left Alexandria on 9 December, arriving in Malta on 14 December and yet again two merchant ships, *Clan Macindoe* and *Erinna* arrived unmolested.

Two Beaufighters belonging to 272 Squadron left Malta at 08.40 on 19 December. They were accompanied by four Spitfires of 249 Squadron. The mission was an offensive reconnaissance. Shortly after 11.00, during their return to Malta, they spotted a DO24 flying boat near Dlimara. One of the Spitfires shot it down, but unfortunately shortly after this one of the Beaufighters crashed into the sea and exploded, killing the crew.

Further supplies arrived on 21 December, having left Port Said on 17 December. Despite the fact that offensive sweeps by the Maltese-based fighters and bombers were commonplace, the month had seen thirty-five enemy air raid alerts and sixty tons of bombs had been dropped on the island.

As the New Year dawned, Malta was adopting a new role. It was no longer besieged, but it would now operate as a bridgehead between the Allied forces gathering in North Africa and the exposed underbelly of the enemy in Sicily and mainland Italy. Victory was still a long way off and privations would still continue on the island. The work was unabated: it was no longer a question of keeping a handful of Hurricanes and Spitfires aloft in an attempt to keep the enemy at bay. Malta had become an armed camp and was fast becoming an island aircraft-carrier, with an offensive capacity to cause enormous damage to the Italians and Germans. The appearance of many German and Italian transport aircraft in the region signalled not the threat of invasion, but desperation on behalf of the enemy. Their shipping losses had been crippling, none of their surface vessels were safe and the few that remained were unwilling to run the gauntlet of Allied aircraft, submarines and surface vessels that now dominated the Mediterranean. The transport aircraft represented the only hope to resupply the dwindling German and Italian effort in North Africa.

January 1943 saw the first month since the outbreak of hostilities when no bombs were dropped on the island of Malta, despite twenty-five air-raid alerts. In the last week of January Tripoli had been captured by the Allies and this was to mark the beginning of the end of enemy resistance in North Africa. Attacks were being launched not only on the Italian mainland, North Africa and Sicily, but also on airfields such as the one on the island of Pantelleria.

The new offensive role of the Spitfires that had so gallantly defended the island brought new challenges to the pilots and their ground crews. A new airfield had been set up on Malta, at Krendi. The new Wing Commander of the two squadrons based there was Sandy Johnstone. They had launched innumerable fighter sweeps over Sicily, hoping to lure German and Italian aircraft into the sky. More often than not the enemy had refused battle. In order to maintain pressure on the enemy, particularly in Sicily, experiments were put into motion to fit a 500 lb bomb under each wing of each Spitfire, effectively transforming the fighter into a fighter bomber.

The first attack went in against a chemical factory at Pochino on Sicily on 16 January 1943. Twenty-four Spitfires were employed in the attack, twelve as conventional fighters and the others as fighter bombers. Johnstone later wrote about his experiences in the attack:

> In each Spitfire, with his 500 lb lethal weapon under each wing, the pilot kept his screaming dive under control while he zeroed the bombs on target by using the normal gun sight. One after the other the bombs ran down on the target area, dropping at regular intervals and exploding with frightening velocity. At least three made direct hits on the factory, sending tons of masonry hurtling through the air to join the twisted metal of the gutted machinery. As the last bomber began its dive I swooped down to ground level with my eleven escorting companions and raced in on the scene of destruction, raking the smoke and flames with cannon and machine-gun fire. The vibrations set up by the firing of the guns was like the tingling of newly awakened nerves. It was a strange overwhelming feeling of excitement that made your mouth dry with the taste of it; your heart beat faster and your body tensed itself in its firm and unrelaxed grip. I swept towards the wreckage of the factory. As I pulled back on the stick to lift the Spitfire above the smoke, there were clear indications that my fire power had struck home. There were signs of a large explosion and judging by the clouds of steam, followed by dense black smoke which billowed from the

tall chimney and burst outwards from several of the factory windows, I was certain that I had hit a massive boiler. Re-forming, the bomber aircraft, now shed of their loads, acted as an escort to the twelve straffers whose ammunition was spent. We set course for Malta and were back on the ground, ready to refuel without any retaliation from the Sicilian-based enemy aircraft.

Although Johnstone's attack met with little in the way of reaction from the enemy, not all operations were so fortunate. Pilot Officer Nesbitt of 185 Squadron failed to return after a morning sweep over south-east Sicily on 4 February. He was seen to bale out at 09.00 some 15 miles north-east of the Grand Harbour. Nesbitt reported:

When returning from a sweep on Sicily, owing to engine failure, I was forced to abandon my aircraft about 15 miles from the island. The air screw revolutions increased to 3,300 and I tried to adjust this by pulling up the nose of my aircraft, closing the throttle and moving the air screw pitch-lever back. Nothing seemed to happen so I straightened out, whereupon the engine cut. Checking the ignition switches and petrol lever, I tried the throttle and also tried priming. As this had no effect I put the air screw into fully coarse and started to glide at 135 ASI from approximately 18,000 ft on a coarse of 220°. I was then between 5 to 10 miles from the coast of Sicily.

Nesbitt finally managed to ditch. He was covered by four Spitfires of 126 Squadron and was in the water for nearly 40 minutes before HSL166 picked him up.

Incidents such as these were an almost daily occurrence. Another Spitfire was lost on 8 February, a Baltimore on 18 February, a Mosquito on 21 February and another Spitfire that had been in a dogfight with Me109s on 26 February. Engine failure was more of a hazard than engagements with enemy aircraft. Ditching into the sea was still a hazardous affair, despite the successes of the Air Sea Rescue launches and seaplane tenders. On 1 March, for example, eight Spitfires of 185 Squadron made a sweep over Sicily at 25,000 ft. They had barely arrived over Sicily when Flight Sergeant Miller's engine stopped and he was forced to bale out some 32 miles to the north of the Grand Harbour. This had occurred shortly before 09.00 hours. Luckily for Miller

HSL107 swiftly picked him up and he was back at his base at 11.40 that day. Miller reported:

> I was flying on a sweep over south-east Sicily with seven other fighters of 185 Squadron. At 08.50 hours, while at 23,000 ft and 15 miles inland over Sicily I was about to participate in an attack on three Me109s when my engine cut without any warning. Having tried unsuccessfully to restart the engine, I released my harness and began to glide towards base. When down to 5,000 ft, I attempted to jettison the hood but was unable to do so, I therefore slid it back and turned the aircraft over. My parachute got wedged by the handle of the hood but managed to get free and, after a short drop, found the toggle and the parachute opened. On my way down I removed my gloves and boots and turned the quick release box. Immediately my feet touched the water I released my parachute. When in the water I first freed the dinghy from its cover and, when it was free of the parachute, pushed the lever on the Mae West to operate the CO_2 bottle, which did not function properly. I then tried to inflate the dinghy manually but did not know that the valve locking-pin had to be removed. As the dinghy was a dead weight and tending to drag me down, I undid the quick release on my Mae West and let the dinghy go free. I then tried to inflate the Mae West by mouth but was only able to do so partially on account of the sea swell and the effort required.

In the first three months of 1943 Malta's bombers and torpedo bombers sunk nine enemy vessels, had fourteen probables and damaged several others. Typical of this type of work was an attack made in mid-March. A Baltimore, on reconnaissance patrol, spotted a convoy that was south-bound in the Gulf of Taranto, protected by a destroyer escort and an air escort of fifteen Me110s and Ju88s. Five hours later nine Beauforts, with Beaufighter cover, discovered the convoy. The Beaufighters made for the aircraft whilst the Beauforts honed in on the largest of the convoy ships, an 8,000 ton tanker. The tanker was hit three times and there was a huge cloud of smoke rising from the ship and smoke pouring across its decks.

Valuable contributions were also being made by Wellington torpedo bombers. They operated against targets at night that were illuminated by Wellingtons equipped with flares and radar. One such example of an attack took place in January 1943 when Flight Sergeant Hornung attacked an enemy cargo vessel, believed to be 4,000 tons, and escorted by a destroyer. Hornung's aircraft weaved through a barrage of anti-aircraft fire from the ships and struck the merchant vessel with a pair of torpedoes. The target immediately burst into flames.

Sergeant W A Fraser had an amazing fortnight at the beginning of February 1943. On 2 February a pair of search aircraft had spotted a convoy off the south-east coast of Italy. When Fraser's Wellington arrived there was only one flare illuminated, which made it difficult for him to make an attack on the tanker and avoid the pair of escorting destroyers. He managed to release the torpedo at 700 yards, hitting the 6,000 ton tanker, which then caught fire and had to be beached. On 7 February he made a successful attack on a 6,000 ton merchant ship, badly damaging it. On 15 February he made an attack on another tanker of 5,000 tons. Despite it being defended by a pair of destroyers and one his crew members being wounded, his torpedo struck the tanker amidships.

By April 1943 the 8th Army had linked up with the Anglo-American troops operating in Algeria and preparations were underway to invade Sicily. By the end of May 1943 the number of Malta's frontline aircraft stood at around 600 compared to just 200 towards the end of 1942. The new arrivals on the island included four Spitfire wings and additional Mosquito and Beaufighter squadrons. The old airfields had been enlarged and new landing fields had been created. Malta could now dominate the central Mediterranean.

The wheel had definitely turned full circle and in September 1943 Faith, one of the three original Gladiators that had faced the Italians more than three years before, was retrieved from the bottom of a quarry where she had lain. She was then presented to the people of Malta by Air Marshal Sir Keith Park. Faith very much represented the courage and the fortitude of the servicemen and the civilians of the island.

In June 1943 Operation Corkscrew was launched against the Italian island of Pantelleria. In effect it would provide a practice for the forthcoming invasion of Sicily and Italy and it would also give the Allies a chance to gauge the impact of bombing on defensive positions. The tiny island, just eight and a half miles by five and a half miles, lay 140 miles to the north-west of Malta. Plans had been drawn up as early as 1940 to take the island, but these had been put off as it was believed that it would be difficult to continue to hold the island and support Malta at the same time. In June 1943 14,203 bombs, which amounted to 4,119 tons, were dropped on the sixteen gun batteries on the island.

There were eighty guns defending the island and the bombing wrecked over half of them. Communications were destroyed, along with air raid shelters and ammunition stores. On D-Day (11 June 1943) surface vessels opened fire on the island an hour before the landing craft reached the beaches. By the time the first British commandos clambered ashore the white flag was already flying.

The Germans had already evacuated the airfield, leaving just a handful of technicians. The Italians, however, had left a garrison of 10,000 men. Within the next two days Lampedusa and Linosa, two other Italian-held islands, were also captured and the route to the invasion of Sicily was now open.

Back on Malta, the Supreme Allied Commander for Europe, General Eisenhower and General Montgomery, Commander of the British 8th Army, established their new headquarters at Valletta, in preparation for Operation Husky, the invasion of Sicily. Some 3,000 ships were being gathered and many of the 600 aircraft based on Malta would provide air cover for the invasion.

The island had received a visit from an American engineer on 25 May 1943. He had come at the invitation of Lord Gort and Air Vice Marshal Sir Keith Park. British and American engineers had surveyed Gozo, looking for a possible site of a new airstrip. Eisenhower was concerned that Malta's airfields were not large enough to deal with the huge amount of aircraft that would be required for the opening of the Italian campaign. Eisenhower said:

> British field engineers, who depended to a great extent upon hand tools and light mechanical equipment, had given up all hope of finishing an airfield there [Gozo] in time for use in the Sicilian campaign.

The arrival of the American engineer, Major Lee Baron Colt, brought new hope to the plan. He believed he could have an airstrip ready in two weeks. All he needed was men and equipment. Company E, 21st Engineer Aviation Regiment was moved to Gozo. They would have to clear cultivated fields and terraces in order to build a runway 4,000 ft in length and 150 ft in width.

There was continued action still, with numerous dogfights taking place over Sicily and the waters between the Italian island and Malta. Almost daily there were losses.

There was intense excitement on 20 June when the rumour that King George VI was about to visit Malta was confirmed at 05.00. He would be arriving in the Grand Harbour onboard the cruiser HMS *Aurora* that morning. All the dignitaries were out in force to greet the monarch, along with thousands of Maltese citizens. The King toured the island, visiting many of the sites of the conflict over the past years. Gort signalled to the King on his departure:

> At the close of a day never to be forgotten in the history of these islands, the armed forces and the people of Malta and Gozo humbly wish Your Majesty God speed. We are deeply sensible of the honour our beloved sovereign has bestowed on his fortress by this personal visit whilst Malta still stands in the van of the forces of the United Nations in the central Mediterranean. As in the past, this colony has only one intention – never to falter in the service of Your Majesty.

The King replied:

> It was with great eagerness that I seized the occasion of my visit to North Africa to come to Malta and bring to the armed forces and to the Maltese people a message of good cheer on behalf of all other peoples of the British Empire. The warmth with which I have been received today has touched me more than I can say. It has been for me one further proof of the loyalty which has inspired the island fortress to withstand the fiercest blows that a cruel enemy could inflict upon her. I thank the people of Malta from my heart and send them my best wishes for the happier times that surely lie ahead.

As for the development of the airfield on Gozo, success was confirmed when seventy-four Spitfires of the 31st Fighter Group, led by Lieutenant Colonel Fred M Dean USAAF were transferred from Tunisia on 30 June. The month had ended with just thirty air raid alerts and not a single bomb had been dropped on Malta.

Malta now braced itself to become part of the invasion effort. Operation Husky was due to be launched on 10 July 1943 and it would be from Malta that Eisenhower would first step foot on enemy-held Europe just two days later. Raids were still necessary prior to the invasion. Each enemy aircraft destroyed in the air or on the ground brought the prospects of the invasion success closer.

According to statistics compiled in England, the total number of enemy aircraft destroyed between 1939 and June 1943 in operations against the RAF and Fleet Air Arm amounted to 3,500 in the Middle East region, which included Malta. This was an incredible amount since the total number of enemy aircraft shot down over Great Britain in the same period was 4,201. RAF losses in the Middle East region amounted to 1,977 aircraft.

Malta's Spitfires were still in action, even after Allied troops had begun their invasion of enemy-held Europe. Daily Maltese Spitfire sweeps led to dogfights over Sicily and beyond.

By 5 August, with British and Canadian troops almost at Mount Etna on Sicily, Eisenhower delivered his own tribute to Malta:

> The epic of Malta is symbolic of the experience of the United Nations in the war. Malta has passed successively through the stage of woeful unpreparedness, tenacious endurance, intensive preparation and the initiation of a fierce offensive. It is resolutely determined to maintain a rising crescendo of attack until the whole task is completed. For this inspiring example the United Nations will be forever indebted to Field Marshal Lord Gort, the fighting services under his command and to every citizen of the heroic island.

The Times of Malta throughout the entire siege had never failed to be published. Mabel Strickland, the editor, writing on 17 August after Sicily had fallen, wrote:

> The hideous German Junkers 88s no longer possess the sky, instead there is the continuous drone of British fighters and bombers, heading out for Italy, speeded on their mission by the Maltese with a fierce and furious delight. They are the first liberators of oppressed Europe.

A greater joy was to come to Malta on 8 September. The remnants of the Italian fleet, just twenty-eight vessels, steamed into the Grand Harbour to surrender. The Germans had tried to sink the surrendering Italian surface fleet and had managed to destroy the Italian battleship and flagship, *Roma*.

On 28 September Marshal Badaoglio signed the Italian surrender at Malta. Admiral Sir Andrew Cunningham sent a telegram of confirmation to London:

> Pleased to inform their lordships that the Italian battle fleet now lies at anchor under the guns of the fortress of Malta.

Malta's staunchest ally and supporter arrived on the island in November 1943. Prime Minister Winston Churchill was later to write:

> The interrelation between Malta and the desert operations was never so plain as in 1942, and the heroic defence of the island in that year formed the keystone of the prolonged struggle for the maintenance of our position in Egypt and the Middle East.

On Wednesday 8 December 1943 Malta played host to President Roosevelt. He commended the islanders for their contribution:

> In the name of the people of the United States of America I salute the island of Malta, its people and defenders, who in the cause of freedom and justice and decency throughout the world have rendered valorious service far above and beyond the call of duty. Under repeated fire from the skies, Malta stood alone but unafraid in the centre of the sea, one tiny bright flame in the darkness, a beacon of hope for the clearer days which have come.

The civilians and servicemen of Malta had suffered enormous losses and privations and many of the vessels that had brought them hope had also been lost. HMS *Eagle*, USS *Wasp* and HMS *Welshman* had all been sunk by the time the war had ended. The USS *Wasp* had been sunk off Guadalcanal in the Pacific by a Japanese submarine on 15 September 1942. HMS *Welshman* had been sunk off Tobruk on 1 February 1943 and HMS *Eagle* had of course been sunk during Operation Pedestal. Four torpedoes, fired from the German submarine U-73 had sunk her in the early morning of 11 August 1942, 70 miles south of Cape Salinas.

Lieutenant General Sir William Dobbie wrote in 1944 of the victory that would have appeared to have been so impossible in 1940:

> It was my privilege to witness these amazing happenings from the vantage point of Malta, which was destined to play a great part in the epic struggle. It is possible that the importance and the role of that island fortress have only been imperfectly understood until recently, but it is very evident now that its importance was so great and its role so vital to our wellbeing in the Mediterranean that its retention in our hands justified any effort and any sacrifice however great. It is no exaggeration

to say that the security of Malta reacted very definitely on the safety of Egypt, and all that those words imply. If Malta had fallen, the safety of Egypt would have been very gravely endangered. It was from Malta that the attacks were launched by sea and air on the enemy's lines of communication between Italy and North Africa. By means of these attacks we were able to exert some influence on the effectiveness of the enemy forces in North Africa, and in this way to reduce the threat on Egypt.

Dobbie went on to describe the perilous position that Malta found itself in at the beginning of hostilities:

Our resources were meagre enough. Especially in the early months of the Italian war, the garrison was unbelievably weak both in men and material, and the enemy undoubtedly knew exactly how weak we were. Our air resources in Malta were practically nil, although the fortress was only a few minutes flying away from the many air bases in Sicily and southern Italy at the disposal of the strong Regia Aeronautica. No wonder the Italians had been boasting that they would overrun the island within a few days of the declaration of war. Their resources were amply adequate to justify them making the attempt, especially in view of our own weakness. But this attempt was never made (just as the attempt to invade Britain was never made), and all other attempts during the two long years and more to reduce the fortress by other means failed. We acknowledge with admiration and gratitude the way the people of Malta, the three fighting services and the Merchant Navy faced the ordeal and willingly paid the price needed to keep Malta safe. But even so the fact that Malta is today still in British hands is a miracle. The miracle of Malta is a part, and a big part, of the Mediterranean miracle.

The war front was gradually leaving Malta in the rear. By December 1943 there had been no air raid alerts over the island, a situation that had existed for at least two months. January 1944 saw two air raid alerts and there were none in February.

By August 1944 the island and the servicemen had settled down to a new, more peaceful routine. On 5 August Gort visited Valletta for the last time. He had been appointed High Commissioner and Commander in Chief in Palestine and would be replaced by Lieutenant General Sir Edmond Acton Schreiber.

The last alert was sounded on 28 August 1944. It began at 20.43 and the all clear was sounded at 2.100 hours. In all, Malta had experienced 3,349 air raid alerts. The island had been under alert for 2,357 hours. Of these 1,206 had been actual bombing raids.

The year 1944 brought more food, security and an end to the terror. There were still huge mounds of broken buildings. Each village and town on the island was scarred and disfigured by the actions of the enemy over the period of the siege. Daily Allied aircraft, not Italian or German raiders, flew overhead. The island was subjected to successive invasions: not by the enemy but by servicemen bringing in supplies and material or in transit to or from the front in Italy. Still alert for any danger, the fighter squadrons and anti-aircraft batteries scoured the skies for the sign of an enemy attack. In the harbours cargo ships and other vessels sailed in and out freely, unmolested by the attentions of Ju87s and Ju88s. In the Grand Harbour there was the wreckage of many of the ships that had brought much needed supplies and reinforcements to the island.

For many years the scars left by the blitz on Malta remained. The countryside was strewn with burned out aircraft, the villages and towns with collapsed buildings. In time the army, the air force and the navy would all leave Malta. To this day the Opera House lies in ruins, the only landmark on the island that has not been rebuilt.

In 1992 the Siege Bell Memorial was built on the site of a Bofors gun emplacement, overlooking the Grand Harbour. At noon each day the bell is rung to remind the islanders and the tourists that the island remains the home of the many airmen that fought and died on Malta and that the island remains their resting place.

TIMELINE OF THE SIEGE
(APRIL 1940–DECEMBER 1942)

Incorporating relevant events before the siege itself

Date	Event
1935	Anti-aircraft defences of the Grand Harbour are strengthened.
20 April 1939	British merchant shipping is banned from operating in the Mediterranean.
July 1939	The Central Committee is created by the governor of Malta's Advisory Council.
September 1939	District Committees are formed in each parish on Malta.
23 April 1940	Creation of the Malta Fighter Fight, with eight volunteer pilots. Twenty-four Royal Navy Gladiators that arrived in March 1939 have been reduced to eighteen. Eight of them are requisitioned for HMS *Glorious* and ten for HMS *Eagle*. In the event, four are to be kept for the Malta Fighter Flight.
29 April 1940	The Malta Flight is dissolved when all ten of the assembled Gladiators are in fact requisitioned by the Royal Navy.
2–3 May 1940	Blackout practice on Malta between 22.00 hours and dawn.
4 May 1940	Malta Fighter Flight re-formed after Royal Navy has a change of plan and only takes three of the ten Gladiators, leaving seven on Malta.
11 May 1940	Air raid warning practice on Malta.

Date	Event
20 May 1940	Volunteers called for, for the Malta Volunteer Defence Force, in Maltese newspapers.
27 May 1940	Emergency hospitals on Malta established and a curfew is introduced between 23.00 and 05.00.
10 June 1940	Italy declares war on Britain at midnight if Malta is not surrendered. At the outbreak of the war Malta had thirty-four heavy anti-aircraft guns instead of an approved 112 and just eight light anti-aircraft guns, instead of sixty. Also on the island are four obsolete Gladiators to operate as fighters and a single radio set.
11 June 1940	The Italians launch their first air raid on Malta at 07.00, attacking Hal Far, Valletta and the Grand Harbour.
12 June 1940	Italian bombers inflict seventeen casualties in four different locations on the island.
13 June 1940	More Italian raids, including bombs dropped over Kalafrana.
14 June 1940	A pair of Italian bombers attacks the Grand Harbour. Refugee settlement centres are established on the island.
15 June 1940	Air raid on Hamrun, killing one person. The Governor of Malta announces that protection officers will work with District Committees.
16 June 1940	Kalafrana hit. More raids launched in the afternoon.
17 June 1940	Five bombers and two fighters attack just after 06.00. Seven Economical Kitchens (or Victory Kitchens) are opened to feed town refugees on the island.
20 June 1940	Malta's first night air-raid.
21 June 1940	Four Italian raids, with bombs falling on Marsa and Gozo.

Date	Event
22 June 1940	First confirmed kill of an Italian aircraft, off Kalafrana.
23 June 1940	Flight Lieutenant Burges in a Gladiator shoots down a Macchi 200.
26 June 1940	Frequent air raids, with twenty-five S79s. One bomb hits a crowded bus at Marsa, killing twenty-one (seven more would later die from their injuries).
27 June 1940	Malta suffers its twenty-eighth air raid in the evening. There are four deaths.
29 June 1940	Six Italian aircraft intercepted and forced back before bombing runs.
30 June 1940	More Italian raids and cars banned from the roads after 24.00 without special permit.
3 July 1940	Eleven Italian aircraft attack. One S79 shot down by a Hurricane five miles out from Kalafrana.
4 July 1940	Low flying machine-gun attack on Kalafrana.
5 July 1940	Malta receives an unexpected reinforcement when a French floatplane reached Kalafrana at 23.00 hours, having flown from Tunisia. Its crew was eventually attached to No. 230 Squadron at Kalafrana.
6 July 1940	Heavy bomb raid on the island but just one casualty. Civilian respirators issued from police stations.
7 July 1940	Italians hit three Maltese villages, killing a number of children and older residents.
10 July 1940	Several attacks by Italian aircraft. One is shot down.
13 July 1940	Flight Lieutenant Burges awarded the Distinguished Flying Cross.

Date	Event
15 July 1940	Bombproof shelters opened in Valletta.
24 July 1940	Raid on Kalafrana at 04.00.
31 July 1940	Gladiators from Hal Far Fighter Flight intercept an S79 escorted by a number of CR42s. One CR42 shot down to the north of the Grand Harbour. Pilot Officer Hartley shot down, but rescued by the Marine Craft Section.
2 August 1940	Twelve Hurricanes arrive in Malta from HMS *Argus* in Operation Hurry.
13–14 August 1940	Nine aircraft of 830 Squadron Fleet Air Arm launch attack on Augusta Harbour. Three aircraft fail to make it back to Malta.
15 August 1940	Ten S79s escorted by nineteen CR42s attack Hal Far. Four Hurricanes are scrambled. Sergeant O'Donnell was shot down by one of the CR42s.
23 August 1940	Several reconnaissance flights launched over the island.
24 August 1940	Six S79s and seventeen CR42s attack Kalafrana and Hal Far. Four Hurricanes manage to shoot down a CR42.
29 August 1940	In Operation Hats convoy sails from Alexandria to Malta, launching attacks on Italian airbases *en route*.
2–3 September 1940	Six Swordfish from HMS *Illustrious* arrive in Malta.
4 September 1940	Five Italian-manned Ju87 Stukas attack Malta, bombing Kalafrana.
5 September 1940	Enemy bombers intercepted over Gozo. Italians machine-gun bus passengers.
7 September 1940	Ten S79s and seventeen CR42s attack Valletta just after 12.00. Most bombs fall in the dockyard area.

Date	Event
14–17 September 1940	Several more Italian raids on Valletta, Kalafrana and Hal Far. On 17 September twelve Italian Stukas, twenty-one CR42s and six Macchi 200s attack Luqa airfield. One Stuka shot down off Filfla.
22 September 1940	Italians attack Luqa, destroying several houses and killing a teenager.
23 September 1940	Unexploded bombs in the Hal Far area are cleared.
9 October 1940	Five S79s attack Kalafrana. A Hurricane night fighter intercepts and shoots one down off Benghisa.
11–12 October 1940	Convoy bringing in food and other supplies arrives from Port Said.
15 October 1940	A French flying boat arrives in Malta, having escaped from Tunisia from the French battleship *Richelieu*.
17 October 1940	More Italian air raids, with one casualty at Zabbar.
31 October 1940	British Wellington bombers, based at Luqa, launch their first bombing raid from the island. The aircraft hit Naples, 350 miles away.
5–6 November 1940	A single CR42 strafes a Sunderland in Marsaxlokk Bay.
12 November 1940	Hurricane shoots down a Macchi 200 in St Thomas Bay.
17 November 1940	Twelve more Hurricanes arrive in Operation White, flown off HMS *Argus*. Of the twelve only four reach Malta: the rest run out of fuel and crash into the sea. More ships arrive with supplies from Egypt.
18 November 1940	Night raids launched by the Italians around the Grand Harbour and Kalafrana. A Hurricane shoots down an S79.

Date	Event
24 November 1940	Low-level attacks made on Luqa airfield.
26 November 1940	A Macchi 200 shot down by a Hurricane. Convoy arrives from Alexandria.
29 November 1940	Convoy codenamed Operation Collar arrives in Malta with 20,000 tons of supplies.
14 December 1940	Several Italian aircraft launch attacks on the island. Little damage is done and they are beaten off by anti-aircraft fire.
20 December 1940	Operation Hide, a convoy from Alexandria delivers supplies on seven merchant ships. An S79 is shot down off Fort Tigne.
9 January 1941	Sixteen Macchi 200s attack Luqa airfield. Nine Italian Ju87s and ten CR42s attack merchant ships in Marsaxlokk Bay and Kalafrana. A Macchi 200 shot down by a Hurricane in St Paul's Bay.
10 January 1941	Operation Excess convoy from Gibraltar arrives in Malta with ammunition and twelve crated Hurricanes. They also deliver 10,000 tons of stores and 500 soldiers and airmen.
15 January 1941	Italian reconnaissance flights over the eastern part of the island.
16 January 1941	First Italian air raid against HMS *Illustrious*. A second raid takes place in the afternoon and a third at night. British claim at least ten enemy aircraft, most of which are German. There is extensive damage in Valletta. This is the first time the Germans launch an assault on the island.
17 January 1941	Several more heavy air raids, but only one casualty.

Date	Event
18 January 1941	Fifty Ju87s and Ju88s, with Macchi 200 escorts, launch continuous waves of attacks for over an hour in the morning. At least eighty bombers hit Luqa and Hal Far airfields. Two British Fulmars shot down. British claim eleven enemy aircraft. Third major air raid takes place but the two enemy formations are engaged out to sea and fail to press home their attack.
19 January 1941	Italian Cant shot down off Valletta. Major raids by Germans against the Grand Harbour in an effort to destroy HMS *Illustrious*. A single Ju88 flies on towards Kalafrana, but is shot down by a Hurricane. Later a CR42 is also shot down near Valletta.
20 January 1941	After a reconnaissance flight by a Ju88 a high level bombing raid is launched on the harbour at night.
21 January 1941	Germans and Italians launch two raids, bombing various targets on the island.
24 January 1941	A Ju88 shot down by a Gladiator and a Cant is shot down by another Malta-based aircraft.
26 January 1941	A Ju88 on a reconnaissance flight is intercepted by two Hurricanes. It disappeared out to sea with smoke pouring out of its engine.
28 January 1941	Six Hurricanes arrive from Egypt, along with some reserve pilots.
4 February 1941	100 enemy aircraft attack Hal Far, Luqa and Kalafrana at dusk. In the previous month sixty-three civilians had been killed.
6 February 1941	Germans and Italians launch dive bombing attacks on Maltese airfields.
7 February 1941	Various alerts but all are reconnaissance flights.

Date	Event
8 February 1941	Several enemy air raids. Six Hurricanes are scrambled at night. They intercept an HE111 above Rabat. The bomber crashed into the sea.
9 February 1941	The British report that to date eighty-five enemy aircraft have been shot down over Malta, twenty-four probable kills and thirty-three more have been damaged.
12 February 1941	First appearance of Messerschmitt Bf109Es, operating out of Sicily. Hurricanes scramble to intercept Ju88s but are attacked by the 109s. One Hurricane is shot down.
16 February 1941	Enemy drops mines close to the harbour entrance.
25 February 1941	A pair of German Dorniers is shot down.
26 February 1941	Heaviest raid to date with thirty-eight Ju87s, twelve Ju88s, ten DO17s, ten HE111s and up to thirty fighters. All attack Luqa. They destroy six Wellingtons on the ground and several Marylands. Eight Hurricanes are scrambled to intercept. RAF loses five Hurricanes and three pilots. British claim five confirmed, four probable and one damaged. Later in the afternoon German fighter attacks fishing boats.
28 February 1941	Parachute mines dropped around Valletta.
1 March 1941	Enemy reconnaissance flights over the island, followed by bombers escorted by fighters.
2 March 1941	Several enemy raids launched.
5 March 1941	At least sixty enemy bombers, escorted by fighters, attack the island. At least one Ju88 and one Ju87 shot down.
6 March 1941	Five Hurricanes and two Wellingtons arrive in Malta from Egypt.
7 March 1941	A Hurricane, flown by Sergeant Jessop, shot down by a German fighter.

Date	Event
9 March 1941	German aircraft raid Valletta. One bomber crash lands on Gozo.
10 March 1941	At midday at least three enemy formations attack the island. Messerschmitt 110s attack Kalafrana. At night anti-aircraft guns claim a German bomber.
11 March 1941	Indiscriminate bombing, mainly on Sliema.
15 March 1941	German aircraft attack Maltese airfields and an enemy mine blows up a Gozo boat.
22 March 1941	Ten Ju88s, escorted by Bf109s, intercepted by Hurricanes. Five Hurricanes are shot down and four of the pilots are lost.
23 March 1941	Day and night time raids on the island. Up to twelve enemy aircraft claimed. Convoy arrives from Haifa.
24 March 1941	Ju88s, escorted by German fighters, drop bombs in the Grand Harbour.
29 March 1941	Night raids by German aircraft across the island.
3 April 1941	Operation Winch sees twelve Hurricanes arrive from HMS *Ark Royal*. An Italian S79, escorted by CR42 fighters, attempts to attack an RAF launch. Later in the day Ju87s, escorted by fighters, attack two minesweepers off Filfla.
8 April 1941	The mooring lighter *Moor* is sunk in the Grand Harbour. The explosion causes damage to the surrounding area and many casualties.
11 April 1941	Twelve Macchi 200s, six CR42s and Bf109s appear over the island. Hurricanes are scrambled and shoot down one German fighter. British also lose aircraft in the dogfight over the island. By this stage the Germans and Italians have lost 132 aircraft, with forty-four probable and fifty-eight damaged. British losses to date twenty-nine fighters.

Date	Event
13 April 1941	The 500th alert on the island. There are four raids. Flight Officer Mason shoots down a Bf109 but three others shoot him down. He is later picked up by HSL 107.
14 April 1941	Successive waves of Ju87s and 88s attack the island.
15–19 April 1941	Several more raids of lessening intensity.
20 April 1941	Italian S79s and CR42s, supported by Bf109s, attack the eastern parts of the island.
21 April 1941	A parachute mine lands near a large air raid shelter but fails to inflict casualties.
22 April 1941	German aircraft attack at night using flares. They drop bombs and mines around Valletta.
23 April 1941	Hurricane shot down off Hal Far.
27 April 1941	Twenty-three of twenty-four Hurricanes arrive from HMS *Ark Royal* in Operation Dunlop. German fighters attack and destroy a Sunderland at Kalafrana. Wellington bombers leave for Egypt, to be replaced by Blenheims, arriving from England via Gibraltar.
29 April 1941	Six Ju88s attack Valletta in the early evening. Seventeen Hurricanes are scrambled and they shoot down one Ju88.
30 April 1941	Heavy raids against the Grand Harbour and Valletta. The cathedral and a Greek Orthodox Church are destroyed.
2 May 1941	Twenty-one crated Hurricanes and other supplies, due to arrive on the cargo ship *Parracombe* in Operation Temple, are lost when the vessel hits a mine off Cape Bon.

Date	Event
4 May 1941	The parish church of St Publius is severely damaged after a raid.
6 May 1941	Major German attacks on the island. Several Hurricanes shot down.
9 May 1941	Convoy Operation Tiger arrives from Alexandria. Ju87s attack as they enter the Grand Harbour but they are chased off by Hurricanes that claim a kill.
10 May 1941	German fighters engaged by Hurricanes. One German aircraft destroys a Sunderland in Marsaxlokk Bay.
11 May 1941	German fighters machine-gun seaplane bases and Valletta is bombed.
13 May 1941	Hurricane shot down by German aircraft.
15–20 May 1941	Enemy air raids against Valletta and Zabbar.
21 May 1941	Operation Splice sees forty-eight Hurricanes due to be launched from HMS *Ark Royal* and HMS *Furious*. Forty-one actually take off and forty reach Malta, along with five Fulmar aircraft.
25 May 1941	Enemy raids claim one casualty at Naxxar.
31 May 1941	Raids damage the former Courts of Justice and block Kingsway. The Law Courts building collapses.
3 June 1941	Two raids on the island. In the second raid a German Ju52 is shot down. Signposts are removed for fear of enemy airborne attack. An S79 is shot down by a Hurricane off Gozo.
6 June 1941	In Operation Rocket forty-three Hurricanes safely arrive on Malta from HMS *Ark Royal* and HMS *Furious*.
7 June 1941	Night raids by HE111s.

Date	Event
9 June 1941	*Luftwaffe* leaves Sicily. Off Malta four Italian S79s are intercepted by four Hurricanes: one S79 is shot down.
11 June 1941	An S79, escorted by seventeen Macchi 200s, is intercepted off Valletta in the early morning. The bomber is shot down.
12 June 1941	An S79, escorted by thirty Macchi 200s, is intercepted by eighteen Hurricanes. An unspecified number of Italian fighters are shot down. In the afternoon a Cant and a CR42 are also shot down. Later Hurricanes claim another Cant but a Hurricane, flown by Sergeant Walker, is shot down by a CR42 forty-five miles north of Valletta. Italians press attacks on Mosta.
14 June 1941	Forty-eight Hurricanes and four Hudsons arrive from HMS *Ark Royal* and HMS *Victorious* in Operation Tracer. Four Hurricanes run out of fuel and crash *en route*.
15–18 June 1941	Enemy air attacks on Tarxien and Marsa. On June 18 a Macchi 200 is shot down.
23 June 1941	An HE115 float plane, flown by a Norwegian, arrives from England. It will undertake special operational work.
25 June 1941	An S79, escorted by thirty-six Macchi 200s, is intercepted by nine Hurricanes. Two enemy aircraft are shot down.
27 June 1941	In Operation Railway One, twenty-one of twenty-two Hurricanes arrived on Malta from HMS *Ark Royal*. One Hurricane ditches *en route*. There are two raids in the morning, one S79 and two Macchi 200s are intercepted by nine Hurricanes. One Macchi is shot down and another ditches into the sea.

Date	Event
30 June 1941	Forty-two Hurricanes are due to launch from HMS *Ark Royal* and HMS *Furious* in Operation Railway Two. After a Hurricane crash on HMS *Furious* only thirty-five take off, all of which reach Malta. In the afternoon Hurricanes engage a number of Macchi 200s and one Macchi is shot down.
4 July 1941	A Cant on a reconnaissance flight, escorted by thirty-eight Macchi 200s, is intercepted by four Hurricanes. One Macchi is shot down and one Hurricane of No. 126 Squadron, out of Safi, fails to return.
5 July 1941	Enemy raids on Hamrun, killing three children.
7 July 1941	More raids, this time on Paola, killing several civilians.
8 July 1941	A Fiat BR20 is shot down by anti-aircraft fire. Fighters intercept Macchi 200s and seaplanes and scare them off.
9 July 1941	Kalafrana is targeted at night by two raids.
11 July 1941	At least forty Macchi 200s attack in the afternoon. A group of them attacks Luqa airfield. Three enemy fighters are shot down.
12 July 1941	Enemy raids kill several civilians at Hamrun and Marsa.13 July 1941. Malta will now only face Italian aircraft for the time being, as the Germans are shifted to the Russian front.
17–18 July 1941	Enemy fighters and reconnaissance aircraft launch more raids and one civilian is killed.
25 July 1941	65,000 tons of supplies arrive on cargo ships in Operation Substance. HMS *Ark Royal*, as part of the operation despatches seven Swordfish to the island. Twenty-two Hurricanes intercept a reconnaissance Cant and forty Macchi 200s. Three enemy aircraft are shot down.

Date	Event
26 July 1941	The Italian navy X-MAS flotilla launches a raid on the Grand Harbour and Marsamxett. The attack was repelled and in the pursuit a Hurricane was shot down 30 miles north of the island.
1 August 1941	Throughout the previous month thirty-nine civilians had been killed and the island had faced 800 alerts.
3–7 August 1941	Italian raids at Sliema and other targets. At least four enemy aircraft shot down.
14–21 August 1941	Several raids against Hamrun, Zejtun and Sliema. Incendiaries also dropped.
26–28 August 1941	Incendiaries and air raids, particularly on Naxxar, killing six civilians, including five children.
4 September 1941	A large group of Macchi 200s were engaged by Hurricanes. At least six Italian aircraft are claimed. There are several more raids during the night. The Italians lose Lieutenant Carlo Romagnoli.
7 September 1941	RAF aircraft engage Italian fighters.
8–9 September 1941	Five Italian Ju87s attack Valletta. A BR20M attacks Hal Far and nine Z1007bis also attack. A pair of Hurricanes intercept and a Cant is shot down. HMS *Ark Royal* despatches fourteen Hurricanes in Operation Status One.
12 September 1941	Anti-aircraft crews shoot down a pair of BR20s.
13 September 1941	Forty-five of forty-six Hurricanes arrive safely on Malta from HMS *Ark Royal* and HMS *Furious* in Operation Status Two.
29 September 1941	Five Hurricane fighter bombers of No. 185 Squadron attack Comiso airfield. They are intercepted by the new Macchi 202 fighters. One Hurricane, flown by Pilot Officer Lintern, is shot down north of Gozo.

Date	Event
1 October 1941	Macchi 202s launch their first sortie over Malta. There are seven that are intercepted by eight Hurricanes. Another Hurricane is shot down.
4 October 1941	Another Hurricane, flown by Pilot Officer Veitch, is believed to have been shot down by Macchi 202s.
14 October 1941	Six Macchi 202s attack Luqa airfield just before dawn. Five Hurricanes are scrambled followed by six more. Pilot Officer Barnwell is shot down.
17–18 October 1941	Several air raids are launched, claiming five civilians. On 18 October HMS *Ark Royal* in Operation Callboy delivers eleven Albacores and two Swordfish. One of the Swordfish is lost *en route*.
22 October 1941	Fourteen Macchi 202s attack Luqa airfield on two occasions. Nine Hurricanes intercept and Sergeant Owens' aircraft is shot down.
24 October 1941	Bombing raid on Gozo.
31 October 1941	Night raids launched and a Cant Z1007 is shot down.
1 November 1941	In the early hours four BR20M night bombers are intercepted and one is shot down. Nonetheless the Italians bomb Valletta and Marsa.
8–12 November 1941	Raids and bombings on three successive days from 8 November. On 12 November Hurricanes of Nos 126 and 249 Squadrons attack Gela airfield. They are intercepted by Macchi 202s and one Hurricane is lost. HMS *Ark Royal* and HMS *Argus* deliver thirty-four Hurricanes and a Swordfish. This is the last reinforcement of aircraft in 1941.
22 November 1941	A Macchi 202 is shot down by a Hurricane of No. 249 Squadron.

Date	Event
5 December 1941	*Luftwaffe Fliegerkorps* II moves to Messina on Sicily with the aim of destroying Malta's offensive power and preparing her for invasion.
8 December 1941	Intensive air raids across the island.
10 December 1941	More attacks on Malta and Maltese volunteers are requested for training as pilots and observers in the RAF.
12–17 December 1941	Incessant daily raids, with six alerts on 15 December alone.
18 December 1941	The cargo ship *Breconshire* arrives in Malta from Alexandria.
19 December 1941	In the morning three Ju88s, escorted by Macchis, attack the airfields and the Grand Harbour. One bomber damaged and another shot down over Gozo. In the afternoon German fighters shoot down a Hurricane flown by the American Pilot Officer Steele.
20 December 1941	Two formations of bombers, supported by fighters, scatter bombs across the island.
21 December 1941	Four Ju88s and twenty BF109s and Macchi 202s launch a raid in the late morning. Eighteen Hurricanes are scrambled. One Hurricane of No. 185 Squadron is shot down, as is one Macchi and a probable second.
22 December 1941	Enemy fighters attack fishing boats off the Grand Harbour. One of the intercepting Hurricanes is shot down; a Ju88 fails to return to base, as does a No. 18 Squadron Blenheim on reconnaissance.
24 December 1941	Ju88s, escorted by fighters, attack several positions on Malta. Four Ju88s bomb the Grand Harbour in the morning. One bomber shot down and possibly a second. German aircraft claim one Hurricane.

Date	Event
27 December 1941	Three Ju88s and twenty BF109s spotted off Kalafrana. One bomber shot down. After dusk another Ju88 is shot down over the island.
28 December 1941	Early afternoon sees Ju88s and escorts approaching. Hurricanes scrambled. One Hurricane shot down. Anti-aircraft defences claim a bomber and Hurricanes claim a second.
29 December 1941	One of the heaviest raids since the return of the *Luftwaffe*. Thirty-six enemy aircraft involved in morning raid. Two Hurricanes collide in mid-air. Later, eighteen Hurricanes intercept twenty-four enemy aircraft, claiming one. Four Hurricanes scrambled to intercept German fighters over Gozo and two Hurricanes are lost. German aircraft also attack Luqa airfield, destroying fifteen aircraft on the ground.
30 December 1941	Ten Hurricanes scrambled to intercept five Ju88s approaching the island. A single Ju88 shot down.
2 January 1942	Heavy raids claim numerous civilian lives.
3 January 1942	Twenty-two Hurricanes intercept Ju88s and BF109s. One Ju88 and one BF109 shot down, but a Hurricane is also shot down by anti-aircraft fire.
4 January 1942	Two early morning raids. Enemy attacking Luqa lose one bomber.
5 January 1942	Stukas launch continuous attacks on Malta's airfields. This is repeated the next day.
11–14 January 1942	Incessant raids on various targets across the island.
15 January 1942	Seventeen alerts in 24 hours, with heavy bombing.
16 January 1942	Since the Italian declaration of war Malta has endured 1,285 air alerts.

Date	Event
18–22 January 1942	Up to eleven alerts each day. Waves of bombers and fighters almost continually over the island. On night of 19 January a Ju88 shot down.
25 January 1942	Four Hurricanes shot down over Kalafrana by BF109s, escorting Ju88s intent on hitting an inbound convoy.
27 January 1942	*Breconshire* arrives from Alexandria. Hurricane lost.
28–31 January 1942	Several raids each day. One Hurricane lost on 28 January.
2 February 1942	Raid on Kalafrana.
3 February 1942	Raid on Hal Far and Kalafrana.
4 February 1942	Several civilians killed across the island.
5–6 February 1942	Enemy raids on Sliema and two enemy aircraft destroyed on 6 February.
7 February 1942	Sixteen alerts in the past 24 hours.
8 February 1942	Enemy attack Kalafrana.
9–11 February 1942	Several civilians killed in widespread raids.
12 February 1942	Attacks begin at dawn. Two inbound Beaufighters shot down. Later a Ju88 is lost, as is a Hurricane. Several cargo vessels arrive, escorted by cruisers and destroyers.
15 February 1942	Four daylight raids. One of seven Ju88s attacking Luqa shot down. Beaufighter lost in second raid. BF109 lost in third raid. Evening casualties include a Hurricane and a Maryland.
20–22 February 1942	Several raids each day.
23 February 1942	Ju88 shot down by anti-aircraft fire. Later another BF109 lost.

Date	Event
24 February 1942	Airfield raids see loss of two Hurricanes.
27 February 1942	Ju88 attack on the Grand Harbour leads to the loss of a Ju88 and three Me109s.
1 March 1942	*Luftwaffe* attacks Grand Harbour and other targets. Hurricane lost at midday.
4 March 1942	One Me109 shot down off the island.
5 March 1942	Six Hurricanes intercept five Ju88s and ten Me109s. One Hurricane lost. Luqa is heavily bombed.
7 March 1942	Fifteen Spitfires arrive safely on Malta after a 700 mile flight. They launch from HMS *Eagle* in Operation Spotter.
9 March 1942	Ju88s and Me109s hit Luqa, Safi and Hal Far. Hurricanes claim one bomber and anti-aircraft a second. This is the last time that Hurricanes alone face the enemy.
10–13 March 1942	Daily raids with some civilian deaths.
14 March 1942	Me109 shot down; four Spitfires engage 109s over Gozo and shoot another one down.
17 March 1942	Heavy air raids kill many civilians across the island.
18 March 1942	One Spitfire, two Hurricanes and an Me109 lost in dogfights over the island.
20 March 1942	Heavy raids. Spitfires claim another Me109.
21 March 1942	Nine more Spitfires arrive on the island in Operation Picket, flown in from HMS *Eagle*. Several waves of Ju88s attack the island. This is the largest single attack since the *Luftwaffe* returned in December 1941. There are many civilian casualties.

Date	Event
22 March 1942	Several cargo ships safely arrive. Spitfires shoot down three Ju88s. One enemy attack believed to have used at least seventy bombers.
24 March 1942	Heavy attacks on the island, inflicting widespread casualties.
25 March 1942	*Breconshire* badly hit by German fighters. In the afternoon Grand Harbour hit by nearly seventy German aircraft. This is believed to be one of the biggest air battles fought over the island.
26–28 March 1942	Continued attacks claim more civilian lives.
29 March 1942	Seven Spitfires arrive from HMS *Eagle* in Operation Picket Two.
1 April 1942	Three Me109s and two Ju88s shot down. Later two Stukas are lost as they attack Kalafrana and Hal Far.
2 April 1942	Two Spitfires fail to return after being scrambled in the morning. Kalafrana bombed.
3–6 April 1942	Heavy raids on each day, particularly on 6th.
7 April 1942	Malta's 2,000th alert. Several more civilian casualties.
8 April 1942	Several Ju88s and 109s attack Kalafrana.
9 April 1942	Forty or more Ju88s, sixteen Ju87s and forty Me109s hit the airfields at midday. Sixty Ju88s and twelve Ju87s involved in afternoon raids. One Hurricane lost.
10–14 April 1942	Daily raids, with eighty bombers involved on 12 April. Daily civilian casualties. Me109 shot down on 14 April.
15 April 1942	Fighter defence down to around six aircraft due to losses and damage to airfields and also fuel shortages.

Date	Event
18 April 1942	Kalafrana hit by several raids throughout the day. Several military personnel killed.
19 April 1942	Grand Harbour raided and ships set on fire. Many civilian casualties.
20 April 1942	Valletta, Hal Far and Kalafrana hit by seventy Ju88s and twenty Ju87s.
21–22 April 1942	More raids from first light until dusk. Ju88 shot down on 22 April.
23 April 1942	Forty Ju88s, fifteen Ju87s and fighter escorts hit the island. One Ju87 destroyed.
24 April 1942	Several raids with the largest on the Grand Harbour by thirty Ju88s and twenty Me109s.
25 April 1942	Eight-five Ju88s and fifteen Ju87s attack Luqa. Similar numbers return midday.
26 April 1942	Large raid on Kalafrana and Valletta by seventy enemy aircraft. Anti-aircraft claim a Ju88.
28–30 April 1942	Numerous raids. Two enemy aircraft shot down on 30 April, bringing anti-aircraft tally for the month to 102 downed.
2 May 1942	Widespread bombing inflicts numerous civilian casualties.
4 May 1942	Ferryboat *Royal Lady* machine-gunned on her way to Gozo.
5 May 1942	Six Hurricanes arrive from Gambut. Evening air raid by enemy fighter bombers with fighter escorts.
6 May 1942	*Royal Lady* sunk. One Hurricane lost.
8 May 1942	Ju88 and Me109 and a Ju87 lost in morning raid. Several civilian bombing casualties.
9 May 1942	In Operation Bowery sixty new Spitfires arrive, one crashing on landing. Enemy raids the Grand Harbour.

Date	Event
10 May 1942	More attacks on Grand Harbour. RAF scrambles thirty-seven Spitfires and thirteen Hurricanes. Claims of up to sixty-three enemy aircraft shot down. More raids in the afternoon and evening by Italian aircraft.
12 May 1942	Two Spitfires lost. Evening raid intercepted and one S84 shot down.
13 May 1942	Sixteen German bombers and twenty Me109s intercepted. One Me109 shot down.
14 May 1942	Twenty-eight Spitfires intercept Ju88s and fighter escorts attacking Luqa and Ta'Qali. One Spitfire lost.
17 May 1942	Nine enemy aircraft shot down by RAF and anti-aircraft fire.
18 May 1942	In Operation LB seventeen new Spitfires arrive from HMS *Eagle*.
19 May 1942	Four Italian aircraft and six German fighters destroyed in dogfights.
25 May 1942	Numerous air raids over Malta, but Valletta streets now reopened after removal of debris.
26–27 May 1942	Several air raid attacks, including those on Hamrun and Luqa.
2 June 1942	Three Italian S84 bombers, twenty-four RE2000s and thirty-two Macchi 202s intercepted by twenty Spitfires off Kalafrana. One Spitfire lost.
3 June 1942	Thirty-two Spitfires arrive from HMS *Eagle* in Operation Style. Four lost *en route* and one crashes on take-off.
7 June 1942	Five Italian fighters, an Italian floatplane and two German bombers shot down.
8 June 1942	Me109s shoot down one of nine Spitfires flown by Rhodesian Pilot Officer Barlow (603 Squadron).

Date	Event
9 June 1942	Thirty-one Spitfires arrive from HMS *Eagle* in Operation Salient.
10 June 1942	By this stage Malta has endured 2,537 alerts, 492 daytime raids and 574 night attacks. Spitfire lost but pilot recovered.
15 June 1942	Several enemy attacks on airfields. Single Spitfire lost.
16 June 1942	Cargo ships and escorts arrive in Malta in Operation Harpoon, bringing airmen and supplies.
22 June 1942	Large scale night raids.
23 June 1942	Evening raids by Italians. One Macchi 202 shot down and one Spitfire lost.
26 June 1942	Bombing raids claim several civilians across the island.
27 June 1942	Four Spitfires engage eight Me109s. One Spitfire lost. Later Beaufighters shoots down a pair of Ju88s.
1 July 1942	Ta'Qali airfield hit in the evening. One Spitfire interceptor lost.
2 July 1942	Cant bombers with Macchi 202s and RE2001 escorts *en route* to Safi and Kalafrana are intercepted by Spitfires. Unconfirmed kills.
3 July 1942	Cant bombers and Macchi 202s try again but once more are beaten off.
4 July 1942	Three S84s and twenty-two Macchi 202s plus up to seventeen additional fighters intercepted in the early morning. Two S84s shot down.
5 July 1942	Similar size raid but this time scared off by Spitfires. Spitfires claim a number of kills. Germans attack in the evening and twenty Spitfires are scrambled. Two bombers are shot down.

Date	Event
7 July 1942	Very heavy raids. Around twelve enemy aircraft shot down, mainly German. Several others badly damaged. One Spitfire also lost.
8 July 1942	Spitfires intercept German bombers, escorted by German and Italian fighters. One Spitfire lost.
9 July 1942	Germans target Ta'Qali. Twenty-seven Spitfires are scrambled and one is lost. Two German aircraft are destroyed.
10–11 July 1942	Widespread bombing. British claim eighty-two enemy aircraft over the last ten days: upwards of eight a day.
13 July 1942	Early morning raid sees one Spitfire lost.
14 July 1942	Heavy enemy raids. A number of unconfirmed enemy losses.
15 July 1942	Thirty-one new Spitfires arrive in Operation Pinpoint from HMS *Eagle*.
17–20 July 1942	Incessant raids. A number of Me109s claimed and a Ju88 on 20 July.
21 July 1942	Twenty-eight Spitfires safely reach Malta from HMS *Eagle* in Operation Insect.
24 July 1942	Enemy raids on numerous targets across the island.
26 July 1942	Today Malta marked its 2,800th alert.
27 July 1942	Up to thirteen enemy aircraft claimed by anti-aircraft defences.
28 July 1942	Spitfire and a Ju88 lost in the morning. Several children killed by bombing.
30 July 1942	Spitfire shot down in St Paul's Bay.
31 July 1942	Two Spitfires lost in dogfights with Me109s and Macchi 202s.

Date	Event
3 August 1942	Spitfire lost in dogfight with Me109s.
9 August 1942	Spitfire lost in mid afternoon.
11 August 1942	HMS *Furious* delivers thirty-seven Spitfires to Malta in Operation Bellows.
15 August 1942	Operation Pedestal arrives in Gibraltar, with cargo ships and escorts. One Me109 and one Spitfire lost in dogfight.
17 August 1942	Ju88s attempt to attack Grand Harbour but make off. HMS *Furious* delivers twenty-eight more Spitfires in Operation Baritone. One Me109 shot down at midday.
19 August 1942	Heavy raids resume.
26 August 1942	German and Italian fighters in sweep over Malta but are dispersed.
31 August 1942	Lighter raids on island.
5 September 1942	Me109 shot down to the south-east of Kalafrana.
6 September 1942	Two Beaufighters lost and an unclear number of enemy aircraft shot down.
8 September 1942	Spitfire shot down as Me109s make reconnaissance sorties over the island.
17 September 1942	Numerous 109s seen over Zonqor Point and to the north-east of Grand Harbour. One enemy aircraft shot down. Later Spitfire is also lost.
19 September 1942	Two Italian seaplanes shot down by Spitfires in the evening.
24–25 September 1942	Several raids greeted by heavy anti-aircraft fire. Two enemy aircraft claimed on 25 September.
29 September 1942	Generally believed to be the day in which Britain gained air superiority over Malta. Enemy aircraft attacking today are driven off before they reach the island.

Date	Event
10 October 1942	Ju88s target Gozo, killing a number of civilians.
11 October 1942	The opening of the last blitz on Malta. Seven Ju88s, twenty-five Macchi 202s and four Me109s are intercepted by nineteen Spitfires. Britain claims seven bombers, five German fighters and three Italian fighters. Several more are reported damaged.
12 October 1942	Five air raids launched. Two British aircraft lost.
13 October 1942	One of the heaviest raids since May. In the fourth raid alone seven Ju88s, thirty Macchi 202s and forty-two Me109s attack. By the end of the day Britain claimed twenty-two enemy aircraft destroyed.
14 October 1942	Four raids launched. Four Spitfires lost in return for a number of enemy aircraft.
15 October 1942	Four more raids. Several claims and counterclaims made on kills.
16 October 1942	Similar pattern, as *Luftwaffe* tries to knock out the airfields. Several aircraft lost by both sides.
17 October 1942	More large scale attacks. Spitfire destroyed in head-on collision with Ju88. Two more Ju88s shot down at midday. In the evening fifteen bombers hit Kalafrana.
20 October 1942	Daylight raids on Maltese airfields.
21 October 1942	Britain claims that up to this point over 1,000 enemy aircraft have been destroyed, but admits that 6,704 buildings on Malta have either been destroyed or badly damaged.
22 October 1942	Ju88 shot down.
23 October 1942	A German and then an Italian raid in the evening kills a number of civilians.

Date	Event
25 October 1942	Two more fighter bomber raids. Me109 shot down in first raid and Spitfire lost in the second.
26 October 1942	One of thirty-six enemy aircraft shot down in early morning raid. Three more Me109s lost later in the day.
29 October 1942	Twenty-nine Spitfires arrive from HMS *Furious* in Operation Train. This will be the last reinforcement of fighter aircraft by aircraft carrier.
3 November 1942	Bomb raids against three targets on the island.
13 November 1942	Beaufighters of No. 227 Squadron intercept formation of German and Italian troop carriers. Four Ju52s and two SM81s shot down.
20 November 1942	Convoy delivers 35,000 tons of supplies in Operation Stoneage.
22 November 1942	Two more German transport aircraft destroyed, along with three Italian transports.
24 November 1942	Enemy fighters carry out sweep across the island. Malta now permanently on the offensive, rather than defensive. By the end of the month only thirty air raid alerts occurred and just 12 tons of bombs were dropped on the island.
5 December 1942	Enemy aircraft launch sporadic raids.
9 December 1942	More enemy troop carriers intercepted and shot down.
10 December 1942	Four Beaufighters intercept more enemy troop carriers *en route* from Tunisia to Sicily.
31 December 1942	Throughout the month thirty-five air raid alerts have been sounded and 60 tons of bombs have been dropped on the island. The air battle for Malta is now considered won and raids are becoming less common.

PICK-UPS BY RAF AIR SEA RESCUE AND MARINE CRAFT SECTION
(JUNE 1940 AUGUST 1944)

Date	Craft	Number Recovered	Alive or Dead	Nationality	Aircraft Type	Crew Names (If Known)
31/07/40	ST280	1	Alive	Allied	Gladiator	Hartley
14/08/40	ST280	2	Alive	Allied	Swordfish	Hall and Brooks-Walford
16/09/40	ST280	2	1 alive, 1 dead	Italian	Ju87	Catani (alive), Di Giorgi (dead)
18/11/40	HSL107	2	Alive	Allied	Swordfish	Not known
12/01/41	HSL107	5	Alive	Allied	Wellington	Not known
12/02/41	HSL107	1	Alive	Allied	Hurricane	Thacker
25/02/41	HSL107	1	Alive	Allied	Hurricane	Walsh
26/02/41	HSL107	2	Alive	German	Ju87	Heil and Stamm
07/03/41	HSL107	1	Alive	Allied	Hurricane	Jessop
11/04/41	HSL107	1	Dead	Allied	Hurricane	Kennett
12/04/41	HSL107	1	Alive	Allied	Hurricane	Mason
06/05/41	HSL107	1	Alive	Allied	Hurricane	Gray

Date	Craft	Number Recovered	Alive or Dead	Nationality	Aircraft Type	Crew Names (If Known)
27/05/41	ST224	1	Dead	Allied	Unknown	Unknown
09/06/41	HSL107	2	Alive	Allied	Swordfish	Jopling and wireless operator
09/06/41	HSL107	1	Alive	Allied	Hurricane	Rex
09/06/41	HSL107	1	Alive	Italian	S79	Fabbri
11/06/41	HSL107	1	Dead	Italian	Unknown	Unknown
12/06/41	HSL107	2	Alive	Allied	Fulmar	Sabey and Manning
12/06/41	HSL107	1	Alive	Allied	Hurricane	Saunders
14/06/41	HSL107	1	Alive	Allied	Hurricane	Campbell
25/07/41	HSL107	1	Alive	Italian	Macchi 200	De Giorgi
26/07/41	HSL107	2	Alive	Italian	E-boat	Paratore and Zaniboni
07/08/41	HSL107	1	Dead	Italian	Unknown	Unknown
03/09/41	ST280	2	Alive	Allied	Fulmar	Unknown
09/09/41	ST338	5	Alive	Italian	Cant Z1007bis	Unknown
29/09/41	HSL107	2	Alive	Allied	Swordfish	Eyres and Furlong
22/10/41	ST280	1	Alive	Allied	Hurricane	Owen
01/11/41	HSL129	1	Alive	Italian	BR20M	Marcantonio
15/11/41	HSL128	6	Alive	Allied	Wellington	Duncan, Popper, Cameron, Barlow, Leonard and Welch
29/11/41	HSL128	3	Alive	Allied	Wellesley	Taylor, Cunnison and Scholar

Date	Craft	Number Recovered	Alive or Dead	Nationality	Aircraft Type	Crew Names (If Known)
28/12/41	HSL129	1	Alive	Allied	Hurricane	Owen
29/12/41	HSL129	1	Alive	Allied	Hurricane	Andrews
15/02/42	ST338	4	Alive	Allied	Maryland	Lowery, Rasmussen, Durrant and Bosley
01/03/42	HSL107	1	Dead	Allied	Hurricane	Harvey
12/03/42	ST253	1	Alive	German	Unknown	Unknown
18/03/42	HSL128	1	Alive	Allied	Hurricane	Lester
01/04/42	ST338	1	Alive	German	Ju87	Gunther
02/04/42	HSL128	1	Alive	Allied	Spitfire	McLeod
09/04/42	HSL128	1	Alive	Allied	Hurricane	Pauley
14/04/42	HSL128	1	Alive	Allied	Spitfire	Kelly
14/04/42	HSL128	1	Dead	Allied	Beaufort	Beveridge
08/05/42	HSL107	2	1 alive, 1 dead	Allied	Submarine HMS *Olympus*	Unknown
10/05/42	HSL128	1	Alive	German	Me109	Heiner
10/05/42	HSL107	1	Alive	Allied	Spitfire	Dickson
12/05/42	HSL128	1	Dead	Allied	Spitfire	Graysmark
12/05/42	HSL128	1	Dead	Italian	S84	Rivolta
12/05/42	HSL128	1	Alive	Allied	Spitfire	Conway
18/05/42	HSL128	1	Alive	German	Me109	Lompa
18/05/42	HSL128	1	Alive	Allied	Spitfire	Fowlow
20/05/42	HSL128	1	Alive	Italian	E-boat	Spy Borg Pisani

Date	Craft	Number Recovered	Alive or Dead	Nationality	Aircraft Type	Crew Names (If Known)
21/05/42	HSL128	1	Alive	German	Me109	Beitz
01/06/42	HSL128	6	Alive	Allied	Wellington	Curtiss, Dowse, Paterson, Fugar, Marshall and Moore
01/06/42	HSL128	1	Dead	Allied	Spitfire	McNaughton
02/06/42	ST338	1	Alive	Allied	Spitfire	Halford
10/06/42	HSL107	1	Alive	Allied	Spitfire	Innes
15/06/42	HSL128	1	Alive	Allied	Spitfire	Allen-Rowlandson
16/06/42	HSL128	2	Alive	Allied	Spitfire	McNamara and Vineyard
23/06/42	HSL128	1	Alive	Allied	Spitfire	Mitchell
29/06/42	HSL128	1	Alive	Allied	Spitfire	Barbour
01/07/42	HSL107	1	Alive	Allied	Spitfire	Ballantyne
02/07/42	HSL107	1	Alive	Italian	Macchi 202	Chierici
03/07/42	HSL107	1	Alive	Allied	Spitfire	Thomas
04/07/42	HSL128	1	Alive	Italian	S84	Pelleschi
06/07/42	HSL128	1	Dead	Italian	Cant Z1007bis	Antoroise
06/07/42	HSL128	3	Alive	German	Ju88	Stiller, Krumbachner and Albrecht
07/07/42	HSL128	3	Alive	Allied	Spitfire	Middlemiss, Davey and De Nancrede
07/07/42	HSL128	1	Dead	Allied	Spitfire	Haggas
08/07/42	HSL128	1	Alive	German	Ju88	Queisser

Date	Craft	Number Recovered	Alive or Dead	Nationality	Aircraft Type	Crew Names (If Known)
09/07/42	HSL128	1	Alive	Allied	Spitfire	Ballantyne
10/07/42	HSL128	1	Alive	Maltese	Fishing boat	Tonna-barthet
13/07/42	HSL128	1	Alive	Allied	Spitfire	Willie
14/07/42	HSL128	1	Alive	Allied	Spitfire	Stoop
17/07/42	HSL128	1	Alive	German	Me109	Sauer
18/07/42	HSL107	1	Alive	Allied	Spitfire	McLean
20/07/42	HSL107	2	Alive	German	Ju88	Mulen and Blass
23/07/42	HSL128	1	Alive	Italian	Macchi 202	Di Pauli
28/07/42	ST338	2	Alive	German	Ju88	Frick and Bauer
28/07/42	HSL107	1	Alive	Allied	Spitfire	Brown
29/07/42	HSL107	5	Alive	Italian	Cant Z506B	Mastrodicasa, Chifari, Losi, Schisano and Scarciella
29/07/42	HSL107	4	Alive	Allied	Cant Z506B	Strever, Wilkinson, Dunsmore and Brown
31/07/42	HSL128	1	Alive	Allied	Spitfire	Livingstone
03/08/42	HSL107	1	Alive	Allied	Spitfire	Knox-Williams
10/08/42	ST338	1	Alive	German	Me109	Schmidt
10/08/42	HSL107	1	Alive	Allied	Spitfire	Ritchie
11/08/42	HSL107	2	Alive	Allied	Beaufighter	Bing and Fumerton
14/08/42	HSL128	1	Alive	Allied	Spitfire	Hogarth
15/08/42	HSL128	1	Alive	Allied	Spitfire	Tarbuck

Date	Craft	Number Recovered	Alive or Dead	Nationality	Aircraft Type	Crew Names (If Known)
17/08/42	HSL128	1	Alive	Allied	Spitfire	Stenborg
20/08/42	HSL128	1	Alive	Allied	Beaufighter	Eyre
21/08/42	HSL128	4	Alive	Allied	Beaufort	Moody, Griffith, Pritchard and Gill
27/08/42	HSL128	1	Dead	Italian or German	Unknown	Unknown
08/09/42	HSL128	1	Alive	Allied	Spitfire	Roberts
17/09/42	HSL128	1	Alive	German	Me109	Schneider
17/09/42	HSL107	1	Alive	Allied	Spitfire	Farmer
05/10/42	HSL128	3	Alive	Allied	Beaufighter	Wigmore, Crow and Briffett
11/10/42	HSL128	1	Alive	German	Ju88	Grams
12/10/42	HSL128	3	Alive	German	Ju88	Lang, Zettlemaier and Kobszinowski
12/10/42	HSL100	1	Alive	Allied	Spitfire	Knox-Williams
12/10/42	HSL128	1	Alive	Italian	Macchi 202	Radini
12/10/42	ST280	1	Alive	Allied	Spitfire	Stephens
14/10/42	ST280	1	Alive	Allied	Spitfire	Long
14/10/42	HSL128	2	Alive	Allied	Spitfires	Nash and Beurling
15/10/42	ST253	1	Alive	Allied	Spitfire	Smith
15/10/42	HSL128	2	Alive	Allied	Spitfires	Farquarson and Bryden
16/10/42	ST338	2	Alive	German	Ju88	Wallenburger and Wehner

Date	Craft	Number Recovered	Alive or Dead	Nationality	Aircraft Type	Crew Names (If Known)
17/10/42	HSL128	3	Alive	German	Ju88	Seibt, Borner and Futterknecht
17/10/42	HSL107	2	Alive	German	Ju88	Unknown
22/10/42	HSL128	4	Alive	German	Ju88	Neuffer, Ekehant, Stern and Hinter
26/10/42	HSL100	1	Alive	German	Unknown	Unknown
06/11/42	HSL128	9	Alive	Allied	Wellington	Ritter, McLeod, Sadler, Whitlock, Powell, Cooper, Lilly, McInnes and Baxter
13/11/42	HSL107	1	Alive	Allied	Spitfire	Unknown
20/11/42	HSL128	2	Alive	Allied	Swordfish	Jones and Moon
17/12/42	HSL128	1	Alive	Allied	Spitfire	Fuller
18/12/42	HSL107	1	Dead	Allied	Spitfire	Harrison
25/12/42	HSL100	1	Alive	Allied	Beaufighter	Campbell
26/12/42	HSL107	5	Alive	Allied	Wellington	Unknown
10/01/43	HSL166	6	Alive	Allied	Wellington	Earle, Liveridge, Whale, Cooper, Turner and Milne
17/01/43	HSL166	2	Alive	Allied	Beaufighter	Colman and Lynehale
28/01/43	HSL107	1	Alive	Allied	Spitfire	Goodwin
28/01/43	HSL166	2	Alive	Allied	Beaufighter	Freer and Holdman
30/01/43	HSL166	1	Alive	Allied	Spitfire	Heppell
04/02/43	HSL166	1	Alive	Allied	Spitfire	Nesbitt

Date	Craft	Number Recovered	Alive or Dead	Nationality	Aircraft Type	Crew Names (If Known)
01/03/43	HSL107	1	Alive	Allied	Spitfire	Miller
02/03/43	HSL128	1	Alive	Allied	Spitfire	Hanson-Lester
03/03/43	HSL166	1	Alive	Allied	Spitfire	Billing
03/03/43	HSL107	1	Alive	Allied	Spitfire	Taggart
03/03/43	HSL107	1	Alive	Allied	Spitfire	Stark
17/03/43	HSL166	2	Alive	Allied	Beaufighter	Frazee and Sandrey
25/03/43	HSL128	1	Alive	Allied	Spitfire	Stovel
04/04/43	HSL128	4	Alive	Allied	Wellington	Harris, Jolicoeur, Hargreaves and Haddock
14/04/43	HSL128	2	Alive	Allied	Albacore	Stewart and Townsend
28/04/43	HSL166	9	Alive	Allied	Liberator	Freemyer, Petke, Savaria, Mirock, McKilley, Johnson, O'Brien, Brock and Nance
03/05/43	ST338	2	Alive	Allied	Albacore	Barr and Chalker
06/05/43	HSL128	3	Alive	Allied	Liberator	Widinmier, Hood and Brown
06/05/43	HSL107	1	Alive	Allied	Spitfire	Mercer
08/05/43	ST338	6	Alive	Allied	Liberator	Chilcott, Rutledge, Williamson, Brown, Bullock and Robinson
25/05/43	HSL107	1	Alive	Allied	Spitfire	Hodges

Date	Craft	Number Recovered	Alive or Dead	Nationality	Aircraft Type	Crew Names (If Known)
01/06/43	HSL166	1	Alive	Allied	Spitfire	Chandler
06/06/43	HSL128	1	Alive	Allied	Beaufighter	Hawksley
08/06/43	HSL107	1	Alive	Allied	Spitfire	McKenzie
12/06/43	HSL128	2	1 alive, 1 dead	German	HE111	Gerhard and unknown dead
13/06/43	HSL107	1	Alive	Allied	Spitfire	Jones
03/07/43	HSL107	1	Alive	German	Me109	Reinicke
05/07/43	HSL107	7	Alive	Allied	Mitchell	Unknown
06/07/43	ASRP1254	1	Alive	Allied	Spitfire	Symons
07/07/43	ASRP1244	1	Alive	Allied	Spitfire	Armstrong
18/07/43	ST338	1	Alive	Allied	Warhawk	Fourneaugh
19/07/43	HSL2598	1	Alive	Allied	B17	Unknown
26/07/43	HSL107	1	Dead	Allied	Mosquito	Martin
03/08/43	ASRP1246	6	Alive	Allied	Wellington	Marson, Tomlinson, Aldridge, Browne, Black and Cosh
22/08/43	HSL107	3	Alive	German	Ju88	Kluszmann, Hopfner and one other
25/10/43	HSL128	1	Alive	Allied	Kittyhawk	Whitehead
23/02/44	HSL128	1	Alive	Allied	Spitfire	Schooling
23/07/44	HSL128	1	Alive	Allied	Spitfire	Unknown

RAF SQUADRONS BASED ON THE ISLAND

Squadron Number	Base	From	To
23	Luqa	December 1942	May 1944
39	Luqa	August 1942	June 1943
40	Luqa	October 1941	February 1942
69	Luqa	January 1941	April 1944
104	Luqa	October 1941	January 1942
107	Luqa	September 1941	January 1942
108	Luqa/Hal Far	June 1943	July 1944
126	Luqa/Safi/Ta'Qali	June 1941	September 1943
148	Luqa	December 1940	March 1941
185	Hal Far/Qrendi	April 1941	September 1943
221	Luqa	January 1943	March 1944
227	Luqa/Ta'Qali	August 1942	March 1943
229	Ta'Qali/Qrendi/Hal Far	August 1942	January 1944
249	Qrendi/Hal Far	May 1941	October 1943
256	Luqa	October 1943	April 1944
261	Luqa	August 1940	May 1941
272	Ta'Qali	November 1942	September 1943
283	Hal Far	April 1944	August 1945

BIBLIOGRAPHY

Attard, Joseph. *The Battle of Malta: An Epic True Story of Suffering and Bravery*. Progress Press. 1988.

Austin, Douglas. *Churchill and Malta*. Spellmount. 2006.

Baker, E C R. *The Fighter Aces of the RAF*. Kimber. 1962.

Bradford, Ernle. *Siege: Malta 1940–1943*. Pen & Sword Books. 2003.

Clayton, Tim and Phil Craig. *End of the Beginning: From the Siege of Malta to the Victory at Alamein*. Coronet Books. 2003.

Cull, Brian and Frederick Galea. *Hurricanes over Malta*. Grub Street. 2002.

Cull, Brian and Frederick Galea. *Spitfires over Malta*. Grub Street. 2002.

Douglas-Hamilton, James. *The Air Battle for Malta*. Airlife Publishing. 2000.

Forty, George. *The Battle for Malta*. Ian Allan. 2003.

Galea, Frederick R. *Call-Out*. Malta at War Publications. 2002.

Galea, Michael. *Malta: Diary of a War*. Publishers Enterprises Group. 1992.

McAulay, Lex. *Against All Odds*. Hutchinson. 1989.

McCaffery, Dan. *Hell Island*. James Lorimer. 1998.

Ministry of Information. *The Air Battle of Malta*. HMSO. 1944.

Hogan, George. *Malta: The Triumphant Years 1940 – 1943*. Progress Press, Malta, 1988.

Holland, James. *Fortress Malta*. Orion. 2003.

Leighton, Frank. *Frayed Lifelines: A Siege Survivor's Story*. Trafford. 2003.

Lucas, Laddie. *Malta: The Thorn in Rommel's Side*. Stanley Paul. 1992.

Roger, Anthony. *Battle Over Malta*. Sutton. 2000.

Roger, Anthony. *185: The Malta Squadron*. The History Press. 2005.

Williamson, David G. *Malta Besieged 1940 – 1942*. Pen & Sword Military. 2007.

Wragg, David. *Malta: The Last Great Siege*. Leo Cooper. 2003.

INDEX